Contemporary Composition

Contemporary

PRENTICE-HALL, INC.
Englewood Cliffs, New Jersey

Composition

Charles L. Cherry
Villanova University

Caroline L. Cherry
Eastern Baptist College

CONTEMPORARY COMPOSITION
by Charles L. Cherry and Caroline L. Cherry

© 1970 by PRENTICE-HALL, INC.
ENGLEWOOD CLIFFS, N.J.

Library of Congress Catalog Card No.: 71-112449
13-169789-7

Current Printing (*last digit*)
10   9   8   7   6   5   4   3   2   1

Printed in the United States of America

PRENTICE-HALL INTERNATIONAL, INC., *London*
PRENTICE-HALL OF AUSTRALIA, PTY. LTD., *Sydney*
PRENTICE-HALL OF CANADA, LTD., *Toronto*
PRENTICE-HALL OF INDIA PRIVATE LIMITED, *New Delhi*
PRENTICE-HALL OF JAPAN, INC., *Tokyo*

Preface

I became increasingly frustrated at not being able to express what I wanted to convey in letters that I wrote, especially those to Mr. Elijah Muhammad. In the street, I had been the most articulate hustler out there—I had commanded attention when I said something. But now, trying to write simple English, I not only wasn't articulate, I wasn't even functional. How would I sound writing in slang, the way I would *say* it, something such as, "Look, daddy, let me pull your coat about a cat, Elijah Muhammad—"[1]

Once aware of the differences between speaking and writing, Malcolm X proceeded to gain full control of language. A "new world" opened up to him. "In fact," he says, "up to then, I never had been so truly free in my life." Many, like Malcolm X, wish to move and communicate beyond their present levels, yet find it difficult to adjust to formal writing. *Contemporary Composition* assists in such an adjustment.

Our own classroom experience has governed the choice of most materials and the various approaches. We assume that many students learn little when alone with their text. They need the competition and interplay of an active class. Therefore all of the sections are structured for classroom work. Our own commentary in the text is minimal; the

[1] *The Autobiography of Malcolm X* (New York: Grove Press, Inc., 1966), p. 171. Copyright © 1964 by Alex Haley and Malcolm X. Copyright © 1965 by Alex Haley and Betty Shabazz. Reprinted by permission of the publisher.

emphasis is always on student interaction. The accompanying *Teacher's Manual,* with its suggestions on how to generate and guide such interaction, is equally as important to the teacher as the text itself. *It must be read.*

The text contains four major sections which, though directly related to each other, are self-contained units. Two of these, *Mechanics of Style* and *Essay Development,* briefly review the essential principles of grammar and style. However, we try to avoid being just another grammar or rhetoric text. We feel that the student can profit from a review of these basic principles, but a review in a briefer, simpler, more interesting context that engages the mind as well as the memory. We offer a number of new approaches to these traditional problems and take most illustrations from student writing. A third section, *Student Papers,* offers a still wider range of sample papers as accessible models for criticism or imitation.

Finally, a section on *Critical Thinking* contains a variety of material—fiction, poetry, editorials, pictures, essays—selected to involve and interest the student, to provide materials for logical analysis, and to suggest subject matter for writing assignments. The major criterion for the selection of these materials, as with the other sections, is *usefulness.*

We acknowledge the valuable assistance of the following: Eric Nelson of St. Olaf's College for writing several chapters; John Monro, Freshman English Director at Miles College, for ideas and teaching material; Louis Phillips of the New York Maritime College, Murray Suid of the Curriculum Center of the Philadelphia Public Schools, Eileen McCarthy and Gerard Mulligan of Shaw University, Joseph Da Crema of Villanova University, and Leroy Martin of the University of North Carolina for important suggestions; Barbara Keane and Robert Pigeon for invaluable aid; and Villanova University for a typing grant.

Contents

PART

2 *Critical Thinking* 35

Contemporary Composition

General Introduction

"Would you tell me please, which way I ought to go from here?"

"That depends a good deal on where you want to get to," said the Cat.

"I don't much care where—" said Alice.

"Then it doesn't matter which way you go," said the Cat.

"—So long as I get somewhere," Alice added as an explanation.

"Oh, you're sure to do that," said the Cat, "if you only walk long enough."[1]

At a Work-Study Institute held in Waveland, Mississippi, in February–March, 1965, Stokely Carmichael conducted a class entitled "Stokely's speech class." He placed eight sentences on the blackboard, with a line separating them:

I digs wine.	I enjoy drinking cocktails.
The peoples wants freedom.	The people want freedom.
Whereinsoever the policemens goes they causes troubles.	Anywhere the officers of the law go, they cause trouble.
I wants to reddish to vote.	I want to register to vote.

CARMICHAEL. What do you think about these sentences? Such as— The peoples wants freedom?

ZELMA. It doesn't sound right.

---

[1] Lewis Carroll, *Alice in Wonderland*.

1

CARMICHAEL.   What do you mean?

ZELMA.   "Peoples" isn't right.

CARMICHAEL.   Does it mean anything?

MILTON.   People means everybody. Peoples means everybody in the world.

ALMA.   Both sentences are right as long as you understand them.

HENRY.   They're both okay, but in a speech class you have to use correct English.

(*Carmichael writes "correct English" in corner of blackboard.*)

ZELMA.   I was taught at least to use the sentences on the right side.

CARMICHAEL.   Does anybody you know use the sentences on the left?

CLASS.   Yes.

CARMICHAEL.   Are they wrong?

ZELMA.   In terms of English, they are wrong.

CARMICHAEL.   Who decides what is correct English and what is incorrect English?

MILTON.   People made rules. People in England, I guess.

CARMICHAEL.   You all say some people speak like on the left side of the board. Could they go anywhere and speak that way? Could they go to Harvard?

CLASS.   Yes . . . No. (*Disagreement.*)

CARMICHAEL.   Does Mr. Turnbow speak like on the left side?

CLASS.   Yes.

CARMICHAEL.   Could Mr. Turnbow go to Harvard and speak like that? "I wants to reddish to vote."

CLASS.   Yes.

CARMICHAEL.   Would he be embarrassed?

CLASS.   Yes . . . No!

ZELMA.   He wouldn't be, but I would. It doesn't sound right.

CARMICHAEL.   Suppose someone from Harvard came to Holmes County and said, "I want to register to vote"? Would they be embarrassed?

ZELMA.   No.

CARMICHAEL.   Is it embarrassing at Harvard but not in Holmes County? The way you speak?

MILTON.   It's inherited. It's depending on where you come from. The people at Harvard would understand.

CARMICHAEL.   Do you think the people at Harvard should forgive you?

MILTON. The people at Harvard should help teach us correct English.

ALMA. Why should we change if we understand what we mean?

SHIRLEY. It is embarrassing.

CARMICHAEL. Which way do most people talk?

CLASS. Like on the left.

(*He asks each student. All but two say "left." One says that Southerners speak like on the left, Northerners on the right. Another says the Southerners speak on the left, but the majority of people speak like on the right.*)

CARMICHAEL. Which way do television and radio people speak?

CLASS. Left.

(*There was a distinction made by the class between Northern commentators and local programs. Most programs were local and spoke like on the left, they said.*)

CARMICHAEL. Which way do teachers speak?

CLASS. On the left, except in class.

CARMICHAEL. If most people speak on the left, why are they trying to change these people?

GLADYS. If you don't talk right, society rejects you. It embarrasses other people if you don't talk right.

HANK. But Mississippi society, ours, isn't embarrassed by it.

SHIRLEY. But the middle class wouldn't class us with them.

HANK. They won't accept "reddish." What is reddish? It's Negro dialect and it's something you eat.

CARMICHAEL. Will society reject you if you don't speak like on the right side of the board? Gladys said society would reject you.

GLADYS. You might as well face it, man! What we gotta do is go out and become middle-class. If you can't speak good English, you don't have a car, a job, or anything.

CARMICHAEL. If society rejects you because you don't speak good English, should you learn to speak good English?

CLASS. No!

ALMA. I'm tired of doing what society says. Let society say "reddish" for a while. People ought to just accept each other.

ZELMA. I think we should be speaking just like we always have.

ALMA. If I change for society, I wouldn't be free anyway.

ERNESTINE. I'd like to learn correct English for my own sake.

SHIRLEY. I would, too.

ALMA. If the majority speaks on the left, then a minority must rule society? Why do we have to be accepted by the minority group? (*Lunchtime.*)[2]

Mr. Carmichael's point is well taken, and this text will not presume to deny the originality and strengths of the Negro idiom or that of any other cultural dialect. Any language able to "give me five" for shake hands, discuss a "main squeeze" for best girl, categorize a policeman as "Dudley do right," or term a talkative person "gabagonious" displays a rich flexibility and colloquial inventiveness. And certainly, as Milton claims, our speech is conditioned to an extent by our backgrounds and social heritage: we smile at an ex-president's pronunciation of "Cuber"; many Baltimoreans speak of washing their dishes in the "zink" or pronounce the name of their home city as if it had two syllables—"Balmore"; in the New York area you will hear "foist" and "thoid"; and, of course, when a Southerner mentions "I" it sounds to an outsider like a person having his throat examined.

Though realizing these natural influences which shape our speech, we should still heed the words of Langston Hughes:

> I play it cool
> And dig all jive.
> That's the reason
> I stay alive.
>
> My motto,
> As I live and learn is:
> *Dig and be dug*
> *In return.*[3]

The doctor who cures your head colds and who mends those broken bones spends eight years beyond college learning the complex "jive" of his trade. The plumber who gets the toilet unstopped learns another kind of "jive." "Soul Music" is transmitted by musicians who have learned the language or "jive" of sounds—what a triple beat

---

[2] "Notes about a Class Held by Stokely Carmichael" from Paul Jacobs and Saul Landau, *The New Radicals* (New York: Random House, Inc., 1966), pp. 131–35. Copyright © 1964 by The Student Nonviolent Coordinating Committee. Reprinted by permission of the Student National Coordinating Committee.

[3] "Motto" from Langston Hughes, *The Panther and the Lash* (New York: Alfred A. Knopf, Inc., 1951). Copyright © 1951 by Langston Hughes. Reprinted by permission of the publisher.

means or a quarter-time. Still another important jive, one needed by all of us just to watch TV, or listen to the radio, or read the newspaper, is a form of the English language known as American English. Aside from cultural additions, what each of us contributes to the language, there is a basic storehouse of agreed-upon symbols for expression and communication. Thus we in America refer to a large, solid-hoofed herbivorous mammal as "horse," whereas to our French counterparts it is *le cheval* and to our German friends, *das Pferd*. Also, we have agreed that when writing we should indicate questions by the figure "?". Why couldn't we just as easily use "!" or "$"?

We see that language, like society, has basic rules which must be learned and adhered to in order to prevent breakdowns in communication and ultimate chaos. As Northrop Frye, a literary critic, says:

> English means . . . the mother tongue. As that, it's the most practical subject in the world: you can't understand anything or take any part in your society without it. Wherever illiteracy is a problem, it's as fundamental a problem as getting enough to eat or a place to sleep. The native language takes precedence over every other subject of study; nothing else can compare with it in usefulness.[4]

Any language, especially a written one, has rules and we need to learn these; we live in America and need to learn standard American English (Mr. Carmichael realizes this and uses it when addressing college audiences). But language rules are not simply straightjackets. Once controlled, they can develop and not repress, can free and not confine; our language gives shape to our imagination and expresses our individuality. A famous philosopher said: "The limits of my language mean the limits of my world." It is not surprising then, that Malcolm X, a man so concerned with freedom, admired James Baldwin for his control of language. For, just as in a good swing of the bat or the golf club, control gives power. An ability to handle language properly opens closed doors, enables us to create new worlds.

It does matter which way you go; you must decide this and how far you wish to travel. This textbook proposes to help your teacher give some direction and purpose to your journey. It hopes to help you write good expository prose and better handle the "jive" of the

[4] Northrop Frye, *The Educated Imagination* (Bloomington, Ind.: Indiana University Press, 1964), pp. 14–15.

English language. Secondly, using materials related to things happening in the world around you, it hopes to expand and stretch your mind so that it can never return to its original position. Such a trip requires determination on your part, but it *can* bring you to new worlds.

Essay Development

INTRODUCTION

Have you ever considered just how language began, how early man formulated an organized means of communication? Linguists have tackled this problem in many ways and have come up with some interesting theories. One, called the "bow-wow" theory, proposes that language arose from early man's attempt to duplicate the sounds made by animals. The "ding-dong" theory, on the other hand, states that man first designated items by echoing the sound made when one struck that item. Thus, when "talking" about a tree or block of wood, early man would say "thud" or "konk." Another is the "yo-he-ho" theory. According to this belief, communication arose from rhythmic chants made when men pulled and tugged together.

These are but a few of the theories proposed. They do not satisfy everyone and the search still continues for the beginning of language. In any event, man did eventually associate certain words with objects. The word "tree" became identified with the tall plants which afforded early man shade and sometimes food, "rock" for the hard material used in constructing his home or for attacking his enemies, "woman" for the long-haired creature who cooked his food and bore his children. Gradually our ancestors began to combine words in such a way as to make statements: "woman and rock at tree." Of course we have come a long way, so much so that it is not rare for a man to write a 1,000-page book employing a vocabulary of over 50,000 words.

A later section, *Mechanics of Style,* deals with word problems within the individual sentences and sets certain rules to be followed in writing formal prose. Just as we preserve a certain order in our system of communication by designating rules to be followed in the organization of individual sentences, so too do we employ common patterns in longer pieces. What we call here "Essay Development" is sometimes called "rhetoric." We may think of it in terms of building blocks. Individual words are the blocks which combine to form sentences; sentences, in turn, unite to form paragraphs which, by extension, become themes of several paragraphs or longer essays or even books of considerable length. Of course, we do not expect each of you to write a book; our aim is more modest. It is to aid you in the structure of paragraphs and the organization of several such paragraphs into competent themes. Rhetoric, then, is as *Webster's New World Dictionary* defines it, "the art or science of literary composition." Good writing does not require genius or great gifts of imagination; hard work and proper organization will do the trick.

You have probably noticed that there are different kinds of prose. A glance at the reading section of the corner drugstore confirms this, for there you can find newspapers, comic books, novels, magazines—all language mediums—which employ either narrative, descriptive, or expository prose, or combinations of these. Narrative prose tells a story:

> Long before daylight, I was called to go and rub, curry, and feed the horses. I obeyed, and was glad to obey. But whilst thus engaged, whilst in the act of throwing down some blades from the loft, Mr. Covey entered the stable with a long rope; and just as I was half out of the loft, he caught hold of my legs, and was about tying me. As soon as I found what he was up to, I gave a sudden spring, and as I did so, he holding to my legs, I was brought sprawling on the stable floor. Mr. Covey seemed now to think he had me, and could do what he pleased; but at this moment—from whence came the spirit I don't know—I resolved to fight; and, suiting my action to the resolution, I seized Covey hard by the throat; and as I did so, I rose. He held on to me, and I to him. My resistance was so entirely unexpected, that Covey seemed taken all aback. He trembled like a leaf. . . .[1]

---

[1] Frederick Douglass, *Narrative of the Life of Frederick Douglass* (Garden City, N.Y.: Doubleday & Company, Inc., 1963), pp. 72–73.

Descriptive prose gives a verbal picture of an object or person:

> The schoolhouse was a log hut, where Colonel Wheeler used to shelter his corn. It sat in a lot behind a rail fence and thorn bushes, near the sweetest of springs. There was an entrance where a door once was, and within, a massive rickety fireplace; great chinks between the logs served as windows. Furniture was scarce. A pale blackboard crouched in the corner. My desk was made of three boards, reinforced at critical points, and my chair, borrowed from the landlady, had to be returned every night. Seats for the children [were] . . . rough plank benches without backs, and at times without legs. They had the one virtue of making naps dangerous, possibly fatal, for the floor was not to be trusted.[2]

Expository prose explains:

> The ballpoint is a writing instrument in which a small rolling ball, housed in a socket at the tip, transfers a viscuous ink on to the writing surface. The ball is lubricated by the ink, which moves downward in the reservoir chiefly by the action of gravity. When the pen is not in use the ball is therefore not moving, it seals the end of the reservoir and thus prevents the ink from drying out. The ink is a viscuous liquid containing either an oil-soluble dye or a spirit-soluble dye. The ball is usually made of steel, but in some pens, synthetic sapphire balls have been used. Most manufacturers use a ball 1 mm (0.04 in.) in diameter.[3]

It is the latter form, expository prose, on which this section will focus. Most prose in our society is expository. We read it in the newspapers, in textbooks, in business letters or reports, in legal briefs, in cookbooks. Although it may employ some narration and description, expository prose usually relies more heavily, not on the writer's imagination and vocabulary range, but on sound, logical structure. We establish a certain point that we wish to make and then proceed

---

[2] W. E. B. DuBois, *The Souls of Black Folk* (New York: Fawcett Publications, Inc., 1961), p. 57. Copyright © 1961 by Fawcett Publications, Inc. Reprinted by permission of the publisher.

[3] *The Way Things Work* (New York: Simon and Schuster, Inc., 1967). Published by George Allen and Unwin Ltd. as *The Universal Encyclopedia of Machines* (London, 1967).

through carefully organized sentences and paragraphs to make it. Thus, by its very nature, expository prose can be mastered by most students; it is all a question of putting one's blocks in order.

I. THE PARAGRAPH

A paragraph attempts to deal with a specific subject and to make some significant remarks concerning that subject. It should be a unified, properly developed block, an organized grouping of sentences which develops a basic idea. As such, the paragraph is a most important foundation in the larger structure of the theme and essay; you must be able to handle the single blocks before going on to larger works.

The parts of any paragraph are the *topic sentence* and the *paragraph content*. The topic sentence states the central theme or idea of the paragraph. It is the heart of any paragraph and focuses your reader's attention on the central point you wish to make. The paragraph content is the material used to clarify, illustrate, or explain the topic sentence. All of the content sentences should develop or be associated with the topic sentence; this gives unity to your paragraph.

Remember when writing paragraphs to keep in mind the various stylistic difficulties covered later in the *Mechanics of Style* section, but it is just as important to widen your sights from the individual sentences to the entire structure of several sentences. This would be like watching the precision and teamwork of five basketball players from a distance rather than focusing on the moves and shots of one particular player. Keep your general structure in mind.

Compare the following paragraphs:

A.   The job I held this summer had an influence on my mental and emotional growth. I dreaded the first day that I had to go to work. I was afraid of the new things that I would have to face. This was the first time that I really had a responsibility which depended on me alone. The thought of the people I would work with frightened me. They were people from different backgrounds and I did not know how I would be able to get along with them. I did not know if these people would help me and become my friends or if they would ignore me.

As time progressed I found that I had been silly to think such thoughts. These people helped me as much as they could. They made my work seem like play instead of work. I found that I was always happy to be around them. I wanted to be around them. I began to look forward each day to go to my job.

B. While a surgeon at Provident Hospital, one day Dr. Williams performed an operation that was immediately heralded by newspapers and written about in medical journals around the world. It was the first time in history that such an operation had ever been done successfully. One day a man was brought into the emergency ward with a deep stab wound in the chest, bleeding profusely. Dr. Williams was called. He attended to the man. But the next day when he went to his bedside to see him, the man was worse, and still bleeding internally. To find out why this should be, Dr. Williams opened the wound and extended it so that he might discover the source of the trouble. He found that the man had literally been stabbed to the heart, and that there was a puncture in that vital organ. No one expected the man to live, but Dr. Williams decided to try to save him. The walls of the vessel surrounding the heart were cut and, while other doctors with forceps held these walls open, Dr. Williams carefully sewed up the knife wound in the man's heart. Then he replaced the walls of his heart while it continued beating. To do this required great skill, daring, and very steady nerves. The man lived. And the operation became a famous one in medical history.[4]

How would you evaluate these two paragraphs in terms of topic sentence, unity, and content? What grade or remarks would you place on these papers? One way of answering such questions is to formulate a checklist of essential criteria:

1. TOPIC SENTENCE.
    A. "The job I held this summer had an influence on my mental and emotional growth."—a direct statement that establishes a clear topic for development.
    B. "While a surgeon at Provident Hospital, one day Dr. Williams performed an operation that was immediately heralded by newspapers and written about in medical journals around the world."—same as A.

[4] "Daniel Hale Williams" from Langston Hughes, *Famous American Negroes* (New York: Dodd, Mead & Company, 1954), p. 59. Copyright © 1954 by Langston Hughes. Reprinted by permission of the publisher.

2. UNITY.

A. It appears that all of the sentences develop the topic sentence and that no new subjects not included in the topic sentence are introduced.

B. Same as A.

Thus we see that in terms of mechanics both A and B are proper paragraphs. It is in the third quality, however, that we might make distinctions between the two pieces, and thus rate paragraph B a better paper.

3. CONTENT.

A. Fails to create much interest since the author is seldom concrete. For instance, he never does mention the type of job, where he held it, the kind of people he worked with, etc.

B. The author accompanies the expository explanation of the operation with interesting, concrete narration and description. There is also greater sentence variety and clearer transitions between sentences.

EXERCISE

In a similar fashion, evaluate the following paragraphs to determine which is superior and if there are any breakdowns that need to be corrected.

I. A. The most important sense that an individual has is his sense of smell. The reason I think smelling is the most important is that you can smell the beautiful spring air and good food. I like to smell fresh air, food, grass, flowers, and sweet-smelling perfume. I think smelling is the most essential sense an individual can possess.

B. The sense of sight is a very important sense in that the sense of sight out of all the other ones is used most. I would say this is true because in the world today things are happening so fast a person really has to be on the lookout. The freeways and expressways have signs that must be read quickly to tell where you are going. Cars are one of the most important means of transportation today. So you see the sense of sight is important.

II. A. Both past and present-day westerns give the viewer an idea of the "old days," but the methods of acting have changed considerably. The first western stars performed their stunts as part of the job of acting. Present-day actors seldom place themselves in such dangerous positions. Stunt men and substitutes take the necessary risks which frequent westerns these days. The first westerns used the stereotype plot, the good guy versus the bad guy, but producers of today try to include something for every member of the family. The popularity of the western, however, has given way to many of the modern adventure stories characteristic of our age.

B.   Upon careful investigation of its components, one can easily discern the vast dissimilarities between the traditional western and the contemporary western. The western of a decade ago usually has a superhero who is perfect in every way. He is clean-shaven, handsome, and is dressed immaculately. Of course, his antagonist, dressed in filthy black, consists of the lowest form of humanity. The plot of this type of western is relatively easy to follow, having only a surface meaning. The moral of the story, if any, is that good always conquers evil. The modern western, on the other hand, places more emphasis on the plot and the motives behind the actions of the characters, rather than on the characters themselves. Although the plots are usually very simple, contained in every "adult" western is a moral or a thought-provoking chain of events. Good often wins, but this is not necessary. Another basic difference between the old and new western is the character of the hero. Unlike his predecessor, today's hero usually has one or more faults. One finds cardsharps, drunks, thieves, and bums being portrayed as heroes. Another keynote of today's western is its reality. Unlike the ancient western, in which a cowboy will engage in a fight and his clothes remain unspoiled, the modern western tends to strive toward realism. Consequently, in the span of a decade, one may observe a complete transformation in the western.

III. A.   My bedroom is the most beautiful room in my house. The colors in my room are pale blue and white. On one side of my room there are two beautiful twin beds and a table in the middle of them. The color of the spreads on the beds are pale blue with white pillows. On the other side of the room there are two large dresser drawers which have pretty scarfs on them. And on the floor there is a big white rug which covers the whole floor. My room reminds me of a picture on a postcard.

B.   The Student Union Building is a big brick building with three different parts. It has an upstairs where students go up and play cards and cop those jazzie sounds. When you step in the door it is big on one side. They have card tables where the students play cards most of the time, but in the middle of the room they have a sofa and about two chairs where you can sit down and start a conversation if you want to. Downstairs is the cafeteria. There is a rockola where students eat and listen to music.

II. DEVELOPMENT BY DETAIL

Can you identify the objects being discussed in the following papers?

A.   They are found everywhere around campus, in every building, on every street, and in every dormitory. They are loathed by all students although they are indispensable, for without them we couldn't get to the library, to English class, to the cafeteria, or to the football game. Besides their intended use, people have devised new ones. The practice of cleaning muddy shoes is the first that comes to mind. Toddlers have invented games on them which they play while waiting for their mothers. People sit on them reading, studying, or just watching others go by.

Sitting on them can be a bad practice, for they tend to be eternally dirty. Their physical characteristics are rather difficult to describe, for they vary both in dimension and composition. Ranging in lengths from three feet to thirty yards, they are as little as two inches or as tall as ten and are generally constructed of brick, metal, wood, concrete, or stone. While some are small and almost avoid notice, others are quite imposing with a certain grandeur. Those found in our gym are old and filled with ruts in contrast to those in the new science building which are almost white and geometrically perfect from a distance.

One thing about them that lends them personality is their age and degree of wear. Some on campus are one hundred years old and are part of a national monument, for they served the first students of the university as much as they do now. At the dining hall as at the gym, ruts have been carved by erosion of bricks over the years of usage. Such ruts and dips give them their own certain personality when one considers the famous alumni that have used them.

Whether long or short, high or low, old or new, worn or not they are easily recognized. Someday their use may be obsolete and then abandoned, but until then they remain an integral part of our campus.

B.   While striding semiconsciously from school one day, I decided to take a seat on one of the many green benches in the park. As I sat there gazing around, an ordinary object attracted my attention. Focusing my thoughts on the object, I reflected what it might signify and exactly what it was.

It could symbolize the growth of anything mighty, for example,

America. Yet, it could also stand for a long hard struggle like the education of youth. To many, it means high school, college, and maturity or the growth of the mind. It would seem that an object with these connotations would be large, but its size is deceiving.

It is a little larger than the average marble, dirty brown to almost bronze in color, and has a rigid oval construction. It is nearly beyond all comprehension that locked in its tiny shell is the power to tear up highways, reroute pathways, stop strong winds, and bring countless hours of pleasure for some. It can withstand the harshness of winter cold, wind, and rain, yet it consumes the hot summer sun as if it were an unfed child or a mind yearning for knowledge.

My thoughts were instantly interrupted while a pair of fat squirrels paused under my bench. Before I could react one of the furry beasts lifted my sacred object from its resting place and with a chirp of satisfaction and mockery it scampered up a tree. There it would probably devour it out of my sight or place it in its home for security during the winter's long months.

Your answer, of course, depends on how you interpret the facts given you by the writer. You must relate the facts to each other. Thus the writer has a responsibility to provide you with enough clear, concise details, so that you may determine what is his subject.

Details are important. They are used often for their own sake to gain your reader's interest and attention. In addition, they are used to inform your reader. If you apply for a job, a prospective employer expects a clear summary of your education, your abilities, your references, and so on. So too in any paper your reader demands specific facts. Always keep in mind that facts without generalization is pedantry and that generalization without facts is nonsense.

Discuss the use of details in the following papers:

A. The best time of the year for me is Christmas. Many relatives and friends drop by the house to see our tree and to eat with us. I especially like the great meals that Mother prepares for us at this time. Everyone has plenty to eat, and after spending much time with that knife and fork, I can barely push myself away from the table. It really is a great day. I am only sorry it comes just once a year.

B. They fed stupendously. Eugene began to observe the food and the seasons. In the autumn, they barrelled huge frosty apples in the cellar. Gant bought whole hogs from the butcher, returning home early to salt them, wearing a long work-apron, and rolling his sleeves half up his lean hairy arms. Smoked bacons hung in the pantry, the great bins were full of flour, the dark recessed shelves groaned with preserved cherries, peaches, plums, quinces, apples, pears. . . .

In the morning they rose in a house pungent with breakfast cookery, and they sat at a smoking table loaded with brains and eggs, ham, hot biscuit, fried apples seething in their gummed syrups, honey, golden butter, fried steak, scalding coffee. Or there were stacked battercakes, rum-colored molasses, fragrant brown sausages, a bowl of wet cherries, plums, fat juicy bacon, jam. At the mid-day meal, they ate heavily: a huge hot roast of beef, fat buttered lima beans, tender corn smoking on the cob, thick red slabs of sliced tomatoes, rough savory spinach, hot yellow corn bread, flaky biscuits, a deep-dish peach and apple cobbler spiced with cinnamon, tender cabbage, deep glass dishes piled with preserved fruits—cherries, pears, peaches. At night they might eat fried steak, hot squares of grits fried in egg and butter, pork chops, fish, young fried chicken.[1]

C.   It is obvious in Mr. Kunitz's poem "The War Against the Trees" that he conveys a very pessimistic and dejected tone to his audience. He seems to say that the destruction of these simple but living things is disgraceful. The best analysis of his intended tone is seen in the last stanza. Here he expresses a truly strong emotional involvement with all the preceding occurrences. The words which he uses here are much stronger and more meaningful than the ones previously used. His tone and established mood create a really hideous scene filled with terrible reality.

D.   Throughout the "The War Against the Trees" the efforts to destroy the trees are criticized. The bulldozers are described as being "drunk with gasoline" and as "hireling engines" which "charged" their victims. This gives the reader the impression that they are very aggressive and suffer little remorse for their actions. One can almost picture them as a ruthless army annihilating everything in its path. The term "hireling" itself suggests mercenary motives. On the other hand, a more favorable approach is taken towards the trees. They are spoken of as "giants" who are forced "to their knees." They are not just uprooted, but are "ripped from the craters." This gives the feeling that they are rather noble and that their downfall is unjust. The vivid account of their destruction suggests a violent death.

[1] Thomas Wolfe, *Look Homeward, Angel* (New York: Charles Scribner's Sons, 1957), pp. 55–56. Copyright © 1929 Charles Scribner's Sons; renewal copyright © 1957 Edward C. Aswell, C.T.A. and/or Fred W. Wolfe. Reprinted with permission of the publisher.

E.   Mr. Johnny Michaels, my uncle, is a man of very incredible musical talent. Mr. Michaels is twenty-seven years of age, light complexion, slender but muscular features, and six feet, three inches tall. He is capable of playing almost any musical instrument, either with the music or by ear. His favorite instruments are the string instruments, especially the guitar. While playing this instrument, he usually has an indifferent smile on his face, has his head tilted to one side, and moves his lanky fingers over the strings in order to get the feel of the instrument. This especially takes place when he is about to play jazz, his favorite type of music. Yet my uncle is a man who believes that all music is art, whether it is jazz, religious, classical, rock 'n' roll, or folk.

F.   My mother is one of the greatest people in the world. She is a person with a mild temperament. She will do all she can to help others, but will not let anyone take advantage of her. By taking advantage, I mean that she will do all she can to help a person, but she will not help them continue to persuade her to stay in the same rut. She did not finish school, but encourages other children as well as her own to be someone. She has helped us a whole lot and is truly a great person.

III. DEVELOPMENT BY EXAMPLE

When we use details to illustrate a general point they become examples. *Examples* are those concrete elements used to support and clarify and not just to describe or interest. Thus when we say that "Jim Brown was born in Cleveland, Ohio, in 1932 and attended Syracuse University," we are giving some interesting and important details about his life. But when we make the statement "Jim Brown is the greatest runner in the history of the National Football League," we then need to support such a statement with relevant details. To convince you that we are right, we might point out that while a fullback for the Cleveland Browns from 1957–1965, Brown gained over 12,000 yards, led the league in rushing for eight seasons, had an average yards per carry lifetime mark of 5.22, and scored 106 touchdowns in his career. These details become examples. We use them to prove that our assertion is correct.

You can also see how examples are another means of developing a paragraph. The topic sentence (such as "Jim Brown is the greatest runner in the history of football") or other key sentences will often be general statements that must be supported or clarified by specific facts. This is the work of examples.

Let us examine this idea in greater detail in terms of a specific assignment. You are asked to explain what is meant by the word "cool," a word used in a variety of ways to mean different things. Give some thought to this question yourself and then evaluate the following paper:

> "Cool," as it is often used today, is a modern slang word given general meaning by teenagers. To anyone unfamiliar with the moods and passions of the young generation, the word appears to have only a descriptive meaning pertaining to that temperature which is in between cold and comfortable, but the youth of this country have changed and broadened its meaning. They use it to describe the prestige of a thing, event, or person, and its prestige is always highly favorable. Actually, the best description of one who believes he is "cool" is that he is manifesting his innate sense of decorum. He thinks quite a bit of himself and expects others to also. In describing events and objects, the word usually describes amazement and intrigue. Always the connotations of the word to those who understand and use it have been good, and since it covers many meanings, it has been popularly used. Nevertheless, it appears just to be a fad that will soon pass.

Do you find this discussion convincing? Is it interesting to read? How would you improve it? Remember the discussion in the first chapter of this section on the paragraph; use what you learned there to evaluate this paper.

Evaluate the following papers in the same manner:

> A.   "Cool" is just another word that I use for being smart. Smart enough to stay out of trouble. Smart enough to go with girls. I said this because this is the way I play cool. When most of my classmates were drinking wine before going to class every morning, I drank along with them to keep them from calling me chicken. After I had done this for awhile I quit, just before the principal cracked down on the fellows. I played it cool. Another way I play cool is with the girls. I never have a steady girl friend. If we have to break up it never hurts me, because I have many more. Even if I was hurt, nobody would

know, I would go on having fun and dating. This is how I would be playing cool.

B.   What qualities must a man possess to be classed as "cool"? Among all men of the elite group, an air of arrogance is found. This arrogance stems from their ability to be leaders and not followers. Suaveness is also a necessary asset of this type of man; he must know how to act and what to say at all times. The second of these two qualities is the foremost. A knowledge of correct word usage and the ability to say the right thing at the correct time separates a cool person from a peon. It can be seen that these characteristics are not easily obtained, but one should strive for them in the hope of one day being classed as a "cool" man.

C.   "Cool" is the slang expression used mostly by the teenage set to describe certain acts or personality traits. The acts which are designated as "cool" vary with the type of group using the word. Some motorcycle gangs (such as "Hell's Angels") consider it "cool" to beat up a policeman or to rape a young girl. This is exactly opposite of the meaning of the word when used by the more lawful groups. Talking someone into doing your work could be considered as a "cool" act by others. A unique style someone has for playing a sport—such as a left-handed catcher in baseball—could be considered "cool." A lack of expressed emotion also denotes a person as being "cool." A quarterback pulls his team from behind in the last quarter with seemingly no effort at all. A criminal under interrogation by the police shows no excitement or loss of composure. These are examples of a "cool" personality. Thus, there are two types of action that are considered "cool." One is a certain unusual or cunning act. The other type concerns an emotionless personality during times of stress.

IV. DEVELOPMENT BY COMPARISON-CONTRAST

In this type of development one explores the similarities and differences between two things—the Yankees and Dodgers, grade school and high school, the Democratic Party and the Republican Party, city and country.

In discussing any two things you must first decide what are the *bases* of discussion; that is, what elements do the individual subjects

have in common. For instance, when comparing and contrasting base-ball teams, you might deal with batting power, fielding ability, and coaching since these topics are relevant to both teams.

Having chosen the bases of discussion, you must then decide how to organize your ideas. We often do this unconsciously, but there are some set, ordered patterns that can be followed. We can illustrate the two major methods with selections from student papers discussing the following picture:

American Gothic by Grant Wood.
Courtesy of The Art Institute of Chicago.

I. You can consecutively discuss the two subjects within one paragraph or in several paragraphs:

Mr. and Mrs. Walker live in the country, where they work very hard. They have a large farm which is very clean and neat. They raise corn, tomatoes, fruit, vegetables, and many other things. They have been living on this farm all of their lives and they won't leave it.

Mr. Walker seems to be a very easy man. He believes in having nice food and a nice house. He has worked hard all of his life and he seems tired. But Mrs. Walker is a stern person who never gets tired of working. She bosses Mr. Walker around and she tells him what to do. She is very mean and doesn't like children. But Mr. Walker loves children and he would like to have some on his farm. Mrs. Walker thinks they will destroy their fruit and other crops.

I think that when Mr. and Mrs. Walker took that picture they had been to church. Mr. Walker likes to dress casually and neatly. Mrs. Walker thinks that one is supposed to dress up. She seems to like jewelry because she has a necklace around her neck. Mr. Walker's bald head and skinny body means that he is getting old. Mrs. Walker still looks young and has pretty hair.

So I think Mr. and Mrs. Walker are very different from each other. But they love each other.

II. You can discuss the subjects separately in different paragraphs:

Mr. and Mrs. Woods are a strange couple. Their personalities, facial expressions, and dress seem to be an outside appearance of what they are.

Mr. Woods is a very unfriendly man who shows kindness to no one. The glare in his eyes seems to say, "Don't speak to me and I'll turn you the same favor." His lips seem to protrude just enough to keep a harsh word ready to go. His nose seems to be trained to remain turned up at everyone, including his wife. His ears are standing alert for someone to say something, even speak to him, and give him a reason to defy them. His dress indicates that he is a farmer and wants no part of anything else. His entire wardrobe consists of the same thing. He never goes to church or anywhere else, so he needs no more clothes.

Mrs. Woods, however, seems to have once been a mild-mannered, sweet, loving person. However, her contact with her husband has changed all of this. For she has turned into a mean, grouchy, hard-working woman. Deep in her heart, perhaps, some kindness remains, but she knows better than to let it show. Her mouth is set in a thin line which reveals the hurt and heartfelt pity she has seen during the last thirty years. Her golden hair is fixed in the style of a good farmer's wife. Her eyes seem to drift afar with wonder. She wonders if her husband will ever change. She wishes he would reform himself and become a man she could really love. The troubled face of Mrs. Woods has every right to be. Her dress portrays her life of dullness. She always wears conservative colors which she feels appropriate for her situation.

Mr. and Mrs. Woods, this strange couple, are alone in their own world which has no room for anyone else.

EXERCISE

Evaluate the following papers in terms of organization and development.

A.   Wilbur and Ellen Jones were brought up in a small farm town in North Carolina. They have been married for twenty years. As children they had a very strict social upbringing.

Wilbur Jones was born into a very strict low-class family. Wilbur's parents made him stay at home every night, except Sundays when he would call on Ellen. He could square dance a little but never did except at a church social or a barn dance occasionally. He went to the movies once or twice but never to a night club. Once he came home at ten o'clock! His parents made him sleep in the barn that night. He does not drink or smoke, but he does chew tobacco sometimes.

Ellen Jones was born into a very simple family. She was allowed to go to church on Sunday if her mother went. She never went to the movies, a night club, or a carnival. When she was going with Wilbur, she could go to a barn dance only if her mother came too. She was very shy and danced only with Wilbur. Once while she and Wilbur were still engaged, they stayed in the parlor until nine o'clock. Her people were in a rage. They made her stop seeing Wilbur for two months. She enjoys sewing and knitting.

B.   Mr. and Mrs. Woods are a happily married couple. They are celebrating their sixtieth anniversary.

As a gift to their grandchildren, they are having a picture made in front of their home. Mrs. Woods is wearing a blue dress with a white collar and a brown pinafore which was probably worn in 1895. She has blonde hair that reminds you of yellow grass in a meadow. Mrs. Woods has no wrinkles on her ageless face. She looks frightened.

Mr. Woods is an aged man who wears glasses because of poor vision. Over a period of years, the worry of his corn fields has made him bald. The wrinkles upon his once rosy cheeks come from so much stress and strain while working in the fields all hours of the day. The pitchfork in his hand is evidence of a tedious day in the barn pitching hay. The physical features prove that he is ready to lay his weary bones to rest.

C.   Mr. and Mrs. Woods live in the late nineteenth century or the early twentieth century.

Mr. Woods is a man who seems to be concerned only with his work. He seems to be a grouchy and cold-hearted person. His personality has apparently rubbed off on his wife. They both are fuss machines when they are home alone. The Woods have been married thirty years and are childless. Mrs. Woods has often wanted children, but Mr. Woods has often rejected the idea. This is the only time she has opposed her husband during their marriage. The Woods seldom associate with other people, except when they go into town for supplies.

The farm is kept in top condition. Johnny, one of Mr. Woods' neighbors, helps him out in the field.

V. THE THEME

Chapter I dealt with the organization and development of a single paragraph. A *theme* is a union of several paragraphs, ones still guided by the basic principles of topic sentence and paragraph content. Writing a theme requires you to juggle a few more balls than writing a paragraph. You must, for example, be aware of the *introductory paragraph,* the *body* of several paragraphs, and the *concluding paragraph;* all of these elements constitute a well organized theme and should be balanced evenly.

A theme can be constructed in terms of blocks. We have already discussed problems in individual sentences and paragraphs. What we said then is also applicable to themes. In addition, the theme must be more carefully organized since it is a larger unit. One useful way to do this is to think of the paper in terms of blocks as shown on the following page.

Blocks A and E are your introductory and concluding paragraphs, while B, C, and D constitute the body of your paper. We discuss A and E in the following sections, so let us move right into the body of the paper. Examine the following paper:

Mr. Webster defines school as being "an institution for learning." I agree with this. But my definition of a perfect school would be an institution of learning that has the following qualities: proper facilities, good teachers, and the choice of subject matter.

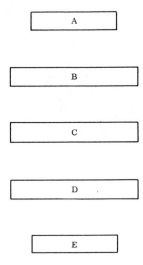

First, proper facilities should include a good snack bar, clean rest rooms, and large classrooms. The reason why I say a good snack bar is that so often we come across schools that don't have anything but a lunchroom, and students tend to go off campus to a nearby store; this can result in trouble. The same holds true with the rest rooms. Some students have brought out the fact that they think the rest rooms are supposed to be the cleanest part of a building because they can be the disease spreader. The classrooms should be designed so that the largest class will be as comfortable as the smallest one. Also, all classrooms should have good lighting in order that the students will not hurt their eyes.

Second, good teachers are needed. These impart knowledge successfully without favoritism and prejudice. Too often teachers favor one student better than another.

Finally, the choice of subject matter is important. A student should be able to choose any subject he wishes to take; of course, the guidance counselor should help him in these decisions. So often a student may be thrown into something he doesn't want and, as a result, may not do his best. His grades may suffer. For example, in the school I attended many students were taking geometry who wanted to take trigonometry, and many in the trigonometry class wanted algebra or advanced mathematics. They unfortunately were not allowed into these classes. The results were apparent at the end of the grading period.

But even with these qualities, the rest is up to the student. He will learn nothing if he does not want to, and no one can make him.

A block diagram of this paper would look something like this:

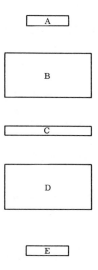

As this diagram indicates, the third paragraph (C) is too brief and does not fit well into the total organization of the paragraph. Try to organize your own paragraphs so that they are of similar length and develop individual topics thoroughly. Newspapers often contain very brief paragraphs, but we are interested in more formal structures.

Outline the block designs of the following themes and then discuss the individual paragraphs:

A. To analyze "The War Against the Trees" intelligently, it is essential that the reader grasp the message that the poet is trying to convey. More important too is an analysis of the manner in which the poet presents his message.

In "The War Against the Trees," the reader is not concerned primarily with who is speaking so much as he is concerned with what is being said. The poet gives a precise description of the destruction of property which takes place throughout the poem. He achieves these images through a delicate choice of words. The poet does not refer merely to bulldozers tearing up the soil. Rather, he describes them as "bulldozers drunk with gasoline." The poet envisions the clearing of the property as a general would envision a battle: "All day the hireling engines charged the trees . . . forcing the giants to their knees." The poet uses words like "gorgons" to describe the roots of a tree which have been torn from the soil. He likens their appearance to the head of Medusa.

Since the poem is written in free verse, the poet has allowed himself the freedom to say what he desires to say without concerning himself with the limitations of a steady rhyme scheme or strict meter. His diction is common, mixed with a few exceptions which enhance the quality of the poem.

The meaning of the poem becomes evident in the last two lines of the poem: "One witness-moment, caught in the rear-view mirrors of the passing cars." This whole sense of destruction which has moved the poet, is hardly noticed by the people driving past in their cars. It is almost as if the people see but don't care enough to stop and take notice.

B.   Throughout "The War Against the Trees" Mr. Kunitz uses personification. The title itself is evidence of this; the idea of waging war implies two sides capable of movement in defense of themselves. Obviously trees cannot defend themselves. Therefore the title attributes to them the human quality of defense.

The first example that occurs in the body of the poem is in the third line: "While the bulldozers, drunk with gasoline." Bulldozers here are given the quality of drunkenness. This line also implies that the bulldozers are acting of their own accord and are not controlled by men. The intoxication of the bulldozers implies that they do not realize what they are doing; man does not realize the wrong he is committing either.

The second personification of the machines appears in line thirteen: "All day the hireling engines charged the trees." Here the word "hireling," which means a person employed to do a job, is applied to the engines, meaning the machines used to clear the land. Here too we see the word "charged," which in the military sense means an attack mounted against the opposition, giving to the engines again the quality of independent action.

Now in reference to things of nature such as trees and soil rather than manufactured goods, there are also many examples of personification that can be seen in this poem.

The first such example appears in line four: "Tested the virtue of the soil." "Virtue" is a word applied to the good qualities of a person, such as his courage or strength. Here the word applies to the strength of the soil. But the use of the word also implies courage to resist the machinery.

The second example appears in line nine: "Against the great-grandfathers of the town." "Great-grandfathers" applies to a person's relationship to his grandson's children. Trees have no children, but it does imply their age. However, it does attribute to the trees the quality of having children, which is obviously a personification.

In the next line "So freshly lopped and maimed" the word "maimed" usually applies to human injury, not that of trees. Again this personification, using a word or phrase that attributes to something not human a human quality.

In conclusion I would like to say that the use of personification in this poem suggests a war of man against himself or man inadvertently working against himself by bringing the trees and the machines to the level of man.

C. The use of imagery in "The War Against the Trees" shows the author's view on what is taking place in the poem. He is not in favor of the destruction of the trees or the childhood dreams they bring back, and his technique of writing makes that clear. It enables him to show this to his audience without directly expressing it.

Throughout the work, the efforts to destroy the trees are criticized. The bulldozers are described as "drunk with gasoline" and as "hireling engines" which "charged" their victims. This gives the reader the impression that they are very aggressive and suffer little remorse for their actions. One can almost picture them as a ruthless army annihilating everything in its path. The term "hireling" itself suggests mercenary motives. On the other hand, a more favorable approach is taken towards the trees. They are spoken of as "giants" who are forced 'to their knees." They are not just uprooted, but are "ripped from the craters." This gives the feeling that they are rather noble and that their downfall is unjust. The vivid account of their destruction suggests a violent death.

By use of these images he has created, the author accomplishes what he desires. He establishes a picture for the reader which is basically favorable to the trees and against the bulldozers. What is significant about this is that he doesn't use direct criticism to do so. That is, he doesn't come right out and say that he is against what the speaker sees, but he implies this in his style of writing. For example, instead of just saying that the roots were torn out of the ground, he writes about "amputated coils" and "pocks and scars." It almost appears as if he is talking about a human being's injuries. This arouses a sense of pity and sympathy. The forces of destruction in the poem are seen in an evil sense, which is the way they are meant to be seen. Just the fact that the reader recognizes that they appear in this manner shows that the author has succeeded in his purpose.

Imagery is used throughout the poem. There are examples of it in each stanza. For the most part, they are figurative in their function. This makes them more effective, because it is easier to present an idea through use of connotations such as the before-mentioned "drunk with gasoline" phrase. It is easier to set a mood and to get a message across by utilizing this style of writing.

VI. INTRODUCTORY PARAGRAPH

The introductory paragraph "introduces" the reader to your topic. Thus, as in an introduction of a friend on the social level, it should be clear and accurate. When writing an introductory paragraph, you have a choice of how to organize it. You can do it one of three ways:

1. A single organizing sentence drawing together your basic topics.
2. A single organizing sentence which then moves into a full discussion of the first part of your paper.
3. A single organizing sentence with a few sentences to clarify it.

For example, apply these suggestions to the following paragraphs. We have printed the first sentence of the second paragraph to indicate the direction in which the paper is moving.

> A. F. Scott Fitzgerald presents *The Great Gatsby* in a fashion similar to Joseph Conrad's short story, "Heart of Darkness." The structure, images, and relations coincide to a great extent. Each author uses a narrator, who presents a brief summary of past events as well as the present situation to the reader.
>
> Another aspect of structure concerns character development.

> B. In *The Great Gatsby,* by Scott Fitzgerald, and "Heart of Darkness" by Joseph Conrad, there are several relationships in structure, character, and meaning. In the structure, the most obvious similarity is the way each story is narrated. In "Heart of Darkness" it is Marlow who tells the story, and in *The Great Gatsby* it is Nick. Both of these men are characters in the story they tell, and each of them tells the story in the first person. Another similarity in structure is the way the climax is reached when the main character is killed. This is Kurtz in the one book and Gatsby in the other.
>
> There are more similarities in the characters of these two stories than in the structure.

> C. In F. Scott Fitzgerald's novel, *The Great Gatsby,* the observant reader finds the use of symbols to be very important. Through the

use of such concrete objects as ash heaps, billboards, wharf lights, and others, Fitzgerald proceeds to weave an intricate web of human relationships characteristic of the Jazz Age. The symbols are used to bring basic concepts and ideas out of the realm of the abstract and into the realm of concrete reality.

Perhaps the most important symbol in the entire novel is the green light illuminating Daisy's wharf.

Notice that paragraph A has one major flaw. After organizing the paper around the topic subdivisions of "structures, images, and relations," the writer moves immediately into a discussion of the structure. This would be fine except that he does not carry through the discussion. This one sentence in no way develops the first part of his topic.

Paragraph B could be more clearly written, but in general it is an acceptable introductory paragraph. The first sentence is the organizing sentence, while the remainder of the paragraph develops the first part of the topic. Notice that the first sentence in the second paragraph provides an effective transition to the second part of the paper.

Paragraph C illustrates the third method. The second sentence establishes the major topic that will be developed. The remainder of the paragraph clarifies what is meant by "symbol."

Discuss the introductory paragraphs in the following papers:

A. Surely in the course of a semester spent at a large university one would expect to be confronted with a number of critical situations, each contributing in its own way toward character development. However, isolating a single experience from the many happenings of the first semester, and asserting it would be extremely difficult, and, at best, mere guesswork. During the past semester I encountered a new way of life in a new environment. I became associated with many new ideas and many new people. I was challenged in ways I had never been challenged before. More important than any single event seems to be the effect or impression left by the sum total of all my experiences. In view of this there is a recent experience, which is somewhat of a summary or continuation of my impressions over the entire first semester, that best bears description here.

Only a couple of times over the entire year had dear old Mom failed to write on schedule, and then she was only a day or two late. In the early fall I had not thought much about her letters, but as the year went on I began to appreciate them. That seems to be generally true about a lot of things. I began to appreciate my parents more.

People and things that I had never really been concerned about became important. I gained an increased awareness of life, and sought a better understanding of it. Often I pondered over the essential questions of life. I found life at the university to be complex and fascinating; yet at times it was disgusting and simple—in short, basically the same as life anywhere.

As always, Tuesday brought a letter from home. But this one was different. There was not the usual gay greeting, and the news of interesting developments in the family and around town. Instead there was a clipping attached to the front of the letter. Somehow, before I had had time to read the headline beneath the picture, I sensed what had happened. Slowly, unwillingly, my eyes confirmed what I had feared. One of my best friends, a boy I had grown up with, gone to school and graduated with, had been killed in Vietnam. For a long while I just sat, stunned. Countless memories flashed through my mind. I considered many thoughts on life and death. Sure, everyone dies sooner or later, and I personally don't fear death at all, but it is nevertheless a moving and profound aspect of life. The death of a friend cannot help but create a rather shocking effect. Yet this effect can also yield rather subtle comments whose application may be beneficial in life.

I don't know in what way this event developed my character, if indeed, it did at all. I do know that it and most of the experiences of the first semester have contributed to broaden the scope of my life.

B. In my estimation the major problems confronting the city in the next decade are high taxes, unemployment, and poor housing. Without a good house especially, you can not really live a good life. My own family has a small apartment for which they pay $90 a month. It is cleaner than most, but we still have some cold days when the heating system breaks down. Also, the plaster is falling apart.

Another problem with the house is that it is on the fifth floor of our building. . . .

C. English 101 has a definite place in the life of many students at Smithfield College. It gives a good background for the development of better writing techniques. It also helps the student to understand and enjoy fiction.

English 101 causes the student to examine his material carefully in order to determine whether or not he can present the facts in a precise manner. The student learns to formulate a plan for writing each individual theme, because he realizes that each different topic needs special attention and that the topic itself may suggest a method for development of the main idea. The student also learns to project his thoughts more clearly through the correct usage of words and grammatical constructions. He learns to delete all nonessential facts and add only those that are absolutely necessary for a better understanding of the subject. By first learning the proper writing techniques through English 101 the student will almost invariably begin to express his opinions more clearly on any question.

English 101 also plays an important part in teaching the student to appreciate the various elements of fiction. It presents stories that are clearly written with a specific purpose in mind. Each of the stories of a particular kind are placed in a group that is characterized by a certain element of fiction. It then shows how that particular element helps to relate to the general understanding and enjoyment of the story.

I highly praise English 101 because it helped me to learn better organization of my themes and a better understanding of fiction.

VII. CONCLUDING PARAGRAPH

Compare the final remarks in the following papers:

A.   Perhaps the most important factor in our world and lives today is the making of decisions. There comes a time in everyone's life when decisions must be made. Some are large and some are small, yet they must be handled carefully.

One of the most intricate decisions that has confronted me was the one in which college before or after marriage was involved. This decision would prove to be the controlling trend of my future life. After a great deal of serious thought, I decided to take college and forget marriage. This was perhaps the most difficult decision to cross my path.

As the world rotates on its axis, decisions are the most important factor. For without them, man could exist no longer.

B.   I decided to enter college because I believed that an education was very important. In today's world an education is important with the modern changes we are having.

After graduation from high school, I enrolled in a junior college. I attended the college for only half a semester and then dropped out. Then I got a job and started working. Most of the people with whom I worked were educated.

This meant a great deal to me, watching the other people who were educated, and knowing that their education didn't take a lifetime.

In the first paper you know that the writer is finished, although she uses an overly elaborate figure of speech to bring the paper to a close. The second paper, though, leaves you hanging; you expect the writer to continue. The addition of one brief sentence—such as "Thus I returned to college"—would have eliminated the abrupt ending and notified the reader that the writer was finished.

Effective conclusions are needed to make the paper a finished whole. As you probably noticed, one can conclude a paper effectively without devoting a full paragraph to it; the length of your conclusion often depends on the length of the paper itself. In general, the concluding paragraph summarizes the basic points or conclusions drawn in the body of the paper. The following paper is a good example:

> Of all the urban problems facing us today, the three most important are inadequate education, inadequate housing, and inadequate job opportunities.
>
> Urban school systems have increasingly admitted their failure to solve the problems of adequate education for students of low-income minority groups. These groups constitute the major population of our urban centers. The educators of these groups fail to take into consideration various environmental and cultural differences. In many cases the teacher's expectation of substandard performance elicits a poor response from the student. Realization of the fact that ghetto students have abilities more than equal to their suburban counterparts (given the proper opportunities) constitutes the first step toward a successful educational system.
>
> One of the prerequisites for elimination of urban problems is adequate housing. Conditions such as five or six families living in a single-family dwelling, and four or five children sleeping in one bed, are known to exist in cities such as Boston, New York, Chicago, Philadelphia, and Los Angeles. These living conditions create worse ones; rats, roaches, and bedbugs are common in urban America. Adequate low-income housing must be provided, preferably on a non-political basis, and rental requirements and building codes must be maintained.
>
> In order to obtain adequate education and adequate living conditions, the members of minority groups must have adequate job opportunities. All individuals, regardless of background, should be

allowed to develop to the full limit of their potential, and should share equally in the benefits that society offers. Many positions are still not available to minority groups. When the father is employed in a responsible position and feels that he is an integral part of society, his children will have an example to emulate.

Only when people have adequate education, adequate housing, and adequate job opportunities can we expect them to act as adequate citizens of society.

Evaluate the conclusions in the following papers:

A.   My sister, Eileen Evans, is eight years old. She is about five feet tall and of average weight. She is a very stubborn person. She does anything to accomplish her means. Although she finds school a very difficult experience, she is a persistent student. Recently she was chosen to participate in a class composed of students from all schools in the city system. She and my small brother, Joseph, are constantly at each other's throats. She will do almost anything to get him in trouble. Every day when my mother comes home, she tries to convince her that my brother played longer than he was supposed to or did not do his chores or something of this nature.

B.   Having just finished dinner, I noticed the salt in front of me and suddenly realized how tasteless food would be without it. Salt, a fine, white crystalline granule, is easily distinguished from sugar—which it closely resembles in appearance—by taste. Salt's flavor is spicy, whereas sugar's is much sweeter, although both have the capacity to excite one's taste buds. Uncommonly referred to as sodium chloride, it is used as a seasoning on meats, vegetables, and fruits; it is also used to cure and preserve fish and pork products. Being so abundant, it is inexpensive and can be found in homes throughout the world. Due to its characteristics of being useful, plentiful, and inexpensive, salt seems to be taken for granted, but these same characteristics suggest that it will not be replaced easily.

C.   Many changes have taken place in my life during the first semester here at school. My thoughts and ideas have gradually changed from what they were before I left home, especially about such things as extracurricular activities, the opposite sex, my family, and my religious and political views. I believe that I have begun to mix well with all kinds of people who give me a broader and somewhat more liberal view of themselves and the world in which we live.

My ideas towards extracurricular activities such as student government and athletics have rather drastically changed. In high school I was very active in these two fields, and now I don't seem to be as interested. I have found that I would rather make better grades and leave some of these other activities alone.

My attitude towards the opposite sex has passed into another stage. I have become better acquainted with females lately and have enjoyed their company more. I now like to think of females with whom I associate as grown women.

Since I have been away from home, I have found that I appreciate it more. My parents, my brother, and his wife all mean more to me now. I miss them and am always glad to get a chance to go home. The love, fellowship, and all the benefits of home look better now than they did before.

My religious and political views are changing and moving farther away from the views of my parents. I think many students in college tend to drift away from the church, and they also take more interest in politics. This has been the case with me.

Critical Thinking

the minister in society

The Minister's Black Veil: A Parable[1]

1.

The sexton stood in the porch of Milford meeting-house, pulling busily at the bell-rope. The old people of the village came stooping along the street. Children, with bright faces, tripped merrily beside their parents, or mimicked a graver gait, in the conscious dignity of their Sunday clothes. Spruce bachelors looked sidelong at the pretty maidens, and fancied that the Sabbath sunshine made them prettier than on week days. When the throng had mostly streamed into the porch, the sexton began to toll the bell, keeping his eye on the Reverend Mr. Hooper's door. The first glimpse of the clergyman's figure was the signal for the bell to cease its summons.

2.

"But what has good Parson Hooper got upon his face?" cried the sexton in astonishment.

3.

All within hearing immediately turned about, and beheld the semblance of Mr. Hooper, pacing slowly his meditative way towards the meeting-house. With one accord they started, expressing more

---

"The Minister's Black Veil: A Parable" from Nathaniel Hawthorne, *Selected Tales and Sketches* (New York: Holt, Rinehart & Winston, Inc., 1964), pp. 123–37.

[1] Another clergyman in New England, Mr. Joseph Moody, of York, Maine, who died about eighty years since, made himself remarkable by the same eccentricity that is here related of the Reverend Mr. Hooper. In his case, however, the symbol had a different import. In early life he had accidentally killed a beloved friend; and from the day till the hour of his own death, he hid his face from men. [Hawthorne's note.]

wonder than if some strange minister were coming to dust the cushions of Mr. Hooper's pulpit.

4.   "Are you sure it is our parson?" inquired Goodman Gray of the sexton.

5.   "Of a certainty it is good Mr. Hooper," replied the sexton. "He was to have exchanged pulpits with Parson Shute, of Westbury; but Parson Shute sent to excuse himself yesterday, being to preach a funeral sermon."

6.   The cause of so much amazement may appear sufficiently slight. Mr. Hooper, a gentlemanly person, of about thirty, though still a bachelor, was dressed with due clerical neatness, as if a careful wife had starched his band, and brushed the weekly dust from his Sunday's garb. There was but one thing remarkable in his appearance. Swathed about his forehead, and hanging down over his face, so low as to be shaken by his breath, Mr. Hooper had on a black veil. On a nearer view it seemed to consist of two folds of crape, which entirely concealed his features, except the mouth and chin, but probably did not intercept his sight, further than to give a darkened aspect to all living and inanimate things. With this gloomy shade before him, good Mr. Hooper walked onward, at a slow and quiet pace, stooping somewhat, and looking on the ground, as is customary with abstracted men, yet nodding kindly to those of his parishioners who still waited on the meeting-house steps. But so wonder-struck were they that his greeting hardly met with a return.

7.   "I can't really feel as if good Mr. Hooper's face was behind that piece of crape," said the sexton.

8.   "I don't like it," muttered an old woman, as she hobbled into the meeting-house. "He has changed himself into something awful, only by hiding his face."

9.   "Our parson has gone mad!" cried Goodman Gray, following him across the threshold.

10.   A rumor of some unaccountable phenomenon had preceded Mr. Hooper into the meeting-house, and set all the congregation astir. Few could refrain from twisting their heads towards the door; many stood upright, and turned directly about; while several little boys clambered upon the seats, and came down again with a terrible racket. There was a general bustle, a rustling of the women's gowns and shuffling of the men's feet, greatly at variance with that hushed repose which should attend the entrance of the minister. But Mr.

Hooper appeared not to notice the perturbation of his people. He entered with an almost noiseless step, bent his head mildly to the pews on each side, and bowed as he passed his oldest parishioner, a white-haired great grandsire, who occupied an arm-chair in the centre of the aisle. It was strange to observe how slowly this venerable man became conscious of something singular in the appearance of his pastor. He seemed not fully to partake of the prevailing wonder, till Mr. Hooper had ascended the stairs, and showed himself in the pulpit, face to face with his congregation, except for the black veil. That mysterious emblem was never once withdrawn. It shook with his measured breath, as he gave out the psalm; it threw its obscurity between him and the holy page, as he read the Scriptures; and while he prayed, the veil lay heavily on his uplifted countenance. Did he seek to hide it from the dread Being whom he was addressing?

Such was the effect of this simple piece of crape, that more than [11.] one woman of delicate nerves was forced to leave the meeting-house. Yet perhaps the pale-faced congregation was almost as fearful a sight to the minister, as his black veil to them.

Mr. Hooper had the reputation of being a good preacher, but not [12.] an energetic one; he strove to win his people heavenward by mild, persuasive influences, rather than to drive them thither by the thunders of the Word. The sermon which he now delivered was marked by the same characteristics of style and manner as the general series of his pulpit oratory. But there was something, either in the sentiment of the discourse itself, or in the imagination of the auditors, which made it greatly the most powerful effort that they had ever heard from their pastor's lips. It was tinged, rather more darkly than usual, with the gentle gloom of Mr. Hooper's temperament. The subject had reference to secret sin, and those sad mysteries which we hide from our nearest and dearest, and would fain conceal from our own consciousness, even forgetting that the Omniscient can detect them. A subtle power was breathed into his words. Each member of the congregation, the most innocent girl, and the man of hardened breast, felt as if the preacher had crept upon them, behind his awful veil, and discovered their hoarded iniquity of deed or thought. Many spread their clasped hands on their bosoms. There was nothing terrible in what Mr. Hooper said, at least, no violence; and yet, with every tremor of his melancholy voice, the hearers quaked. An unsought pathos came hand in hand with awe. So sensible were the audience of some unwonted attribute in their minister, that they longed for a breath of wind to blow aside the veil, almost believing that a stranger's visage would be discovered, though the form, gesture, and voice were those of Mr. Hooper.

13.   At the close of the services, the people hurried out with indecorous confusion, eager to communicate their pent-up amazement, and conscious of lighter spirits the moment they lost sight of the black veil. Some gathered in little circles, huddled closely together, with their mouths all whispering in the centre; some went homeward alone, wrapt in silent meditation; some talked loudly, and profaned the Sabbath day with ostentatious laughter. A few shook their sagacious heads, intimating that they could penetrate the mystery; while one or two affirmed that there was no mystery at all, but only that Mr. Hooper's eyes were so weakened by the midnight lamp, as to require a shade. After a brief interval, forth came good Mr. Hooper also, in the rear of his flock. Turning his veiled face from one group to another, he paid due reverence to the hoary heads, saluted the middle aged with kind dignity as their friend and spiritual guide, greeted the young with mingled authority and love, and laid his hands on the little children's heads to bless them. Such was always his custom on the Sabbath day. Strange and bewildered looks repaid him for his courtesy. None, as on former occasions, aspired to the honor of walking by their pastor's side. Old Squire Saunders, doubtless by an accidental lapse of memory, neglected to invite Mr. Hooper to his table, where the good clergyman had been wont to bless the food, almost every Sunday since his settlement. He returned, therefore, to the parsonage, and, at the moment of closing the door, was observed to look back upon the people, all of whom had their eyes fixed upon the minister. A sad smile gleamed faintly from beneath the black veil, and flickered about his mouth, glimmering as he disappeared.

14.   "How strange," said a lady, "that a simple black veil, such as any woman might wear on her bonnet, should become such a terrible thing on Mr. Hooper's face!"

15.   "Something must surely be amiss with Mr. Hooper's intellects," observed her husband, the physician of the village. "But the strangest part of the affair is the effect of this vagary, even on a soberminded man like myself. The black veil, though it covers only our pastor's face, throws its influence over his whole person, and makes him ghostlike from head to foot. Do you not feel it so?"

"Truly do I," replied the lady; "and I would not be alone with   16.
him for the world. I wonder if he is not afraid to be alone with himself!"

"Men sometimes are so," said her husband.   17.

The afternoon service was attended with similar circumstances.   18.
At its conclusion, the bell tolled for the funeral of a young lady. The
relatives and friends were assembled in the house, and the more
distant acquaintances stood about the door, speaking of the good
qualities of the deceased, when their talk was interrupted by the appearance of Mr. Hooper, still covered with his black veil. It was now
an appropriate emblem. The clergyman stepped into the room where
the corpse was laid, and bent over the coffin, to take a last farewell
of his deceased parishioner. As he stooped, the veil hung straight
down from his forehead, so that, if her eyelids had not been closed
forever, the dead maiden might have seen his face. Could Mr.
Hooper be fearful of her glance, that he so hastily caught back the
black veil? A person who watched the interview between the dead and
living, scrupled not to affirm, that, at the instant when the clergyman's features were disclosed, the corpse had slightly shuddered,
rustling the shroud and muslin cap, though the countenance retained
the composure of death. A superstitious old woman was the only
witness of this prodigy. From the coffin Mr. Hooper passed into the
chamber of the mourners, and thence to the head of the staircase, to
make the funeral prayer. It was a tender and heart-dissolving prayer,
full of sorrow, yet so imbued with celestial hopes, that the music of
a heavenly harp, swept by the fingers of the dead, seemed faintly to be
heard among the saddest accents of the minister. The people trem-
bled, though they but darkly understood him when he prayed that
they, and himself, and all of mortal race, might be ready, as he trusted
this young maiden had been, for the dreadful hour that should snatch
the veil from their faces. The bearers went heavily forth, and the
mourners followed, saddening all the street, with the dead before
them, and Mr. Hooper in his black veil behind.

"Why do you look back?" said one in the procession to his part-   19.
ner.

"I had a fancy," replied she, "that the minister and the maiden's   20.
spirit were walking hand in hand."

"And so had I, at the same moment," said the other.   21.

That night, the handsomest couple in Milford village were to be   22.

joined in wedlock. Though reckoned a melancholy man, Mr. Hooper had a placid cheerfulness for such occasions, which often excited a sympathetic smile where livelier merriment would have been thrown away. There was no quality of his disposition which made him more beloved than this. The company at the wedding awaited his arrival with impatience, trusting that the strange awe, which had gathered over him throughout the day, would now be dispelled. But such was not the result. When Mr. Hooper came, the first thing that their eyes rested on was the same horrible black veil, which had added deeper gloom to the funeral, and could portend nothing but evil to the wedding. Such was its immediate effect on the guests that a cloud seemed to have rolled duskily from beneath the black crape, and dimmed the light of the candles. The bridal pair stood up before the minister. But the bride's cold fingers quivered in the tremulous hand of the bridegroom, and her deathlike paleness caused a whisper that the maiden who had been buried a few hours before was come from her grave to be married. If ever another wedding were so dismal, it was that famous one where they tolled the wedding knell. After performing the ceremony, Mr. Hooper raised a glass of wine to his lips, wishing happiness to the new-married couple in a strain of mild pleasantry that ought to have brightened the features of the guests, like a cheerful gleam from the hearth. At that instant, catching a glimpse of his figure in the looking-glass, the black veil involved his own spirit in the horror with which it overwhelmed all others. His frame shuddered, his lips grew white, spilt the untasted wine upon the carpet, and rushed forth into the darkness. For the Earth, too, had on her Black Veil.

23.   The next day, the whole village of Milford talked of little else than Parson Hooper's black veil. That, and the mystery concealed behind it, supplied a topic for discussion between acquaintances meeting in the street, and good women gossiping at their open windows. It was the first item of news that the tavern-keeper told to his guests. The children babbled of it on their way to school. One imitative little imp covered his face with an old black handkerchief, thereby so affrighting his playmates that the panic seized himself, and he well-nigh lost his wits by his own waggery.

24.   It was remarkable that all of the busybodies and impertinent people in the parish, not one ventured to put the plain question to Mr. Hooper, wherefore he did this thing. Hitherto, whenever there

appeared the slightest call for such interference, he had never lacked advisers, nor shown himself averse to be guided by their judgment. If he erred at all, it was by so painful a degree of self-distrust, that even the mildest censure would lead him to consider an indifferent action as a crime. Yet, though so well acquainted with this amiable weakness, no individual among his parishioners chose to make the black veil a subject of friendly remonstrance. There was a feeling of dread, neither plainly confessed nor carefully concealed, which caused each to shift the responsibility upon another, till at length it was found expedient to send a deputation of the church, in order to deal with Mr. Hooper about the mystery, before it should grow into a scandal. Never did an embassy so ill discharge its duties. The minister received them with friendly courtesy, but became silent, after they were seated, leaving to his visitors the whole burden of introducing their important business. The topic, it might be supposed, was obvious enough. There was the black veil swathed round Mr. Hooper's forehead, and concealing every feature above his placid mouth, on which, at times, they could perceive the glimmering of a melancholy smile. But that piece of crape, to their imagination, seemed to hang down before his heart, the symbol of a fearful secret between him and them. Were the veil but cast aside, they might speak freely of it, but not till then. Thus they sat a considerable time, speechless, confused, and shrinking uneasily from Mr. Hooper's eye, which they felt to be fixed upon them with an invisible glance. Finally, the deputies returned abashed to their constituents, pronouncing the matter too weighty to be handled, except by a council of the churches, if, indeed, it might not require a general synod.

But there was one person in the village unappalled by the awe   25. with which the black veil had impressed all beside herself. When the deputies returned without an explanation, or even venturing to demand one, she, with the calm energy of her character, determined to chase away the strange cloud that appeared to be settling round Mr. Hooper, every moment more darkly than before. As his plighted wife, it should be her privilege to know what the black veil concealed. At the minister's first visit, therefore, she entered upon the subject with a direct simplicity, which made the task easier both for him and her. After he had seated himself, she fixed her eyes steadfastly upon the veil, but could discern nothing of the dreadful gloom that had so overawed the multitude: it was but a double fold of crape, hanging down from his forehead to his mouth, and slightly stirring with his breath.

26.   "No," said she aloud, and smiling, "there is nothing terrible in this piece of crape, except that it hides a face which I am always glad to look upon. Come, good sir, let the sun shine from behind the cloud. First lay aside your black veil: then tell me why you put it on."

27.   Mr. Hooper's smile glimmered faintly.

28.   "There is an hour to come," said he, "when all of us shall cast aside our veils. Take it not amiss, beloved friend, if I wear this piece of crape till then."

29.   "Your words are a mystery, too," returned the young lady. "Take away the veil from them, at least."

30.   "Elizabeth, I will," said he, "so far as my vow may suffer me. Know, then, this veil is a type and a symbol, and I am bound to wear it ever, both in light and darkness, in solitude and before the gaze of multitudes, and as with strangers, so with my familiar friends. No mortal eye will see it withdrawn. This dismal shade must separate me from the world: even you, Elizabeth, can never come behind it!"

31.   "What grievous affliction hath befallen you," she earnestly inquired, "that you should thus darken your eyes forever?"

32.   "If it be a sign of mourning," replied Mr. Hooper, "I, perhaps, like most other mortals, have sorrows dark enough to be typified by a black veil."

33.   "But what if the world will not believe that it is the type of an innocent sorrow?" urged Elizabeth. "Beloved and respected as you are, there may be whispers that you hide your face under the consciousness of secret sin. For the sake of your holy office, do away this scandal!"

34.   The color rose into her cheeks as she intimated the nature of the rumors that were already abroad in the village. But Mr. Hooper's mildness did not forsake him. He even smiled again—that same sad smile, which always appeared like a faint glimmering of light, proceeding from the obscurity beneath the veil.

35.   "If I hide my face for sorrow, there is cause enough," he merely replied; "and if I cover it for secret sin, what mortal might not do the same?"

36.   And with this gentle, but unconquerable obstinacy did he resist all her entreaties. At length Elizabeth sat silent. For a few moments she appeared lost in thought, considering, probably, what new meth-

ods might be tried to withdraw her lover from so dark a fantasy, which, if it had no other meaning, was perhaps a symptom of mental disease. Though of a firmer character than his own, the tears rolled down her cheeks. But, in an instant, as it were, a new feeling took the place of sorrow: her eyes were fixed insensibly on the black veil, when, like a sudden twilight in the air, its terrors fell around her. She arose, and stood trembling before him.

"And do you feel it then, at last?" said he mournfully.   37.

She made no reply, but covered her eyes with her hands, and   38.
turned to leave the room. He rushed forward and caught her arm.

"Have patience with me, Elizabeth!" cried he, passionately. "Do   39.
not desert me, though this veil must be between us here on earth. Be mine, and hereafter there shall be no veil over my face, no darkness between our souls! It is but a mortal veil—it is not for eternity! O! you know not how lonely I am, and how frightened, to be alone behind my black veil. Do not leave me in this miserable obscurity forever!"

"Lift the veil but once, and look me in the face," said she.   40.

"Never! It cannot be!" replied Mr. Hooper.   41.

"Then farewell!" said Elizabeth.   42.

She withdrew her arm from his grasp, and slowly departed, paus-   43.
ing at the door, to give one long shuddering gaze, that seemed almost to penetrate the mystery of the black veil. But, even amid his grief, Mr. Hooper smiled to think that only a material emblem had separated him from happiness, though the horrors, which it shadowed forth, must be drawn darkly between the fondest of lovers.

From that time no attempts were made to remove Mr. Hooper's   44.
black veil, or, by a direct appeal, to discover the secret which it was supposed to hide. By persons who claimed a superiority to popular prejudice, it was reckoned merely an eccentric whim, such as often mingles with the sober actions of men otherwise rational, and tinges them all with its own semblance of insanity. But with the multitude, good Mr. Hooper was irreparably a bugbear. He could not walk the street with any peace of mind, so conscious was he that the gentle and timid would turn aside to avoid him, and that others would make it a point of hardihood to throw themselves in his way. The impertinence of the latter class compelled him to give up his customary walk at sunset to the burial ground; for when he leaned pensively over the gate, there would always be faces behind the gravestones, peeping at his

black veil. A fable went the rounds that the stare of the dead people
drove him thence. It grieved him, to the very depth of his kind heart,
to observe how the children fled from his approach, breaking up their
merriest sports, while his melancholy figure was yet afar off. Their
instinctive dread caused him to feel more strongly than aught else,
that a preternatural horror was interwoven with the threads of the
black crape. In truth, his own antipathy to the veil was known to be
so great, that he never willingly passed before a mirror, nor stopped
to drink at a still fountain, lest, in its peaceful bosom, he should be
affrighted by himself. This was what gave plausibility to the whispers,
that Mr. Hooper's conscience tortured him for some great crime too
horrible to be entirely concealed, or otherwise than so obscurely intimated. Thus, from beneath the black veil, there rolled a cloud into
the sunshine, an ambiguity of sin or sorrow, which enveloped the poor
minister, so that love or sympathy could never reach him. It was said
that ghost and fiend consorted with him there. With self-shudderings
and outward terrors, he walked continually in its shadow, groping
darkly within his own soul, or gazing through a medium that sad-
dened the whole world. Even the lawless wind, it was believed, respected his dreadful secret, and never blew aside the veil. But still
good Mr. Hooper sadly smiled at the pale visages of the worldly
throng as he passed by.

45.   Among all its bad influences, the black veil had the one de-
sirable effect, of making its wearer a very efficient clergyman. By the
aid of his mysterious emblem—for there was no other apparent cause
—he became a man of awful power over souls that were in agony for
sin. His converts always regarded him with a dread peculiar to themselves, affirming, though but figuratively, that, before he brought
them to celestial light, they had been with him behind the black veil.
Its gloom, indeed, enabled him to sympathize with all dark affections.
Dying sinners cried aloud for Mr. Hooper, and would not yield their
breath till he appeared; though ever, as he stooped to whisper consola-
tion, they shuddered at the veiled face so near their own. Such were
the terrors of the black veil, even when Death had bared his visage!
Strangers came long distances to attend service at his church, with
the mere idle purpose of gazing at his figure, because it was forbidden
them to behold his face. But many were made to quake ere they departed! Once, during Governor Belcher's administration, Mr. Hooper
was appointed to preach the election sermon. Covered with his black

veil, he stood before the chief magistrate, the council, and the representatives, and wrought so deep an impression, that the legislative measures of that year were characterized by all the gloom and piety of our earliest ancestral sway.

In this manner Mr. Hooper spent a long life, irreproachable in   46.
outward act, yet shrouded in dismal suspicions; kind and loving, though unloved, and dimly feared; a man apart from men, shunned in their health and joy, but ever summoned to their aid in mortal anguish. As years wore on, shedding their snows above his sable veil, he acquired a name throughout the New England churches, and they called him Father Hooper. Nearly all his parishioners, who were of mature age when he was settled, had been borne away by many a funeral: he had one congregation in the church, and a more crowded one in the churchyard; and having wrought so late into the evening, and done his work so well, it was now good Father Hooper's turn to rest.

Several persons were visible by the shaded candlelight, in the   47.
death chamber of the old clergyman. Natural connections he had none. But there was the decorously grave, though unmoved physician, seeking only to mitigate the last pangs of the patient whom he could not save. There were the deacons, and other eminently pious members of his church. There, also, was the Reverend Mr. Clark, of Westbury, a young and zealous divine, who had ridden in haste to pray by the bedside of the expiring minister. There was the nurse, no hired handmaiden of death, but one whose calm affection had endured thus long in secrecy, in solitude, amid the chill of age, and would not perish, even at the dying hour. Who, but Elizabeth! And there lay the hoary head of good Father Hooper upon the death pillow, with the black veil still swathed about his brow, and reaching down over his face, so that each more difficult gasp of his faint breath caused it to stir. All through life that piece of crape had hung between him and the world: it had separated him from cheerful brotherhood and woman's love, and kept him in that saddest of all prisons, his own heart; and still it lay upon his face, as if to deepen the gloom of his darksome chamber, and shade him from the sunshine of eternity.

For some time previous, his mind had been confused, wavering   48.
doubtfully between the past and the present, and hovering forward, as it were, at intervals, into the indistinctness of the world to come. There had been feverish turns, which tossed him from side to side, and

wore away what little strength he had. But in his most convulsive struggles, and in the wildest vagaries of his intellect, when no other thought retained its sober influence, he still showed an awful solicitude lest the black veil should slip aside. Even if his bewildered soul could have forgotten, there was a faithful woman at this pillow, who, with averted eyes, would have covered that aged face, which she had last beheld in the comeliness of manhood. At length the death-stricken old man lay quietly in the torpor of mental and bodily exhaustion, with an imperceptible pulse, and breath that grew fainter and fainter, except when a long, deep, and irregular inspiration seemed to prelude the flight of his spirit.

49.   The minister of Westbury approached the bedside.

50.   "Venerable Father Hooper," said he, "the moment of your release is at hand. Are you ready for the lifting of the veil that shuts in time from eternity?"

51.   Father Hooper at first replied merely by a feeble motion of his head; then, apprehensive, perhaps, that his meaning might be doubted, he exerted himself to speak.

52.   "Yea," said he, in faint accents, "my soul hath a patient weariness until that veil be lifted."

53.   "And is it fitting," resumed the Reverend Mr. Clark, "that a man so given to prayer, of such a blameless example, holy in deed and thought, so far as mortal judgment may pronounce; is it fitting that a father in the church should leave a shadow on his memory, that may seem to blacken a life so pure? I pray you, my venerable brother, let not this thing be! Suffer us to be gladdened by your triumphant aspect as you go to your reward. Before the veil of eternity be lifted, let me cast aside this black veil from your face!"

54.   And thus speaking, the Reverend Mr. Clark bent forward to reveal the mystery of so many years. But, exerting a sudden energy, that made all the beholders stand aghast, Father Hooper snatched both his hands from beneath the bedclothes, and pressed them strongly on the black veil, resolute to struggle, if the minister of Westbury would contend with a dying man.

55.   "Never!" cried the veiled clergyman. "On earth, never!"

56.   "Dark old man!" exclaimed the affrighted minister, "with what horrible crime upon your soul are you now passing to the judgment?"

57.   Father Hooper's breath heaved; it rattled in his throat: but, with

a mighty effort, grasping forward with his hands, he caught hold of life, and held it back till he should speak. He even raised himself in bed; and there he sat, shivering with the arms of death around him, while the black veil hung down, awful, at that last moment, in the gathered terrors of a lifetime. And yet the faint, sad smile, so often there, now seemed to glimmer from its obscurity, and linger on Father Hooper's lips.

"Why do you tremble at me alone?" cried he, turning his veiled   58. face round the circle of pale spectators. "Tremble also at each other! Have men avoided me, and women shown no pity, and children screamed and fled, only for my black veil? What, but the mystery which it obscurely typifies, has made this piece of crape so awful? When the friend shows his inmost heart to his friend; the lover to his best beloved; when man does not vainly shrink from the eye of his Creator, loathsomely treasuring up the secret of his sin; then deem me a monster, for the symbol beneath which I have lived, and die! I look around me, and, lo! on every visage a Black Veil!"

While his auditors shrank from one another, in mutual affright,   59. Father Hooper fell back upon his pillow, a veiled corpse, with a faint smile lingering on the lips. Still veiled, they laid him in his coffin, and a veiled corpse they bore him to the grave. The grass of many years has sprung up and withered on that grave, the burial stone is moss-grown, and good Mr. Hooper's face is dust; but awful is still the thought that it mouldered beneath the Black Veil!

DISCUSSION QUESTIONS

1. Why does the Reverend Mr. Hooper wear the black veil?

2. Mr. Hooper says: "Know, then, this veil is a type and a symbol. . . ." A symbol is generally understood as that which is meaningful in itself yet which represents or means something else as well. Explain Mr. Hooper's statement in the light of this definition.

3. Did the wearing of the veil have a positive or negative effect on Mr. Hooper's ministry? If you feel it is not simply one or the other, how would you evaluate the consequences of his wearing the veil?

4. The word "parable" appears in the title of the story. A parable is an illustrative story answering a question or indicating a moral lesson. Is

Hawthorne chiefly concerned with providing answers or with asking questions?

5. Why does Hawthorne concern himself with Hooper's relationship with Elizabeth? How do you react to Mr. Hooper's treatment of Elizabeth?

RHETORIC

1. Hooper describes the veil as the "symbol beneath which I have lived, and die!" (paragraph fifty-eight). Write a theme in which you defend or attack the idea of people dying for symbols. Use concrete examples of such symbols (flag, cross, etc.).

2. Transitions (*Mechanics of Style,* Chapter IX. See p. 245.) are especially important in a narrative where the author is moving events forward in time. How does Hawthorne use his transitions in paragraph twenty-two?

3. Discuss Hawthorne's use of details in developing the sixth paragraph. Do the details in the description allow you to form a clear picture of Hooper? Can you improve on the description?

4. Write a comparison-contrast theme on Hooper and another character in a Hawthorne story you might have read (e.g. Dimmesdale in *The Scarlet Letter*) or on Hooper and Martin Luther King, Jr.

5. Using as many details as possible, try to create a death scene similar to that in paragraph forty-eight. Be especially careful that your words create the precise emotional atmosphere (horror? suspense? sadness? curiosity?) you want to convey to your reader.

6. Chapter VII of *Mechanics of Style* (see p. 235) discusses the value of employing different sentence constructions. Analyze paragraph six of Hawthorne's story. List the kinds of sentences contained in this paragraph.

7. Write a theme with five paragraphs which lists three peculiar mannerisms of ministers or religious people that you know.

8. There are images signifying or connected with light and darkness in this story (for example, paragraphs forty-four and forty-five). How do they help structure and intensify the story's meaning?

VOCABULARY

gait (paragraph 1)   venerable (10)
accord (3)   emblem (10)
phenomenon (10)   oratory (12)

ostentatious (13)	fantasy (36)
countenance (18)	instinctive (44)
babbled (23)	pangs (47)
imp (23)	imperceptible (48)
impertinent (24)	feeble (51)
affliction (31)	resolute (54)
obscurity (34)	loathsomely (58)
obstinacy (36)	mutual (59)

Letter from Birmingham Jail[1]

April 16, 1963

My Dear Fellow Clergymen:

 While confined here in the Birmingham city jail, I came across [1.] your recent statement calling my present activities "unwise and untimely." Seldom do I pause to answer criticism of my work and ideas. If I sought to answer all the criticisms that cross my desk, my secretaries would have little time for anything other than such correspondence in the course of the day, and I would have no time for constructive work. But since I feel that you are men of genuine good will and that your criticisms are sincerely set forth, I want to try to answer your statement in what I hope will be patient and reasonable terms.

 I think I should indicate why I am here in Birmingham, since [2.] you have been influenced by the view which argues against "outsiders coming in." I have the honor of serving as president of the Southern Christian Leadership Conference, an organization operating in every southern state, with headquarters in Atlanta, Georgia. We have some

 "Letter from Birmingham Jail—April 16, 1963" from Martin Luther King, Jr., *Why We Can't Wait* (New York: Harper & Row, Publishers, 1964), pp. 76–95. Copyright © 1963 by Martin Luther King, Jr. Reprinted by permission of the publisher.

1 Author's Note: This response to a published statement by eight fellow clergymen from Alabama (Bishop C. C. J. Carpenter, Bishop Joseph A. Durick, Rabbi Hilton L. Grafman, Bishop Paul Hardin, Bishop Holan B. Harmon, the Reverend George M. Murray, the Reverend Edward V. Ramage, and the Reverend Earl Stallings) was composed under somewhat constricting circumstances. Begun on the margins of the newspaper in which the statement appeared while I was in jail, the letter was continued on scraps of writing paper supplied by a friendly Negro trusty, and concluded on a pad my attorneys were eventually permitted to leave me. Although the text remains in substance unaltered, I have indulged in the author's prerogative of polishing it for publication.

eighty-five affiliated organizations across the South, and one of them is the Alabama Christian Movement for Human Rights. Frequently we share staff, educational and financial resources with our affiliates. Several months ago the affiliate here in Birmingham asked us to be on call to engage in a nonviolent direct-action program if such were deemed necessary. We readily consented, and when the hour came we lived up to our promise. So I, along with several members of my staff, am here because I was invited here. I am here because I have organizational ties here.

3.   But more basically, I am in Birmingham because injustice is here. Just as the prophets of the eighth century B.C. left their villages and carried their "thus saith the Lord" far beyond the boundaries of their home towns, and just as the Apostle Paul left his village of Tarsus and carried the gospel of Jesus Christ to the far corners of the Greco-Roman world, so am I compelled to carry the gospel of freedom beyond my own home town. Like Paul, I must constantly respond to the Macedonian call for aid.

4.   Moreover, I am cognizant of the interrelatedness of all communities and states. I cannot sit idly by in Atlanta and not be concerned about what happens in Birmingham. Injustice anywhere is a threat to justice everywhere. We are caught in an inescapable network of mutuality, tied in a single garment of destiny. Whatever affects one directly, affects all indirectly. Never again can we afford to live with the narrow, provincial "outside agitator" idea. Anyone who lives inside the United States can never be considered an outsider anywhere within its bounds.

5.   You deplore the demonstrations taking place in Birmingham. But your statement, I am sorry to say, fails to express a similar concern for the conditions that brought about the demonstrations. I am sure that none of you would want to rest content with the superficial kind of social analysis that deals merely with effects and does not grapple with underlying causes. It is unfortunate that demonstrations are taking place in Birmingham, but it is even more unfortunate that the city's white power structure left the Negro community with no alternative.

6.   In any nonviolent campaign there are four basic steps: collection of the facts to determine whether injustices exist; negotiation; self-purification; and direct action. We have gone through all these steps in Birmingham. There can be no gainsaying the fact that racial in-

justice engulfs this community. Birmingham is probably the most thoroughly segregated city in the United States. Its ugly record of brutality is widely known. Negroes have experienced grossly unjust treatment in the courts. There have been more unsolved bombings of Negro homes and churches in Birmingham than in any other city in the nation. These are the hard, brutal facts of the case. On the basis of these conditions, Negro leaders sought to negotiate with the city fathers. But the latter consistently refused to engage in good-faith negotiation.

Then, last September, came the opportunity to talk with leaders   7. of Birmingham's economic community. In the course of the negotiations, certain promises were made by the merchants—for example, to remove the stores' humiliating racial signs. On the basis of these promises, the Reverend Fred Shuttlesworth and the leaders of the Alabama Christian Movement for Human Rights agreed to a moratorium on all demonstrations. As the weeks and months went by, we realized that we were the victims of a broken promise. A few signs, briefly removed, returned; the others remained.

As in so many past experiences, our hopes had been blasted, and   8. the shadow of deep disappointment settled upon us. We had no alternative except to prepare for direct action, whereby we would present our very bodies as a means of laying our case before the conscience of the local and the national community. Mindful of the difficulties involved, we decided to undertake a process of self-purification. We began a series of workshops on nonviolence, and we repeatedly asked ourselves: "Are you able to accept blows without retaliating?" "Are you able to endure the ordeal of jail?" We decided to schedule our direct-action program for the Easter season, realizing that except for Christmas, this is the main shopping period of the year. Knowing that a strong economic-withdrawal program would be the by-product of direct action, we felt that this would be the best time to bring pressure to bear on the merchants for the needed change.

Then it occurred to us that Birmingham's mayoralty election was   9. coming up in March, and we speedily decided to postpone action until after election day. When we discovered that the Commissioner of Public Safety, Eugene "Bull" Connor, had piled up enough votes to be the run-off, we decided again to postpone action until the day after the run-off so that the demonstrations could not be used to cloud the issues. Like many others, we waited to see Mr. Connor defeated, and to this end we endured postponement after postponement. Having aided in this community need, we felt that our direct-action program could be delayed no longer.

10.   You may well ask: "Why direct action? Why sit-ins, marches, and so forth? Isn't negotiation a better path?" You are quite right in calling for negotiation. Indeed, this is the very purpose of direct action. Nonviolent direct action seeks to create such a crisis and foster such a tension that a community which has constantly refused to negotiate is forced to confront the issue. It seeks so to dramatize the issue that it can no longer be ignored. My citing the creation of tension as part of the work of the nonviolent-resister may sound rather shocking. But I must confess that I am not afraid of the word "tension." I have earnestly opposed violent tension, but there is a type of constructive, nonviolent tension which is necessary for growth. Just as Socrates felt that it was necessary to create a tension in the mind so that individuals could rise from the bondage of myths and half-truths to the unfettered realm of creative analysis and objective appraisal, so must we see the need for nonviolent gadflies to create the kind of tension in society that will help men rise from the dark depths of prejudice and racism to the majestic heights of understanding and brotherhood.

11.   The purpose of our direct-action program is to create a situation so crisis-packed that it will inevitably open the door to negotiation. I therefore concur with you in your call for negotiation. Too long has our beloved Southland been bogged down in a tragic effort to live in monologue rather than dialogue.

12.   One of the basic points in your statement is that the action that I and my associates have taken in Birmingham is untimely. Some have asked: "Why didn't you give the new city administration time to act?" The only answer that I can give to this query is that the new Birmingham administration must be prodded about as much as the outgoing one, before it will act. We are sadly mistaken if we feel that the election of Albert Boutwell as mayor will bring the millennium to Birmingham. While Mr. Boutwell is a much more gentle person than Mr. Connor, they are both segregationists, dedicated to maintenance of the status quo. I have hope that Mr. Boutwell will be reasonable enough to see the futility of massive resistance to desegregation. But he will not see this without pressure from devotées of civil rights. My friends, I must say to you that we have not made a single gain in civil

rights without determined legal and nonviolent pressure. Lamentably, it is an historical fact that privileged groups seldom give up their privileges voluntarily. Individuals may see the moral light and voluntarily give up their unjust posture; but, as Reinhold Niebuhr has reminded us, groups tend to be more immoral than individuals.

13.

We know through painful experience that freedom is never voluntarily given by the oppressor; it must be demanded by the oppressed. Frankly, I have yet to engage in a direct-action campaign that was "well-timed" in the view of those who have not suffered unduly from the disease of segregation. For years now I have heard the word "Wait!" It rings in the ear of every Negro with piercing familiarity. This "Wait" has almost always meant "Never." We must come to see, with one of our distinguished jurists, that "justice too long delayed is justice denied."

14.

We have waited for more than 340 years for our constitutional and God-given rights. The nations of Asia and Africa are moving with jetlike speed toward gaining political independence, but we still creep at horse-and-buggy pace toward gaining a cup of coffee at a lunch counter. Perhaps it is easy for those who have never felt the stinging darts of segregation to say, "Wait." But when you have seen vicious mobs lynch your mothers and fathers at will and drown your sisters and brothers at whim; when you have seen hate-filled policemen curse, kick, and even kill your black brothers and sisters; when you see the vast majority of your twenty million Negro brothers smothering in an airtight cage of poverty in the midst of an affluent society; when you suddenly find your tongue twisted and your speech stammering as you seek to explain to your six-year-old daughter why she can't go to the public amusement park that has just been advertised on television, and see tears welling up in her eyes when she is told that Funtown is closed to colored children, and see ominous clouds of inferiority beginning to form in her little mental sky, and see her beginning to distort her personality by developing an unconscious bitterness toward white people; when you have to concoct an answer for a five-year-old son who is asking: "Daddy, why do white people treat colored people so mean?"; when you take a cross-country drive and find it necessary to sleep night after night in the uncomfortable corners of your automobile because no motel will accept you; when you are humiliated day in and day out by nagging signs reading "white" and "colored"; when your first name becomes "nigger," your middle name becomes "boy" (however old you are), and your last name becomes "John," and your wife and mother are never given the respected title "Mrs."; when you are harried by day and haunted by night by the fact that you are a Negro, living constantly at tiptoe stance, never quite knowing what to expect next, and are plagued with inner fears and outer resentments; when you are forever fighting a degenerating sense of "nobodiness"—then you will understand why we find it difficult to wait. There comes a time when the cup of endurance runs over, and men are no longer willing to be plunged into the abyss of despair. I hope, sirs, you can understand our legitimate and unavoidable impatience.

15.   You express a great deal of anxiety over our willingness to break laws. This is certainly a legitimate concern. Since we so diligently urge people to obey the Supreme Court's decision of 1954 outlawing segregation in the public schools, at first glance it may seem rather paradoxical for us consciously to break laws. One may well ask: "How can you advocate breaking some laws and obeying others?" The answer lies in the fact that there are two types of laws: just and unjust. I would be the first to advocate obeying just laws. One has not only a legal but a moral responsibility to obey just laws. Conversely, one has a moral responsibility to disobey unjust laws. I would agree with St. Augustine that "an unjust law is no law at all."

16.   Now, what is the difference between the two? How does one determine whether a law is just or unjust? A just law is a man-made code that squares with the moral law or the law of God. An unjust law is a code that is out of harmony with the moral law. To put it in the terms of St. Thomas Aquinas: An unjust law is a human law that is not rooted in eternal law and natural law. Any law that uplifts human personality is just. Any law that degrades human personality is unjust. All segregation statutes are unjust because segregation distorts the soul and damages the personality. It gives the segregator a false sense of superiority and the segregated a false sense of inferiority. Segregation, to use the terminology of the Jewish philosopher Martin Buber, substitutes an "I-it" relationship for an "I-thou" relationship and ends up relegating persons to the status of things. Hence segregation is not only politically, economically, and sociologically unsound, it is morally wrong and sinful. Paul Tillich has said that sin is separation. Is not segregation an existential expression of man's tragic separation, his awful estrangement, his ter-

rible sinfulness? Thus it is that I can urge men to obey the 1954 decision of the Supreme Court, for it is morally right; and I can urge them to disobey segregation ordinances, for they are morally wrong.

Let us consider a more concrete example of just and unjust laws. An unjust law is a code that a numerical or power majority group compels a minority group to obey but does not make binding on itself. This is *difference* made legal. By the same token, a just law is a code that a majority compels a minority to follow and that it is willing to follow itself. This is *sameness* made legal. [17.]

Let me give another explanation. A law is unjust if it is inflicted on a minority that, as a result of being denied the right to vote, had no part in enacting or devising the law. Who can say that the legislature of Alabama which set up that state's segregation laws was democratically elected? Throughout Alabama all sorts of devious methods are used to prevent Negroes from becoming registered voters, and there are some counties in which, even though Negroes constitute a majority of the population, not a single Negro is registered. Can any law enacted under such circumstances be considered democratically structured? [18.]

Sometimes a law is just on its face and unjust in its application. For instance, I have been arrested on a charge of parading without a permit. Now, there is nothing wrong in having an ordinance which requires a permit for a parade. But such an ordinance becomes unjust when it is used to maintain segregation and to deny citizens the First-Amendment privilege of peaceful assembly and protest. [19.]

I hope you are able to see the distinction I am trying to point out. In no sense do I advocate evading or defying the law, as would a rabid segregationist. That would lead to anarchy. One who breaks an unjust law must do so openly, lovingly, and with a willingness to accept the penalty. I submit that an individual who breaks a law that conscience tells him is unjust, and who willingly accepts the penalty of imprisonment in order to arouse the conscience of the community over its injustice, is in reality expressing the highest respect for law. [20.]

Of course, there is nothing new about this kind of civil disobedience. It was evidenced sublimely in the refusal of Shadrach, Meshach, and Abednego to obey the laws of Nebuchadnezzar, on the ground that a higher moral law was at stake. It was practiced superbly by the early Christians, who were willing to face hungry lions and the excruciating pain of chopping blocks rather than to submit [21.]

to certain unjust laws of the Roman Empire. To a degree, academic freedom is a reality today because Socrates practiced civil disobedience. In our own nation, the Boston Tea Party represented a massive act of civil disobedience.

22.   We should never forget that everything Adolf Hitler did in Germany was "legal" and everything the Hungarian freedom fighters did in Hungary was "illegal." It was "illegal" to aid and comfort a Jew in Hitler's Germany. Even so, I am sure that, had I lived in Germany at the time, I would have aided and comforted my Jewish brothers. If today I lived in a Communist country where certain principles dear to the Christian faith are suppressed, I would openly advocate disobeying that country's antireligious laws.

23.   I must make two honest confessions to you, my Christian and Jewish brothers. First, I must confess that over the past few years I have been gravely disappointed with the white moderate. I have almost reached the regrettable conclusion that the Negro's great stumbling block in his stride toward freedom is not the White Citizen's Counciler or the Ku Klux Klanner, but the white moderate, who is more devoted to "order" than to justice; who prefers a negative peace which is the absence of tension to a positive peace which is the presence of justice; who constantly says: "I agree with you in the goal you seek, but I cannot agree with your methods of direct action"; who paternalistically believes he can set the timetable for another man's freedom; who lives by a mythical concept of time and who constantly advises the Negro to wait for a "more convenient season." Shallow understanding from people of good will is more frustrating than absolute misunderstanding from people of ill will. Lukewarm acceptance is much more bewildering than outright rejection.

24.   I had hoped that the white moderate would understand that law and order exist for the purpose of establishing justice and that when they fail in this purpose they become the dangerously structured dams that block the flow of social progress. I had hoped that the white moderate would understand that the present tension in the South is a necessary phase of the transition from an obnoxious negative peace, in which the Negro passively accepted his unjust plight, to a substantive and positive peace, in which all men will respect the dignity and worth of human personality. Actually, we who engage in nonviolent direct action are not the creators of tension. We merely bring to the surface the hidden tension that is already alive. We bring it out

into the open, where it can be seen and dealt with. Like a boil that can never be cured so long as it is covered up but must be opened with all its ugliness to the natural medicines of air and light, injustice must be exposed, with all the tension its exposure creates, to the light of human conscience and the air of national opinion before it can be cured.

25. In your statement you assert that our actions, even though peaceful, must be condemned because they precipitate violence. But is this a logical assertion? Isn't this like condemning a robbed man because his possession of money precipitated the evil act of robbery? Isn't this like condemning Socrates because his unswerving commitment to truth and his philosophical inquiries precipitated the act by the misguided populace in which they made him drink hemlock? Isn't this like condemning Jesus because his unique God-consciousness and never-ceasing devotion to God's will precipitated the evil act of crucifixion? We must come to see that, as the federal courts have consistently affirmed, it is wrong to urge an individual to cease his efforts to gain his basic constitutional rights because the quest may precipitate violence. Society must protect the robbed and punish the robber.

26. I had also hoped that the white moderate would reject the myth concerning time in relation to the struggle for freedom. I have just received a letter from a white brother in Texas. He writes: "All Christians know that the colored people will receive equal rights eventually, but it is possible that you are in too great a religious hurry. It has taken Christianity almost two thousand years to accomplish what it has. The teachings of Christ take time to come to earth." Such an attitude stems from a tragic misconception of time, from the strangely irrational notion that there is something in the very flow of time that will inevitably cure all ills. Actually, time itself is neutral; it can be used either destructively or constructively. More and more I feel that the people of ill will have used time much more effectively than have the people of good will. We will have to repent in this generation not merely for the hateful words and actions of the bad people but for the appalling silence of the good people. Human progress never rolls in on wheels of inevitability; it comes through the tireless efforts of men willing to be co-workers with God, and without this hard work, time itself becomes an ally of the forces of social stagnation. We must use time creatively, in the knowledge that the

time is always ripe to do right. Now is the time to make real the promise of democracy and transform our pending national elegy into a creative psalm of brotherhood. Now is the time to lift our national policy from the quicksand of racial injustice to the solid rock of human dignity.

27.   You speak of our activity in Birmingham as extreme. At first I was rather disappointed that fellow clergymen would see my nonviolent efforts as those of an extremist. I began thinking about the fact that I stand in the middle of two opposing forces in the Negro community. One is a force of complacency, made up in part of Negroes who, as a result of long years of oppression, are so drained of self-respect and a sense of "somebodiness" that they have adjusted to segregation; and in part of a few middle-class Negroes who, because of a degree of academic and economic security and because in some ways they profit by segregation, have become insensitive to the problems of the masses. The other force is one of bitterness and hatred, and it comes perilously close to advocating violence. It is expressed in the various black nationalist groups that are springing up across the nation, the largest and best-known being Elijah Muhammad's Muslim movement. Nourished by the Negro's frustration over the continued existence of racial discrimination, this movement is made up of people who have lost faith in America, who have absolutely repudiated Christianity, and who have concluded that the white man is an incorrigible "devil."

28.   I have tried to stand between these two forces, saying that we need emulate neither the "do-nothingism" of the complacent nor the hatred and despair of the black nationalist. For there is the more excellent way of love and nonviolent protest. I am grateful to God that, through the influence of the Negro church, the way of nonviolence became an integral part of our struggle.

29.   If this philosophy had not emerged, by now many streets of the South would, I am convinced, be flowing with blood. And I am further convinced that if our white brothers dismiss as "rabble-rousers" and "outside agitators" those of us who employ nonviolent direct action, and if they refuse to support our nonviolent efforts, millions of Negroes will, out of frustration and despair, seek solace and security in black nationalist ideologies—a development that would inevitably lead to a frightening racial nightmare.

30.   Oppressed people cannot remain oppressed forever. The yearning

for freedom eventually manifests itself, and that is what has happened to the American Negro. Something within has reminded him of his birthright of freedom, and something without has reminded him that it can be gained. Consciously or unconsciously, he has been caught up by the *Zeitgeist,* and with his black brothers of Africa and his brown and yellow brothers of Asia, South America, and the Caribbean, the United States Negro is moving with a sense of great urgency toward the promised land of racial justice. If one recognizes this vital urge that has engulfed the Negro community, one should readily understand why public demonstrations are taking place. The Negro has many pent-up resentments and latent frustrations, and he must release them. So let him march; let him make prayer pilgrimages to the city hall; let him go on freedom rides—and try to understand why he must do so. If his repressed emotions are not released in nonviolent ways, they will seek expression through violence; this is not a threat but a fact of history. So I have not said to my people: "Get rid of your discontent." Rather, I have tried to say that this normal and healthy discontent can be channeled into the creative outlet of non-violent direct action. And now this approach is being termed extremist.

31. But though I was initially disappointed at being categorized as an extremist, as I continued to think about the matter I gradually gained a measure of satisfaction from the label. Was not Jesus an extremist for love: "Love your enemies, bless them that curse you, do good to them that hate you, and pray for them which despitefully use you, and persecute you." Was not Amos an extremist for justice: "Let justice roll down like waters and righteousness like an ever-flowing stream." Was not Paul an extremist for the Christian gospel: "I bear in my body the marks of the Lord Jesus." Was not Martin Luther an extremist: "Here I stand; I cannot do otherwise, so help me God." And John Bunyan: "I will stay in jail to the end of my days before I make a butchery of my conscience." And Abraham Lincoln: "This nation cannot survive half slave and half free." And Thomas Jefferson: "We hold these truths to be self-evident, that all men are created equal . . ." So the question is not whether we will be extremists, but what kind of extremists we will be. Will we be extremists for hate or for love? Will we be extremists for the preservation of injustice or for the extension of justice? In that dramatic scene on Calvary's hill three men were crucified. We must never forget that all three were crucified

for the same crime—the crime of extremism. Two were extremists for immorality, and thus fell below their environment. The other, Jesus Christ, was an extremist for love, truth, and goodness, and thereby rose above his environment. Perhaps the South, the nation, and the world are in dire need of creative extremists.

32.

I had hoped that the white moderate would see this need. Perhaps I was too optimistic; perhaps I expected too much. I suppose I should have realized that few members of the oppressor race can understand the deep groans and passionate yearnings of the oppressed race, and still fewer have the vision to see that injustice must be rooted out by strong, persistent, and determined action. I am thankful, however, that some of our white brothers in the South have grasped the meaning of this social revolution and committed themselves to it. They are still all too few in quantity, but they are big in quality. Some—such as Ralph McGill, Lillian Smith, Harry Golden, James McBride Dabbs, Ann Braden, and Sarah Patton Boyle—have written about our struggle in eloquent and prophetic terms. Others have marched with us down nameless streets of the South. They have languished in filthy, roach-infested jails, suffering the abuse and brutality of policemen who view them as "dirty nigger-lovers." Unlike so many of their moderate brothers and sisters, they have recognized the urgency of the moment and sensed the need for powerful "action" antidotes to combat the disease of segregation.

33.

Let me take note of my other major disappointment. I have been so greatly disappointed with the white church and its leadership. Of course, there are some notable exceptions. I am not unmindful of the fact that each of you has taken some significant stands on this issue. I commend you, Reverend Stallings, for your Christian stand on this past Sunday, in welcoming Negroes to your worship service on a nonsegregated basis. I commend the Catholic leaders of this state for integrating Spring Hill College several years ago.

34.

But despite these notable exceptions, I must honestly reiterate that I have been disappointed with the church. I do not say this as one of those negative critics who can always find something wrong with the church. I say this as a minister of the gospel, who loves the church; who was nurtured in its bosom; who has been sustained by its spiritual blessings; and who will remain true to it as long as the cord of life shall lengthen.

35.

When I was suddenly catapulted into the leadership of the bus protest in Montgomery, Alabama, a few years ago, I felt we would be supported by the white church. I felt that the white ministers, priests, and rabbis of the South would be among our strongest allies. Instead, some have been outright opponents, refusing to understand the freedom movement and misrepresenting its leaders; all too many others have been more cautious than courageous and have remained silent behind the anesthetizing security of stained-glass windows.

36. In spite of my shattered dreams, I came to Birmingham with the hope that the white religious leadership of this community would see the justice of our cause and, with deep moral concern, would serve as the channel through which our just grievances could reach the power structure. I had hoped that each of you would understand. But again I have been disappointed.

37. I have heard numerous southern religious leaders admonish their worshippers to comply with a desegregation decision because it is the law, but I have longed to hear white ministers declare: "Follow this decree because integration is morally right and because the Negro is your brother." In the midst of blatant injustices inflicted upon the Negro, I have watched white churchmen stand on the sideline and mouth pious irrelevancies and sanctimonious trivialities. In the midst of a mighty struggle to rid our nation of racial and economic injustice, I have heard many ministers say: "Those are social issues, with which the gospel has no real concern." And I have watched many churches commit themselves to a completely other-worldly religion which makes a strange, un-Biblical distinction between body and soul, between the sacred and the secular.

38. I have traveled the length and breadth of Alabama, Mississippi, and all the other southern states. On sweltering summer days and crisp autumn mornings I have looked at the South's beautiful churches with their lofty spires pointing heavenward. I have beheld the impressive outlines of her massive religious-education buildings. Over and over I have found myself asking: "What kind of people worship here? Who is their God? Where were their voices when the lips of Governor Barnett dripped with words of interposition and nullification? Where were they when Governor Wallace gave a clarion call for defiance and hatred? Where were their voices of support when bruised and weary Negro men and women decided to rise from the dark dungeons of complacency to the bright hills of creative protest?"

39.   Yes, these questions are still in my mind. In deep disappointment I have wept over the laxity of the church. But be assured that my tears have been tears of love. There can be no deep disappointment where there is not deep love. Yes, I love the church. How could I do otherwise? I am in the rather unique position of being the son, the grandson, and the great-grandson of preachers. Yes, I see the church as the body of Christ. But, oh! How we have blemished and scarred that body through social neglect and through fear of being nonconformists.

40.   There was a time when the church was very powerful—in the time when the early Christians rejoiced at being deemed worthy to suffer for what they believed. In those days the church was not merely a thermometer that recorded the ideas and principles of popular opinion; it was a thermostat that transformed the mores of society. Whenever the early Christians entered a town, the people in power became disturbed and immediately sought to convict the Christians for being "disturbers of the peace" and "outside agitators." But the Christians pressed on, in the conviction that they were "a colony of heaven," called to obey God rather than man. Small in number, they were big in commitment. They were too God-intoxicated to be "astronomically intimidated." By their effort and example they brought an end to such ancient evils as infanticide and gladiatorial contests.

41.   Things are different now. So often the contemporary church is a weak, ineffectual voice with an uncertain sound. So often it is an archdefender of the status quo. Far from being disturbed by the presence of the church, the power structure of the average community is consoled by the church's silent—and often even vocal—sanction of things as they are.

42.   But the judgment of God is upon the church as never before. If today's church does not recapture the sacrificial spirit of the early church, it will lose its authenticity, forfeit the loyalty of millions, and be dismissed as an irrelevant social club with no meaning for the twentieth century. Every day I meet young people whose disappointment with the church has turned into outright disgust.

43.   Perhaps I have once again been too optimistic. Is organized religion too inextricably bound to the status quo to save our nation and the world? Perhaps I must turn my faith to the inner spiritual church, the church within the church, as the true *ekklesia* and the hope of the world. But again I am thankful to God that some noble souls

from the ranks of organized religion have broken loose from the paralyzing chains of conformity and joined us as active partners in the struggle for freedom. They have left their secure congregations and walked the streets of Albany, Georgia, with us. They have gone down the highways of the South on tortuous rides for freedom. Yes, they have gone to jail with us. Some have been dismissed from their churches, have lost the support of their bishops and fellow ministers. But they have acted in the faith that right defeated is stronger than evil triumphant. Their witness has been the spiritual salt that preserved the true meaning of the gospel in these troubled times. They have carved a tunnel of hope through the dark mountain of disappointment.

44.

I hope the church as a whole will meet the challenge of this decisive hour. But even if the church does not come to the aid of justice, I have no despair about the future. I have no fear about the outcome of our struggle in Birmingham, even if our motives are at present misunderstood. We will reach the goal of freedom in Birmingham and all over the nation, because the goal of America is freedom. Abused and scorned though we may be, our destiny is tied up with America's destiny. Before the pilgrims landed at Plymouth, we were here. Before the pen of Jefferson etched the majestic words of the Declaration of Independence across the pages of history, we were here. For more than two centuries our forebears labored in this country without wages; they made cotton king; they built the homes of their masters while suffering gross injustice and shameful humiliation—and yet out of a bottomless vitality they continued to thrive and develop. If the inexpressible cruelties of slavery could not stop us, the opposition we now face will surely fail. We will win our freedom because the sacred heritage of our nation and the eternal will of God are embodied in our echoing demands.

45.

Before closing I feel impelled to mention one other point in your statement that has troubled me profoundly. You warmly commended the Birmingham police force for keeping "order" and "preventing violence." I doubt that you would have so warmly commended the police force if you had seen its dogs sinking their teeth into unarmed, nonviolent Negroes. I doubt that you would so quickly commend the policemen if you were to observe their ugly and inhumane treatment of Negroes here in the city jail; if you were to watch them push and curse old Negro women and young Negro girls; if you were to see them slap and kick old Negro men and young boys; if you were to observe them, as they did on two occasions, refuse to give us food because we wanted to sing our grace together. I cannot join in your praise of the Birmingham police department.

46.   It is true that the police have exercised a degree of discipline in handling the demonstrators. In this sense they have conducted themselves rather "nonviolently" in public. But for what purpose? To preserve the evil system of segregation. Over the past few years I have consistently preached that nonviolence demands that the means we use must be as pure as the ends we seek. I have tried to make clear that it is wrong to use immoral means to attain moral ends. But now I must affirm that it is just as wrong, or perhaps even more so, to use moral means to preserve immoral ends. Perhaps Mr. Connor and his policemen have been rather nonviolent in public, as was Chief Pritchett in Albany, Georgia, but they have used the moral means of nonviolence to maintain the immoral end of racial injustice. As T. S. Eliot has said: "The last temptation is the greatest treason: To do the right deed for the wrong reason."

47.   I wish you had commended the Negro sit-inners and demonstrators of Birmingham for their sublime courage, their willingness to suffer and their amazing discipline in the midst of great provocation. One day the South will recognize its real heroes. They will be the James Merediths, with the noble sense of purpose that enables them to face jeering and hostile mobs, and with the agonizing loneliness that characterizes the life of the pioneer. They will be old, oppressed, battered Negro women, symbolized in a seventy-two-year-old woman in Montgomery, Alabama, who rose up with a sense of dignity and with her people decided not to ride segregated buses, and who responded with ungrammatical profundity to one who inquired about her weariness: "My feets is tired, but my soul is at rest." They will be the young high school and college students, the young ministers of the gospel, and a host of their elders, courageously and nonviolently sitting in at lunch counters and willingly going to jail for conscience' sake. One day the South will know that when these disinherited children of God sat down at lunch counters, they were in reality standing up for what is best in the American dream and for the most sacred values in our Judaeo-Christian heritage, thereby bringing our nation back to those great wells of democracy which were dug deep by the founding fathers in their formulation of the Constitution and the Declaration of Independence.

Never before have I written so long a letter. I'm afraid it is much   ^{48.} too long to take your precious time. I can assure you that it would have been much shorter if I had been writing from a comfortable desk, but what else can one do when he is alone in a narrow jail cell, other than write long letters, think long thoughts and pray long prayers?

If I have said anything in this letter that overstates the truth and   ^{49.} indicates an unreasonable impatience, I beg you to forgive me. If I have said anything that understates the truth and indicates my having a patience that allows me to settle for anything less than brotherhood, I beg God to forgive me.

I hope this letter finds you strong in the faith. I also hope that   ^{50.} circumstances will soon make it possible for me to meet each of you, not as an integrationist or a civil-rights leader but as a fellow clergyman and a Christian brother. Let us all hope that the dark clouds of racial prejudice will soon pass away and the deep fog of misunderstanding will be lifted from our fear-drenched communities, and in some not too distant tomorrow the radiant stars of love and brotherhood will shine over our great nation with all their scintillating beauty.

Yours for the cause of Peace and Brotherhood,
Martin Luther King, Jr.

DISCUSSION QUESTIONS

1. Dr. King, like Mr. Hooper, does something which shocks and bewilders his community, but is what he is trying to do any different from what Hooper is trying to do?

2. "In the midst of a mighty struggle to rid our nation of racial and economic injustices, I have heard many ministers say: 'Those are social issues, with which the gospel has no real concern!' " Should a minister concern himself with social issues? Why or why not?

3. Most of us think of "law" in purely legal terms, but what meanings does Dr. King insist upon for that term?

4. Dr. King asserts that in a society a "power majority group" should not be allowed to force its will arbitrarily on a minority group. Are there any reasons why a society is obligated to protect minority groups?

5. Dr. King says that "Shallow understanding from people of good will is more frustrating than absolute misunderstanding from people of ill

will. Lukewarm acceptance is much more bewildering than outright rejection." Connect this statement with his theory of the creative necessity of crisis in a society.

6. Does the fact of Dr. King's assassination in any way lessen the validity of his ideas on nonviolence?

7. King declares that in America each man has a stake in the freedom of his fellow citizens, that injustice to someone in Alabama should involve everyone, even a farmer in Maine. This he sees as being particularly true of a democracy. There are, however, many ethnic groups which exist partially detached from the main cultural life of America because they do not feel any special identity with it. Relate this situation to King's statement of the interdependence of all people.

RHETORIC

1. King links the word "extremist" in paragraph thirty-one to a number of famous people. Write a 200-word paragraph extending his arguments to embrace similar "extremists." Pay particular attention to your topic sentence (see *Essay Development,* Chapter I, p. 10).

2. An allusion is a figure of speech which refers to a famous historical or literary figure or event. Why does King use the allusions that he does in paragraph three? See also paragraphs twenty-one and twenty-two.

3. King has the difficult task of stating the difference between a just and an unjust law. Paragraphs sixteen through twenty attempt to clarify this problem. These paragraphs are a crucial part of his argument and for this reason he needs to be clear and logical. Study the organization of his argument. What is the topic sentence? How is it developed? How does King use examples?

4. In his "Letter to the North" (*Life,* March 5, 1956), William Faulkner, the novelist, argues that the Federal government should hesitate in forcing integration on the South by legal process. He says: "I don't believe compulsion will work." Write a theme which lists three advantages or three disadvantages of such compulsion.

5. Faulkner urges the blacks to wait, just as the writer mentioned in paragraph twenty-six does. Construct an argumentative theme in favor of Faulkner's ideas and one against his ideas [for an example of the latter, refer to James Baldwin's essay on "Faulkner and Desegregation" in *Nobody Knows My Name* (1961)]. Outline your arguments.

6. Research and then describe in detail the bus incident mentioned by King in paragraph forty-seven.

7. Discuss the organization and sentence structure of paragraph thirty. Relate this paragraph to paragraphs twenty-seven through thirty-one. What devices does King use to keep his train of thought clear?

8. Notice how a parallel structure can have a powerful effect. Just as in the final sentence of paragraph ten, where King uses the parallel phrases of "prejudice and racism" and "understanding and brotherhood," so too in paragraphs fourteen and twenty-three he uses parallelism. Why did he organize his ideas this way? What is its effect on the reader? Is it justified?

VOCABULARY

affiliate (paragraph 2)
cognizant (4)
agitator (4)
grapple (5)
negotiate (6)
moratorium (7)
lamentably (12)
ominous (14)
degrades (16)
rabid (20)
anarchy (20)
lukewarm (23)

unswerving (25)
stagnation (26)
complacency (27)
antidotes (32)
nurtured (34)
blatant (37)
irrelevancies (37)
laxity (39)
ineffectual (41)
vitality (44)
provocation (47)
scintillating (50)

law, justice, responsibility

THE DETROIT RIOT

The Fire This Time

1.   At midnight, Hubert G. Locke, a Negro who is administrative assistant to the police commissioner, left his desk at headquarters and climbed to the roof for a look at Detroit. When he saw it, he wept. Beneath him, whole sections of the nation's fifth largest city lay in charred, smoking ruins. From Grand River Avenue to Gratiot Avenue six miles to the east, tongues of flame licked at the night sky, illuminating the angular skeletons of gutted homes, shops, supermarkets. Looters and arsonists danced in the eerie shadows, stripping a store clean, then setting it to the torch. Mourned Mayor Jerome Cavanagh: "It looks like Berlin in 1945."

2.   In the violent summer of 1967, Detroit became the scene of the bloodiest uprising in half a century and the costliest in terms of property damage in U.S. history. At week's end, there were 41 known dead, 347 injured, 3,800 arrested. Some 5,000 people were homeless (the vast majority Negro), while 1,300 buildings had been reduced to mounds of ashes and bricks and 2,700 businesses sacked. Damage estimates reached $500 million. The grim accounting surpassed that of the Watts riot in Los Angeles where 34 died two years ago and property losses ran to $40 million. More noteworthy, the riot surpassed those that had preceded it in the summers of 1964 and 1965 and 1966 in a more fundamental way. For here was the most sensational expression of an ugly mood of nihilism and anarchy that has ever gripped a small but significant segment of America's Negro minority.

Blind Pig

Typically enough, Detroit's upheaval started with a routine   ³·
police action. Seven weeks ago, in the Virginia Park section of the
West Side, a "blind pig" (afterhours club) opened for business on
Twelfth Street, styling itself the "United Community League for
Civic Action." Along with the afterhours booze that it offered to
minors, the "League" served up black-power harangues and curses
against Whitey's exploitation. It was at the blind pig, on a sleazy
strip of pawnshops and bars, rats and pimps, junkies and gamblers,
that the agony began.

Through an informant, police were kept advised of the League's   ⁴·
activities. At 1:45 A.M. Sunday, the informant, a wino and ex-convict,
passed the word (and was paid 50¢ for it): "It's getting ready to
blow." Two hours later, 10th Precinct Sergeant Arthur Howison led
a raid on the League, arresting 73 Negro customers and the bar-
tender. In the next hour, while squad cars and a paddy wagon ferried
the arrested to the police station, a crowd gathered, taunting the fuzz
and "jiving" with friends who had been picked up. "Just as we were
pulling away," Howison said, "a bottle smashed a squad-car window."
Then it began.

Rocks and bottles flew. Looting, at first dared by only a few, be-   ⁵·
came a mob delirium as big crowds now gathered, ranging through the
West Side, then spilling across Woodward Avenue into the East Side.
Arsonists lobbed Molotov cocktails at newly pillaged stores. Fires
started in the shops, spread swiftly to homes and apartments. Snipers
took up posts in windows and on rooftops. For four days and into the
fifth, mobs stole, burned and killed as a force of some 15,000 city and
state police, National Guardsmen and federal troops fought to
smother the fire. The city was almost completely paralyzed.

It Can't Happen Here

For the last couple of years, city officials had been saying   ⁶·
proudly: "That sort of thing can't happen here." It had seemed a
reasonable enough prediction.

Fully 40% of the city's Negro family heads own their own   ⁷·
homes. No city has waged a more massive and comprehensive

war on poverty. Under Mayor Jerry Cavanagh, an imaginative liberal with a knack for landing Government grants, the city has grabbed off $42 million in federal funds for its poverty programs, budgeted $30 million for them this year alone. Because many of the city's 520,000 Negroes (out of a population of 1,600,000) are unequipped to qualify for other than manual labor, some $10 million will go toward special training and placement programs for the unskilled and the illiterate. A $4,000,000 medical program furnishes family-planning advice, out-patient clinics and the like. To cool any potential riot fever, the city had allotted an additional $3,000,000 for this summer's Head Start and recreation programs. So well did the city seem to be handling its problems that Congress of Racial Equality Director Floyd McKissick excluded Detroit last winter when he drew up a list of twelve cities where racial trouble was likely to flare. . . .

Evil Fruit

1.   "Pillage, looting, murder, and arson have nothing to do with civil rights. They are criminal conduct."

2.   Those are the words used by President Johnson to the American people Monday night as hordes of Detroit Negroes rampaged in riots which threatened to match or surpass those which ravaged Newark last week.

3.   "We will not tolerate lawlessness," the President said. "We will not endure violence. It matters not by whom it is done or under what slogan or banner. It will not be tolerated."

4.   Maybe not. But President Johnson, and before him, President Kennedy, did tolerate an erosion of law and order which inevitably led to the civil strife which today plagues much of the land.

5.   The transition from civil rights demonstrations into criminal riots follows naturally once the idea becomes established that people can disregard or disobey laws they dislike. And that idea has been growing in the minds of countless Negroes throughout the turbulent years since 1960.

"Evil Fruit," *The State* (Columbia, S.C.), July 26, 1967, Sec. A, p. 12, cols. 1–2. Copyright © 1967 by *The State*. Reprinted by permission of the publisher.

The idea was planted by civil rights agitators who sought to grab by force what was slowly coming through recognition and responsibility. It has been nurtured by mealy-mouthed do-gooders, including far too many clergymen (black and white) who prate of the individual's right to reject those laws that he personally finds offensive. [6.]

And the idea of selective disobedience of law (which represents the collective conscience of a community) has been indulged—indeed, almost invited—by self-serving politicians whose greed for votes transcends their obligation to keep the peace, preserve the law, and protect the people. [7.]

What America is witnessing, to its shame but not to its surprise, is criminality in action, and stupid criminality at that. What is going on in city after city is not protest but pillage. [8.]

Roy Wilkins, executive director of the National Association for the Advancement of Colored People, has described the Newark rioting as "criminal in intent." It was not, in his view—or ours—a legitimate civil rights protest. [9.]

It is encouraging to hear President Johnson speak out bluntly and boldly, to pledge that "this nation will do whatever is necessary to suppress or punish those who engage in [lawlessness and violence]." [10.]

Fine words, those, but how much weight do we give them in the light of his Administration's actions and attitudes? We welcome his overdue declaration, but we think the President could well have appended this Byronic footnote to his statement: [11.]

"The thorns which I have reap'd are of the tree I planted—they have torn me—and I bleed! I should have known what fruit would spring from such a seed." [12.]

DISCUSSION QUESTIONS

1. King feels that crisis and confrontation are necessary to keep justice alive in a society. The author of this editorial feels that King's confrontations and crises eventually produced what he considers great "injustices." Discuss these divergent views.

2. Do you agree with the author that King and people like him are responsible for the Detroit riots? If so, explain.

3. Read paragraph six again. What function do such words as "mealy-mouthed do-gooders," "prate," and "personally" perform in this statement?

4. King in his "Letter" states that "I had hoped that the white moderate would understand that law and order exist for the purpose of establishing justice and that when they fail in this purpose they become the dangerously structured dams that block the flow of social progress." Obviously, this is an opinion strongly opposed by the writer of the editorial. Discuss.

RHETORIC

1. The *Time* article simply gives the facts; the newspaper editorial, however, gives opinions about facts. The former attempts to inform, the latter to persuade. Notice the use of details in the one and the number of emotionally charged words in the other. For your theme assignment, write two papers, one in which you list facts about an event (a current baseball game, the plot of a movie, etc.), and a second paper in which you express opinions about your subject (baseball competition is bad for young people, this movie stinks, etc.).

2. What is the topic sentence of the "Evil Fruit" editorial? Does the editorial coherently develop this topic sentence?

3. Read editorials in your local or school newspaper. Do you agree or disagree with the views expressed? If you disagree, see if you can detect any fallacies (errors in logic, facts, etc.) in the argument. Submit a 400-word evaluation of the editorial with a copy of the editorial itself.

4. Write an answer to the "Evil Fruit" editorial based on your reading of King's "Letter."

VOCABULARY

The Fire This Time	*Evil Fruit*
gutted (paragraph 1)	hordes (paragraph 2)
nihilism (2)	rampaged (2)
taunting (4)	prate (6)
delirium (5)	pillage (8)
smother (5)	suppress (10)
allotted (7)	

RESPONSIBILITY OF SOCIETY TO THE INDIVIDUAL

Coalition for Better Cities

1. While commissions to "investigate" urban riots proliferate in Washington, a group of outstanding citizens has decided to take the lead in spurring the country to positive action to improve housing, schools and jobs, the obvious needs to combat despair in the slums.

2. This private initiative pools the energies of such dissimilar Americans as David Rockefeller, Walter P. Reuther, Bayard Rustin, Mayor Lindsay and Gerald Phillipe, chairman of the board of General Electric. They and their associates in a new Urban Coalition plan to mobilize a thousand leaders in religion, education, business, labor, civil rights and municipal government at an emergency convocation in Washington later this month.

3. That meeting could become the generator of as dramatic a goad to the national conscience as was provided by the civil rights march on Washington four years ago. The spread of rioting from one racial ghetto to another has made it plain that the critical problem now is faster progress toward making real the promises of social justice embodied in the laws for which tens of thousands marched in 1963.

4. Unquestionably, no amount of effort, no outlay of funds, no application of public or private resources will eradicate the roots of unrest swiftly enough to guarantee civic tranquillity this year or next. But reliance on repression without a massive readjustment of priorities to tackle the sources of hopelessness merely means a downward spiral of hate, with increasingly violent eruptions as its outrider.

5. The statement of the coalition leaders stresses that lawlessness in all its forms cannot be tolerated, but it reminds the nation that the acceptance of law and order by the minorities demands a clear demonstration by the majority of its belief that "justice, social progress and equality are the right of every citizen."

6. Congress is urged to move without delay on urban problems, es-

pecially in the provision of new training programs and jobs for the unemployed. However, there is no disposition to push the whole burden onto the Government. The coalition calls on every American "to join in the creation of a new political, social, economic and moral climate which will make possible the breaking up of the vicious cycle of the ghetto."

7.   The shortage now is as much of will and ideas as it is of public and private money. A state of guerrilla warfare is developing between many in the white and black communities. The diversity of the elements in the Urban Coalition represents a serious and significant effort to end this drift, even rush, toward an ugly kind of American apartheid. Reconstruction of attitudes and redefinition of priorities are essential precedents to reuniting America's riven cities.

While Cities Burn

1.   The nation has cause for deep concern if the leaders of both political parties are unable to forget political considerations when murder, arson and looting are sweeping some of its major cities. This grave domestic crisis demands a level and a quality of mature leadership that have been shocking in their absence.

2.   Because he holds the highest office and therefore bears the highest responsibility both to act and set an example, President Johnson offended most conspicuously in his pussy-footing response to the debacle in Detroit. He shilly-shallied for several hours in ordering the Army units into action in the city despite the pleas of local officials that troops were urgently needed. And when he did act, Mr. Johnson issued a proclamation and a personal statement both of which were clearly designed to place the entire political responsibility on Governor Romney.

3.   It is no disgrace to either the Governor, a Republican, or to Mayor Cavanagh, a Democrat, that the situation in Detroit slipped out of local and state control. The fact that Governor Romney may

be the Republican Presidential candidate next year may explain but cannot excuse President Johnson's nervous political posturing at this critical time.

But if the President's conduct was hesitant and strangely lacking   4. in the quality of leadership, the statement issued by the Republican Coordinating Committee is a flagrant outrage. It is the most transparent kind of seedy politics to assert that these terribly difficult and complex problems, decades and even centuries in the making, have erupted "since the present Administration took office."

This shabby statement insults the nation's intelligence when it   5. asserts that President Johnson's veto of a loosely drafted "crime-control bill" for the District of Columbia contributed to an upheaval a thousand miles away in Detroit or that the ludicrous anti-rioting bill already passed by the House would do the slightest bit of good.

"The root causes of discontent," the statement declares, "are of   6. immediate and continuing concern to all of us." The Republican leaders nowhere state what those "root causes" are. There is not a single word about jobs, housing, health care, education or other urban problems. Instead, the statement is replete with demagogic tales about unspecified factories manufacturing Molotov cocktails and unidentified riot organizers touring the country.

Because the statement was so misleading and so irresponsible,   7. Senator Dirksen, that thick-skinned, battle-hardened political veteran, evidently could not bring himself to face up to a defense of it to skeptical reporters and ran away from his own press conference. It is no credit to either of them that former Governor Dewey shared in the drafting of this document and that former President Eisenhower associated his name with it.

It now appears that Congress will appoint a bipartisan joint   8. committee to inquire into the riots. More good would be accomplished if the conservatives in both parties would re-examine their consciences and their voting records on the model cities bill, the rent-subsidy program, the rat-control bill, and many other measures before Congress. The new committee can accomplish little if its members from both parties do not rise above the execrable level established by Washington's political leaders in recent days.

No Laughing Matter

"Where there is no vision, the people perish."
—Old Testament, Proverbs 29:18

1.   Only three days before Detroit exploded, the House of Representatives took up the administration's bill allocating $40,000,000 to banish rats from city slums. The House had a lot of fun with this measure, which it finally voted down 207 to 176. There were chuckles and guffaws as members suggested, tongue in cheek, that the program would create a "rat bureaucracy," "rat patronage," and "a high commissioner of rats."

2.   This may be a laughing matter to some of our elected representatives, but how many of them live in the slums? It is no laughing matter when children are menaced night and day by rats carrying filth and disease.

3.   The action of the House was a cruel blow to these poor children. We are pleased to see that three of our five Long Island representatives voted for the bill, but we regret that Congressmen James R. Grover Jr. (R–Babylon) and Otis G. Pike (D–Riverhead) voted against it. A similar measure is shortly to come before the Senate, backed by both senators from New York State. We urge its passage. When the House takes it up again, we hope Congressmen Grover and Pike will join with other Long Island representatives to enact it into law. Rats in the slums are no laughing matter.

DISCUSSION QUESTIONS

1. The assumption in Dr. King's essay is one that exists in our Constitution—that society exists to promote life, liberty, and happiness of all its members. This implies that society has obligations to each man within it. What are these obligations and how far do they extend?

2. What do we see as some of the primary concerns of the political figures discussed? What should their concerns have been?

"No Laughing Matter," *Newsday* (Long Island, New York), July 28, 1967. Copyright © 1967 by Newsday, Inc. Reprinted by permission of the publisher.

3. The author of "Evil Fruit" felt that what "civil rights agitators" were seeking through crises was in the natural process of things "slowly coming through recognition and responsibility." What do we make of this statement in light of the editorial entitled "No Laughing Matter"?

RHETORIC

1. In "While Cities Burn" the author begins with a general statement about political leadership and then gives concrete examples to support his statement. Similarly, make an abstract statement about a topic and give both positive and negative examples. For example, develop the topic sentence: "Wars are a time when the individual shows forth the best and the worst aspects of his human nature."

2. Rewrite the introductory and concluding paragraphs of "Coalition for Better Cities" without changing the basic meaning. Refer to Chapters VI (p. 28) and VII (p. 31) in *Essay Development*.

3. The quotation which prefaces "No Laughing Matter" illustrates the relevance of the Bible to the modern world. Provide your own quotation from the Bible or another source and relate it to contemporary events.

4. What are the connotations of "pussy-footing" and "shilly-shallied" in paragraph two of "While Cities Burn"? Do they convey the author's meaning better than such standard terms as "delayed" or "avoided the issue"?

VOCABULARY

Coalition	*While Cities Burn*	*No Laughing Matter*
mobilize (paragraph 2)	mature (paragraph 1)	banish (paragraph 1)
goad (3)	posturing (3)	allocating (1)
eradicate (4)	flagrant (4)	guffaws (1)
priorities (4)	shabby (5)	menaced (2)
cycle (6)	ludicrous (5)	enact (3)
diversity (7)	demagogic (6)	
apartheid (7)	skeptical (7)	
	execrable (8)	

RESPONSIBILITY OF THE INDIVIDUAL TO SOCIETY

Rule of Law

1. In a country ruled by law, maintenance of civil authority and protection of life and order are absolute requisites, the premises on which the social fabric rests. While suppression is obviously no cure for the root causes of the rioting that has shaken Detroit, Newark, and other American cities in recent days, the arsonists and the looters have to be dealt with as the criminals they are. And if Federal troops have to be called in, as they were to the Detroit area, then there can be no hesitation in calling them to restore and preserve the peace.

2. The firebombers and snipers—and the leaders of radical Negro organizations who provoke and excuse lawbreaking—are harming not only innocent white persons and their homes but the majority of Negroes trying to break out of the slum life, turning back in suicidal anger the forward thrust of community confidence and civil rights legislation, damning themselves and their larger cause.

3. The fires must be extinguished, the rifles taken from the hands of rioters, and punishment meted out to fit the crimes. While stores burn and rocks are thrown at firemen, the cries of police brutality sound feeble as excuses for inexcusable criminal conduct. Police and firemen must be supported in their painful assignments—and responsible Negroes, it should be pointed out, have protected them in some neighborhoods.

*　　　　*　　　　*

4. But it was the irresponsible Negroes who prevailed at the National Conference on Black Power in Newark—and sent forth a drumbeat of hostility around the country. The violent elements there preached hatred, separatism and revolution. They have seriously harmed the constructive aims—economic self-improvement and full exercise of political rights—of the black power movement itself. They have betrayed the potential of that conference as a positive force for good.

Here is where an immediate need exists for responsible Negro   5.
leadership in the United States to speak forth quickly and uncom-
promisingly. The Negro leaders who have labored in the ghettos of
the Northern cities, on the marches in the Deep South, and in the
vineyards of Congress and the Supreme Court now have the responsibility to condemn the violence and the lawbreaking. The saner
voices of the Negro community must be heard with greater fervor
than those of the sick nationalists, first, to support the forces of law
and, second, to recapture the nonviolent leadership that is the only
course for a genuinely forward advance of the Negro people.

Lack of equality and opportunity in jobs, housing, education   6.
are underlying causes of social unrest. Governor Rockefeller under-
scored this theme yesterday while condemning the violence.

"We have to understand the causes of this frustration and eradi-   7.
cate them," he declared. "When a child of a Negro family has his nose
and ears chewed up by rats, the family loses hope in the society. . . .
At its deepest and most fundamental level, this is a human problem
and must be met with a human effort."

But until the rule of law—and, as important, respect for the law   8.
as the strongest weapon in safeguarding rights of Americans regardless of color—prevails in riot-torn cities, the basic and essential human effort to improve these conditions can only be distracted,
distorted and delayed.

Havana: Stokely Carmichael's Game

Havana, Aug. 1—Stokely Carmichael is playing a miserable   1.
game down here. He is not only condemning his own country abroad,
but he is misleading Fidel Castro and the other revolutionary Communists from Latin America about the condition and power of the
Negroes in America.

The facts are fairly plain. His Black Power Policy has not gained   2.
popular support among the Negro community in the United States.
He has lost his base as head of the Student Nonviolent Coordinating

James Reston, "Havana: Stokely Carmichael's Game," *The New York Times,* August 2, 1967, p. 36, cols. 5–8. Copyright © 1967 by The New York Times Company. Reprinted by permission of the publisher.

Committee. He has come here from Communist Europe without a legal passport to take part in a viciously anti-U.S. meeting of the most revolutionary fragments of the Latin-American Communist parties, and he is strutting around Havana as a symbol of the American Negroes, most of whom have rejected his leadership.

A Bit of Confusion

3.   He is clearly operating now not only outside the legal framework of the United States Government but outside the structure of the Negro protest movement in the United States as well. Even the official Communist newspapers in Havana are confused about him. One of them referred to him not as an advocate of racial separation and Black Power, but as a leader of the integrationist movement in the United States. One of his aides remarked: "They obviously haven't got Stokely's message."

4.   Carmichael is too intelligent and cynical not to know what he is doing. He has given up on trying to persuade the Negroes at home to follow his Black Power thesis and, either consciously or unconsciously, is making an alliance with the radical revolutionary Communists in Latin America. He is using them, and they in turn are using him, probably to the detriment of both the American Negroes and the militant Latin-American Communists.

Yankees Excluded

5.   Carmichael does not even pretend that he is trying to make an objective case for his argument. At least he is apparently not willing to submit it to questioning. He called a press conference here in Havana today, and excluded everybody from the United States. He had two lists for the press conference—not only of those invited, but those excluded—and even the representative of the U.S. Communist party press was not allowed to attend.

6.   Nevertheless, Castro seems very pleased with Stokely's adventure. He had not only introduced Carmichael publicly to half a million Cubans and the entire Havana diplomatic corps as "one of the most distinguished pro-civil rights leaders in the United States," but has taken him off on a two-day tour of eastern Cuba alone.

Even Castro's most sympathetic supporters in the diplomatic   7.
corps think this dramatic liaison between Stokely and Fidel is very
odd. It obviously does not help the Negro struggle in the United States
to have Castro identifying it as one "front" in the Communist war
against "U.S. imperialism." And it does not help Castro to follow the
Carmichael thesis that "in the event of serious trouble between the
United States and Cuba, the American Negroes will oppose their own
Government."

Yet this is the impression that is being given here by Carmi-   8.
chael's visit to Havana, and Castro's emphasis on the significance of
Stokely's presence here. The Cuban Government has gathered here
for a meeting of the Organization of Latin-American Solidarity, an
astonishing collection of Communist revolutionaries who are more
militant than most of the established Communist parties of the hemisphere. The theme of the conference is that the way to frustrate and
defeat American imperialism is to have a number of armed revolts
against the established governments, including especially the United
States Government, and the Negro revolt in the United States is included in these revolts, with the support of Carmichael.

He is quite blunt about it. He told this reporter the other day in   9.
Santiago de Cuba: "If the United States gets into serious trouble with
Cuba, the white boys are going to fight it out alone. And the rest of us
will be fighting against any U.S.-Cuban battle at home."

The Irreconcilables

Castro may not believe Stokely, but he is obviously using him,   10.
and this is highly ironical. For whatever else Cuba is, it is not a racist
state. There is probably less antiracial and antireligious feeling here
than in any other nation in the hemisphere. Carmichael, with his
policy of racial separation and Black Power, could not be further from
Castro's policy of total racial integration. But Stokely is here, repre-
senting little more than himself, and Castro is playing him up as if he
had the support of the entire Negro community in the United States.
It is a squalid business, which hurts everybody concerned: Carmichael
especially, Castro, the revolutionary movement in the hemisphere and
particularly, and sadly, the American Negro.

A Negro Assays the Negro Mood

1.   The fact that American Negroes rioted in the United Nations while Adlai Stevenson was addressing the Assembly shocked and baffled most white Americans.

2.   Stevenson's speech, and the spectacular disturbance in the gallery, were both touched off by the death in Katanga, the day before, of Patrice Lumumba. Stevenson stated in the course of his address that the United States was "against" colonialism.

3.   God knows what the African nations, who are twenty-five per cent of the voting stock in the United Nations, were thinking—they may, for example, have been thinking of the United States abstention when the vote on Algeria had been before the Assembly—but I think I have a fairly accurate notion of what the Negroes in the gallery were thinking. I had intended to be there myself.

4.   My first reaction to the news of Lumumba's death was curiosity about the impact of this political assassination on Negroes in Harlem, for he had—has—captured the popular imagination there. Then I wanted to know if this most sinister of recent events would elicit from "our" side in the United Nations anything more than the usual well-meaning rhetoric. And I was curious about the African reaction.

5.   However, the chaos on my desk prevented me from being in the United Nations gallery. Had I been there, I, too, in the eyes of many Americans, would have been merely a pawn in the hands of the Communists.

6.   The climate and the events of the last decade, and the steady pressures of the cold war, have given Americans yet another means of avoiding self-examination; thus it was decided that the riots were Communist-inspired. Nor was it long, naturally, before prominent Negroes rushed forward to assure the Republic that the United Nations rioters did not represent the real feeling of the Negro community.

7.   According, then, to what I take to be the prevailing view, these rioters were merely a handful of irresponsible, Kremlin-corrupted *provocateurs.*

James Baldwin, "A Negro Assays the Negro Mood," *The New York Times Magazine*, CX, No. 37 (March 12, 1961), 25. Copyright © 1961 by James Baldwin. Reprinted by permission of Robert Lantz-Candida Donadio Literary Agency, Inc. in conjunction with The New York Times Company.

I find this view amazing. It is a view which even a minimal effort   8.
at observation would immediately contradict. One has only, for
example, to walk through Harlem and ask oneself two questions:
Would *I* like to live here? and, Why don't those who now live here
move out?

The answer to both questions is immediately obvious. Unless one   9.
takes refuge in the theory—however disguised—that Negroes are,
somehow, different from (i.e., inferior to) white people, I do not see
how one can escape the conclusion that the Negro's status in this
country is a cruel injustice and a grave national liability.

Now, I do not doubt that, among the people at the United Na-   10.
tions that day, there were pro-Communists and professional revolu-
tionists acting out of the most cynical motives. Wherever there is great
social discontent, these people are to be found sooner or later.

Their presence in not as frightening as the discontent which   11.
creates their opportunity. What I find appalling—and really dangerous—is the American assumption that the Negro is so contented with
his lot here that only the cynical agents of a foreign power can rouse
him to protest.

This is a notion which contains gratuitous insult, implying, as it   12.
does, that Negroes can make no move unless they are manipulated. It
forcibly suggests that the Southern attitude toward the Negro is also,
essentially, the national attitude. When the South has trouble with its
Negroes—when they refuse to remain in their "place"—it blames
"outside" agitators and "Northern interference." When the nation has
trouble with the Northern Negro, it blames the Kremlin.

This, by no means incidentally, is a hazardous thing to do. We   13.
give credit to the Communists for attitudes and victories which are
not theirs. We make of them the champions of the oppressed, and they
could not, of course, be more delighted.

If, as is only too likely, one prefers not to visit Harlem and ex-   14.
pose oneself to the anguish there, one has only to consider the two
most significant movements among Negroes in this country today.

At one end of the pole is the Negro student movement. The   15.
people who make up this movement really believe in the America of
"liberty and justice for all." They really believe that the country is
anxious to become what it claims to be.

We, therefore, all of us, have a grave responsibility to these   16.
young people. Our failure, now, to rise to the challenge they represent

can only result in the most unimaginable demoralization among them, and among their children; and I would rather not think of the probable effects of such demoralization on the life of this country and on the role we play in the Western world.

17.   The movement does not have as its goal the consumption of overcooked hamburgers and tasteless coffee at various sleazy lunch counters. Neither do Negroes, who are the principal proof and issue of miscegenation, share the white man's helplessly hypocritical attitudes toward the time-honored and universal mingling. The goal of the student movement is nothing less than the liberation of the entire country from its most crippling attitudes and habits. It is of the utmost importance for white people to see the Negroes as people like themselves. Otherwise, the whites will not be able to see themselves as they are.

18.   At the other pole is the Nation of Islam movement, which, daily, becomes more powerful. It is not the only Muslim group in the city or the nation, but it seems to be the best-organized and the most articulate.

19.   The Muslims do not expect anything at all from the white people of this country. They do not believe that the American professions of democracy or equality have ever been remotely sincere. They insist on the total separation of the races.

20.   This separation is to be achieved by the acquisition of land from the United States. The land is owed the Negroes, say the Muslims, as "back wages" for the labor wrested from them when they were slaves, and for their unrecognized and unhonored contributions to the wealth and power of this country.

21.   The student movement depends, at bottom, on an act of faith, an ability to see, beneath the cruelty and hysteria and apathy of white people, their bafflement and pain and essential decency. This is superbly difficult. It demands a perpetually cultivated spiritual resilience, for the bulk of the evidence contradicts the vision.

22.   But the Muslim movement has all the evidence on its side. Unless one supposes that the ideal of black supremacy has virtues denied to the idea of white supremacy, one cannot possibly accept the deadly conclusions a Muslim draws from this evidence. On the other hand, it is quite impossible to argue with a Muslim concerning the actual state of Negroes in this country; the truth, after all, is the truth.

This is the great power a Muslim speaker has over his audience.   ^{23.}
His listeners have not heard the truth about their daily lives honored
by anyone else. Almost all others, black or white, prefer to soften the
truth, and point to a new day which is coming in America.

But this "new day" has been coming for nearly one hundred   ^{24.}
years. Viewed solely in the light of this country's moral professions,
the lapse is inexcusable. Even more important, however, is the fact
that there is desperately little in the record to indicate that white
America ever seriously desired—or desires—to see this day arrive.

Usually, for example, those white people who are in favor of   ^{25.}
integration prove to be in favor of it later, in some other city, some
other town, some other building, some other school. The rationaliza-
tions with which they attempt to disguise their panic cannot be respected.

Northerners proffer their indignation about the South as a kind   ^{26.}
of badge, as proof of good intentions; they never suspect that they
thus increase, in the heart of the Negro they address, a kind of helpless pain and rage—and pity.

Negroes know how little most white people are prepared to im-   ^{27.}
plement their words with deeds, how little, when the chips are down,
they are prepared to risk. And this long history of moral evasion has
had an unhealthy effect on the total life of the country, and has eroded
whatever respect Negroes may once have felt for white people.

We are beginning, therefore, to witness in this country a new   ^{28.}
thing. "I am not at all sure," states one prominent Negro, who is *not*
a Muslim, "that I *want* to be integrated into a burning house."

"I might," says another, "consider being integrated into some-   ^{29.}
thing else, an American society more real and more honest—but *this?*
No, thank you, man, who *needs* it?"

And this searching disaffection has everything to do with the   ^{30.}
emergence of Africa: "At the rate things are going here, all of Africa
will be free before we can get a lousy cup of coffee."

Of course, it is easy to say—and true enough, as far as it goes—   ^{31.}
that the American Negro deludes himself if he imagines that he is
capable of loyalty to any other country other than the United States.
He is an American, too, and he will survive or perish with the country.

This seems an unanswerable argument. But, while I have no   ^{32.}
wish whatever to question the loyalty of American Negroes, I think

this argument may be examined with some profit. It is used, I think, too often and too glibly. It obscures the effects of the passage of time, and the great changes that have taken place in the world.

33.   In the first place, as the homeless wanderers of the twentieth century prove, the question of nationality no longer necessarily involves the question of allegiance. Allegiance, after all, has to work two ways; and one can grow weary of an allegiance which is not reciprocal. I have the right and the duty, for example, to vote in my country; but it is my country's responsibility to protect my right to vote.

34.   People now approaching or past middle age, who have spent their lives in such struggles, have thereby acquired an understanding of America and a belief in her potential which cannot now be shaken. (There are exceptions to this, however—W. E. B. DuBois, for example. It is easy to say he was duped by the Communists, but it is more interesting to consider just why so intelligent a man became so disillusioned.)

35.   But I very strongly doubt that any Negro youth, now approaching maturity and with the whole, vast world before him, is willing, say, to settle for Jim Crow in Miami, when he can—or, before the travel ban, *could*—feast at the welcome table in Havana. And he need not, to prefer Havana, have any pro-Communist—or, for that matter, pro-Cuban, or pro-Castro—sympathies: he need merely prefer not to be treated as a second-class citizen.

36.   These are extremely unattractive facts, but they are facts, and no purpose is served by denying them. Neither, as I have already tried to indicate, is any purpose served by pretending that Negroes who refuse to be bound by this country's peculiar attitudes are subversive. They have every right to refuse to be bound by a set of attitudes that are now as useless and obsolete as the pillory.

37.   Finally, the time is forever behind us when Negroes could be expected to "wait." What is demanded now is not that Negroes continue to adjust themselves to the cruel racial pressures of life in the United States, but that the United States readjust itself to the facts of life in the present world.

38.   One of these facts is that the American Negro can no longer, nor will he ever again, be controlled by white America's image of him. This fact has everything to do with the rise of Africa in world affairs.

39.   At the time that I was growing up, Negroes in this country were taught to be ashamed of Africa. They were taught it bluntly by being

told, for example, that Africa had never contributed "anything" to civilization.

40. Or one was taught the same lesson more obliquely, and even more effectively, by watching nearly naked, dancing, comic-opera cannibalistic savages in the movies. They were nearly always all bad, sometimes funny, sometimes both. If one of them was good, his goodness was proven by his loyalty to the white man.

41. A baffling sort of goodness, particularly as one's own father, who certainly wanted one to be "good," was more than likely to come home cursing—cursing the white man.

42. One's hair was always being attacked with hard brushes and combs and vaseline; it was shameful to have "nappy" hair. One's legs and arms and face were always being greased, so that one would not look "ashy" in the wintertime. One was always being mercilessly scrubbed and polished, as though in the hope that a stain could thus be washed away. I hazard that the Negro children, of my generation, anyway, had an earlier and more painful acquaintance with soap than any other children anywhere.

43. The women were forever straightening and curling their hair, and using bleaching creams. And yet it was clear that none of this effort would release one from the stigma and danger of being a Negro; the effort merely increased the shame and rage.

44. There was not, no matter where one turned, any acceptable image of oneself, no proof of one's existence. One had the choice either of "acting just like a nigger" or not "acting just like a nigger"— and only those who have tried it know how impossible it is to tell the difference.

45. My first hero was Joe Louis. I was ashamed of Father Divine. Haile Selassie, shown in a newsreel, was the first black emperor I had ever seen; he was pleading vainly with the West to prevent the rape of his country. And the extraordinary complex of tensions thus set up in the breast, between hatred of whites and contempt for blacks, is very hard to describe. Some of the most energetic people of my generation were destroyed by this interior warfare.

46. But none of this is so for those who are young now. The power of the white world to control their identities was crumbling as these young Negroes were born and by the time they were able to react to the world, Africa was on the stage of history.

47. This could not but have an extraordinary effect on their own

morale, for it meant that they were not merely the descendants of slaves in a white, Protestant, and Puritan country; they were also related to kings and princes in an ancestral homeland, far away. And this has proven to be a great antidote to the poison of self-hatred.

48.   It also signals, at last, the end of the Negro situation in this country as we have known it thus far. Any effort, from here on out, to keep the Negro in his "place" can only have the most extreme and unlucky repercussions. This being so, it would seem to me that the most intelligent effort we can now make is to give up this doomed endeavor and study how we can most quickly end the division in our house.

49.   The Negroes who rioted in the United Nations are but a very small echo of the black discontent now abroad in the world. If we are not able, and quickly, to face and begin to eliminate the sources of this discontent in our own country, we will never be able to do it in the world at large.

DISCUSSION QUESTIONS

1. "One who breaks an unjust law must do so openly, lovingly, and with a willingness to accept the penalty. I submit that an individual who breaks a law that conscience tells him is unjust, and who willingly accepts the penalty of imprisonment in order to arouse the conscience of the community over its injustice, is in reality expressing the highest respect for law." Discuss Dr. King's statement in terms of the editorial on "Rule of Law."

2. Discuss Carmichael's actions in terms of the perspective of Reston and Baldwin.

3. Discuss Baldwin's essay in terms of our duties as citizens to bear arms in defense of our country.

RHETORIC

1. If some of the names in Baldwin's article are unfamiliar (such as Adlai Stevenson, Patrice Lumumba, W. E. B. DuBois), research their backgrounds in the library. Then, using the facts found in the research, write a brief biography of one of these figures.

2. What is the central thesis of the "Rule of Law" editorial and what is the method of its development?

3. Point out at least three examples of parallel structure in Baldwin's essay.

4. All three papers in this section deal with past events. Write a comparison-contrast theme based on any changes made since these papers were written.

5. The version of Baldwin's essay reprinted here first appeared in *New York Times Magazine*. It has so many brief paragraphs because newspaper and magazine editors prefer that their writers, for the sake of reader interest, place their material in small units. Baldwin later tightened up the structure of his essay and joined paragraphs together when it was published in *Nobody Knows My Name* (under the title "East River, Downtown: Postscript to a Letter from Harlem"). For instance, the first four paragraphs were fused into a single unit. Examine the following groups of paragraphs and then decide how they can best be united without destroying the coherence and development of the entire essay: paragraphs fourteen through twenty-four; thirty-one through forty-five.

VOCABULARY

Rule of Law	*Havana*	*A Negro Assays the Negro Mood*
requisites (paragraph 1)	strutting (paragraph 2)	colonialism (paragraph 2)
arsonists (1)	alliance (4)	impact (4)
preserve (1)	detriment (4)	pawn (5)
thrust (2)	excluded (5)	liability (9)
fervor (5)	liaison (7)	implying (12)
distracted (8)	imperialism (8)	demoralization (16)
	blunt (9)	hypocritical (17)
	squalid (10)	glibly (32)
		reciprocal (33)
		obsolete (36)
		stigma (43)
		morale (47)
		repercussions (48)

the human heart

Mending Wall

Something there is that doesn't love a wall,
That sends the frozen-ground-swell under it,
And spills the upper boulders in the sun;
And makes gaps even two can pass abreast.
The work of hunters is another thing: 5
I have come after them and made repair
Where they have left not one stone on a stone,
But they would have the rabbit out of hiding,
To please the yelping dogs. The gaps I mean,
No one has seen them made or heard them made,   10
But at spring mending-time we find them there.
I let my neighbor know beyond the hill;
And on a day we meet to walk the line
And set the wall between us once again.
We keep the wall between us as we go.   15
To each the boulders that have fallen to each.
And some are loaves and some so nearly balls
We have to use a spell to make them balance:
"Stay where you are until our backs are turned!"
We wear our fingers rough with handling them.   20
Oh, just another kind of outdoor game,
One on a side. It comes to little more:
There where it is we do not need the wall:
He is all pine and I am apple orchard.
My apple trees will never get across   25
And eat the cones under his pines, I tell him.
He only says, "Good fences make good neighbors."
Spring is the mischief in me, and I wonder
If I could put a notion in his head:

"*Why* do they make good neighbors? Isn't it 30
Where there are cows? But here there are no cows.
Before I built a wall I'd ask to know
What I was walling in or walling out,
And to whom I was like to give offense.
Something there is that doesn't love a wall, 35
That wants it down." I could say "Elves" to him,
But it's not elves exactly, and I'd rather
He said it for himself. I see him there
Bringing a stone grasped firmly by the top
In each hand, like an old-stone savage armed. 40
He moves in darkness as it seems to me,
Not of woods only and the shade of trees.
He will not go behind his father's saying,
And he likes having thought of it so well
He says again, "Good fences make good neighbors." 45

The Monsters Are Due on Maple Street

Hysterical people are apt to see things that they never saw before.

It was Saturday afternoon on Maple Street and the late sun re- 1.
tained some of the warmth of a persistent Indian summer. People
along the street marveled at winter's delay and took advantage of it.
Lawns were being mowed, cars polished, kids played hopscotch on the
sidewalks. Old Mr. Van Horn, the patriarch of the street, who lived
alone, had moved his power saw out on his lawn and was fashioning
new pickets for his fence. A Good Humor man bicycled in around
the corner and was inundated by children and by shouts of "Wait a
minute!" from small boys hurrying to con nickels from their parents.
It was 4:40 P.M. A football game blared from a portable radio on a
front porch, blending with the other sounds of a Saturday afternoon in
October. Maple Street. 4:40 P.M. Maple street in its last calm and
reflective moments—before the monsters came.

Steve Brand, fortyish, a big man in an old ex-Marine set of 2.

dungarees, was washing his car when the lights flashed across the sky. Everyone on the street looked up at the sound of the whoosh and the brilliant flash that dwarfed the sun.

3.   "What was that?" Steve called across at his neighbor, Don Martin, who was fixing a bent spoke on his son's bicycle.

Martin, like everyone else, was cupping his hands over his eyes, to stare up at the sky. He called back to Steve, "Looked like a meteor, didn't it? I didn't hear any crash though, did you?"

4.   Steve shook his head. "Nope. Nothing except that roar."

Steve's wife came out on the front porch. "Steve?" she called. "What was that?"

Steve shut off the water hose. "Guess it was a meteor, honey, came awful close, didn't it?"

"Much too close for my money," his wife answered. "Much too close."

5.   She went back into the house, and became suddenly conscious of something. All along Maple Street people paused and looked at one another as a gradual awareness took hold. All the sounds had stopped. All of them. There was silence now. No portable radio. No lawn mowers. No clickety-click of sprinklers that went round and round on front lawns. There was silence.

6.   Mrs. Sharp, fifty-five years of age, was talking on the telephone, giving a cake recipe to her cousin at the other end of town. Her cousin was asking Mrs. Sharp to repeat the number of eggs when her voice clicked off in the middle of the sentence. Mrs. Sharp, who was not the most patient of women, banged furiously on the telephone hook, screaming for an operator.

7.   Pete Van Horn was right in the middle of sawing a 1×4 piece of pine when the power saw went off. He checked the plug, the outlet on the side of the house and then the fuse box in his basement. There was just no power coming in.

8.   Steve Brand's wife, Agnes, came back out on the porch to announce that the oven had stopped working. There was no current or something. Would Steve look at it? Steve couldn't look at it at the moment because he was preoccupied with a hose that suddenly refused to give any more water.

9.   Across the street Charlie Farnsworth, fat and dumpy, in a loud Hawaiian sport shirt that featured hula girls with pineapple baskets on their heads, barged angrily toward the road, damning any radio outfit

that manufactured a portable with the discourtesy to shut off in the middle of a third-quarter forward pass.

Voices built on top of voices until suddenly there was no more silence. There was a conglomeration of questions and protests; of plaintive references to half-cooked dinners, half-watered lawns, half-washed cars, half-finished phone conversations. Did it have anything to do with the meteor? That was the main question—the one most asked. Pete Van Horn disgustedly threw aside the electric cord of his power saw and announced to the group of people who were collected around Steve Brand's station wagon that he was going on over to Bennett Avenue to check and see if the power had gone off there, too. He disappeared into his back yard and was last seen heading into the back yard of the house behind his. *10.*

Steve Brand, his face wrinkled with perplexity, leaned against his car door and looked around at the neighbors who had collected. "It just doesn't make sense," he said. "Why should the power go off all of a sudden *and* the phone line?" *11.*

Don Martin wiped bicycle grease off his fingers. "Maybe some kind of an electrical storm or something."

Dumpy Charlie's voice was always unpleasantly high. "That just doesn't seem likely," he squealed. "Sky's just as blue as anything. Not a cloud. No lightning. No thunder. No nothin'. How could it be a storm?" *12.*

Mrs. Sharp's face was lined with years, but more deeply by the frustration of early widowhood. "Well, it's a terrible thing when a phone company can't keep its line open," she complained. "Just a terrible thing."

"What about my portable radio," Charlie demanded. "Ohio State's got the ball on Southern Methodist's eighteen-yard line. They throw a pass and the damn thing goes off just then." *13.*

There was a murmur in the group as people looked at one another and heads were shaken.

Charlie picked his teeth with a dirty thumb nail. "Steve," he said in his high, little voice, "why don't you go downtown and check with the police?"

"They'll probably think we're crazy or something," Don Martin said. "A little power failure, and right away we get all flustered and everything."

14.   "It isn't just the power failure," Steve answered. "If it was, we'd still be able to get a broadcast on the portable."

There was a murmur of reaction to this and heads nodded.

Steve opened the door to his station wagon. "I'll run downtown. We'll get this all straightened out."

He inched his big frame onto the front seat behind the wheel, turned on the ignition and pushed the starter button. There was no sound. The engine didn't even turn over. He tried it a couple of times more, and still there was no response. The others stared silently at him. He scratched his jaw.

15.   "Doesn't that beat all? It was working fine before."

"Out of gas?" Don offered.

Steve shook his head. "I just had it filled up."

"What's it mean?" Mrs. Sharp asked.

Charlie Farnsworth's piggish little eyes flapped open and shut. "It's just as if—just as if everything had stopped. You better *walk* downtown, Steve."

"I'll go with you," Don said.

Steve got out of the car, shut the door and turned to Don. "Couldn't be a meteor," he said. "A meteor couldn't do *this*."

He looked off in thought for a moment, then nodded. "Come on, let's go."

16.   They started to walk away from the group, when they heard the boy's voice. Tommy Bishop, aged twelve, had stepped out in front of the others and was calling out to them.

"Mr. Brand! Mr. Martin. You better not leave!"

Steve took a step back toward him.

"Why not?" he asked.

"They don't want you to," Tommy said.

Steve and Don exchanged a look.

"*Who* doesn't want us to?" Steve asked him.

Tommy looked up toward the sky. "Them," he said.

"Them?" Steve asked.

"Who are 'them'?" Charlie squealed.

"Whoever was in that thing that came by overhead," Tommy said intently.

Steve walked slowly back toward the boy and stopped close to him. "What, Tommy?" he asked.

"Whoever was in that thing that came over," Tommy repeated.   17. "I don't think they want us to leave here."

Steve knelt down in front of the boy. "What do you mean, Tommy? What are you talking about?"

"They don't want us to leave, that's why they shut everything off."

"What makes you say that?" Irritation crept into Steve's voice. "Whatever gave you *that* idea?"

Mrs. Sharp pushed her way through to the front of the crowd. "That's the craziest thing I have ever heard," she announced in a public-address-system voice. "Just about the craziest thing I ever did hear!"

Tommy could feel the unwillingness to believe him. "It's always   18. that way," he said defensively, "in every story I've ever read about a spaceship landing from outer space!"

Charlie Farnsworth whinnied out his derision.

Mrs. Sharp waggled a bony finger in front of Tommy's mother. "If you ask me, Sally Bishop," she said, "you'd better get that boy of yours up to bed. He's been reading too many comic books or seeing too many movies or something."

Sally Bishop's face reddened. She gripped Tommy's shoulders tightly. "Tommy," she said softly. "Stop that kind of talk, honey."

Steve's eyes never left the boy's face. "That's all right, Tom. We'll   19. be right back. You'll see. That wasn't a ship or anything like it. That was just a—a meteor or something, likely as not—" He turned to the group, trying to weight his words with an optimism he didn't quite feel. "No doubt it did have something to do with all this power failure and the rest of it. Meteors can do crazy things. Like sun spots."

"That's right," Don said, as if picking up a cue. "Like sun spots.   20. That kind of thing. They can raise cain with radio reception all over the world. And this thing being so close—why there's no telling what sort of stuff it can do." He wet his lips nervously. "Come on, Steve. We'll go into town and see if that isn't what's causing it all."

Once again the two men started away.

"Mr. Brand!" Tommy's voice was defiant and frightened at the same time. He pulled away from his mother and ran after them. "Please, Mr. Brand, please don't leave here."

There was a stir, a rustle, a movement among the people. There   21.

was something about the boy. Something about the intense little face. Something about the words that carried such emphasis, such belief, such fear. They listened to these words and rejected them because intellect and logic had no room for spaceships and green-headed things. But the irritation that showed in the eyes, the murmuring and the compressed lips had nothing to do with intellect. A little boy was bringing up fears that shouldn't be brought up; and the people on Maple Street this Saturday afternoon were no different from any other set of human beings. Order, reason, logic were slipping, pushed by the wild conjectures of a twelve-year-old boy.

22.   "Somebody ought to spank that kid," an angry voice muttered.

Tommy Bishop's voice continued defiant. It pierced the murmurings and rose above them. "You might not even be able to get to town," he said. "It was that way in the story. *Nobody* could leave. Nobody except—"

"Except who?" Steve asked.

"Except the people they'd sent down ahead of them. They looked just like humans. It wasn't until the ship landed that . . . "

His mother grabbed him by the arm and pulled him back. "Tommy," she said in a low voice. "Please, honey . . . don't talk that way."

23.   "Damn right he shouldn't talk that way," came the voice of the man in the rear again. "And we shouldn't stand here listening to him. Why this is the craziest thing I ever heard. The kid tells us a comic-book plot and here we stand listening . . ."

His voice died away as Steve stood up and faced the crowd. Fear can throw people into a panic, but it can also make them receptive to a leader and Steve Brand at this moment was such a leader. The big man in the ex-Marine dungarees had an authority about him.

24.   "Go ahead, Tommy," he said to the boy. "What kind of a story was this? What about the people that they sent out ahead?"

"That was the way they prepared things for the landing, Mr. Brand," Tommy said. "They sent four people. A mother and a father and two kids who looked just like humans. But they weren't."

There was a murmur—a stir of uneasy laughter. People looked at one another again and a couple of them smiled.

"Well," Steve said, lightly but carefully, "I guess we'd better run a check on the neighborhood, and see which ones of us are really human."

His words were a release. Laughter broke out openly. But soon
it died away. Only Charlie Farnsworth's horse whinny persisted over
the growing silence and then he too lapsed into a grim quietness, until all fifteen people were looking at one another through changed eyes.
A twelve-year-old boy had planted a seed. And something was growing out of the street with invisible branches that began to wrap themselves around the men and women and pull them apart. Distrust lay
heavy in the air.

Suddenly there was the sound of a car engine and all heads
turned as one. Across the street Ned Rosen was sitting in his con-
vertible trying to start it, and nothing was happening beyond the
labored sound of a sick engine getting deeper and hoarser and finally
giving up altogether. Ned Rosen, a thin, serious-faced man in his
thirties, got out of his car and closed the door. He stood there staring
at it for a moment, shook his head, looked across the street at his
neighbors and started toward them.

"Can't get her started, Ned?" Don Martin called out to him.

"No dice," Ned answered. "Funny, she was working fine this
morning."

Without warning, all by itself, the car started up and idled
smoothly, smoke briefly coming out of the exhaust. Ned Rosen
whirled around to stare at it, his eyes wide. Then, just as suddenly as
it started, the engine sputtered and stopped.

"Started all by itself!" Charlie Farnsworth squealed excitedly.

"How did it do that?" Mrs. Sharp asked. "How could it just start
all by itself?"

Sally Bishop let loose her son's arm and just stood there, shaking her head. "How in the world . . ." she began.

Then there were no more questions. They stood silently staring
at Ned Rosen who looked from them to his car and then back again.
He went to the car and looked at it. Then he scratched his head again.

"Somebody explain it to me," he said. "I sure never saw anything
like that happen before!"

"He never did come out to look at that thing that flew overhead.
He wasn't even interested," Don Martin said heavily.

"What do you say we ask him some questions," Charlie Farnsworth proposed importantly. "I'd like to know what's going on here!"

There was a chorus of assent and the fifteen people started across
the street toward Ned Rosen's driveway. Unity was restored, they had

a purpose, a feeling of activity and direction. They were doing something. They weren't sure what, but Ned Rosen was flesh and blood—askable, reachable and seeable. He watched with growing apprehension as his neighbors marched toward him. They stopped on the sidewalk close to the driveway and surveyed him.

30.   Ned Rosen pointed to his car. "I just don't understand it, any more than you do! I tried to start it and it *wouldn't* start. You saw me. All of you saw me."

His neighbors seemed massed against him, solidly, alarmingly.

"I don't understand it!" he cried. "I swear—I don't understand. What's happening?"

Charlie Farnsworth stood out in front of the others. "Maybe you better tell us," he demanded. "Nothing's working on this street. Nothing. No lights, no power, no radio. Nothing except one car—*yours!*"

31.   There were mutterings from the crowd. Steve Brand stood back by himself and said nothing. He didn't like what was going on. Something was building up that threatened to grow beyond control.

"Come on, Rosen," Charlie Farnsworth commanded shrilly, "let's hear what goes on! Let's hear how you explain your car startin' like that!"

32.   Ned Rosen wasn't a coward. He was a quiet man who didn't like violence and had never been a physical fighter. But he didn't like being bullied. Ned Rosen got mad.

"Hold it!" he shouted. "Just hold it! You keep your distance. All of you. All right, I've got a car that starts by itself. Well, that's a freak—I admit it! But does that make me some sort of a criminal or something? I don't know why the car works—it just does!"

33.   The crowd was neither sobered nor reassured by Rosen's words, but they were not too frightened to listen. They huddled together, mumbling, and Ned Rosen's eyes went from face to face till they stopped on Steve Brand's. Ned knew Steve Brand. Of all the men on the street, this seemed the guy with the most substance. The most intelligent. The most essentially decent.

"What's it all about Steve?" he asked.

34.   "We're all on a monster kick, Ned," he answered quietly. "Seems that the general impression holds that maybe one family isn't what we think they are. Monsters from outer space or something. Different from us. Fifth columnists from the vast beyond." He couldn't keep the sarcasm out of his voice. "Do you know anybody around here who might fit that description?"

Rosen's eyes narrowed. "What is this, a gag?" He looked around the group again. "This a practical joke or something?" And without apparent reason, without logic, without explanation, his car started again, idled for a moment, sending smoke out of the exhaust, and stopped.

A woman began to cry, and the bank of eyes facing Ned Rosen looked cold and accusing. He walked to his porch steps and stood on them, facing his neighbors.

"Is that supposed to incriminate me?" he asked. "The car engine goes on and off and that really does it, huh?" He looked down into their faces. "I don't understand it. Not any more than you do."

He could tell they were unmoved. This couldn't really be happening, Ned thought to himself.

"Look," he said in a different tone. "You all know me. We've lived here four years. Right in this house. We're no different from any of the rest of you!" He held out his hands toward them. The people he was looking at hardly resembled the people he'd lived alongside of for the past four years. They looked as if someone had taken a brush and altered every character with a few strokes. "Really," he continued, "this whole thing is just . . . just weird—"

"Well, if that's the case, Ned Rosen," Mrs. Sharp's voice suddenly erupted from the crowd—"maybe you'd better explain why—" She stopped abruptly and clamped her mouth shut, but looked wise and pleased with herself.

"Explain what?" Rosen asked her softly.

Steve Brand sensed a special danger now. "Look," he said, "let's forget this right now—"

Charlie Farnsworth cut him off. "Go ahead. Let her talk. What about it? Explain what?"

Mrs. Sharp, with an air of great reluctance, said, "Well, sometimes I go to bed late at night. A couple of times—a couple of times I've come out on the porch, and I've seen Ned Rosen here, in the wee hours of the morning, standing out in front of his house looking up at the sky." She looked around the circle of faces. "That's right, looking up at the sky as if—as if he was waiting for something." She paused for emphasis, for dramatic effect. "As if he was looking for something!" she repeated.

The nail on the coffin, Steve Brand thought. One dumb, ordinary, simple idiosyncrasy of a human being—and that probably was all it would take. He heard the murmuring of the crowd rise and saw

35.

36.

37.

38.

39.

40.

Ned Rosen's face turn white. Rosen's wife, Ann, came out on the porch. She took a look at the crowd and then at her husband's face.

"What's going on, Ned?" she asked.

41.   "I don't know what's going on," Ned answered. "I just don't know, Ann. But I'll tell you this. I don't like these people. I don't like what they're doing. I don't like them standing in my yard like this. And if any one of them takes another step and gets close to my porch—I'll break his jaw. I swear to God, that's just what I'll do. I'll break his jaw. Now go on, get out of here, all of you!" he shouted at them. "Get the devil out of here."

42.   "Ned," Ann's voice was shocked.

"You heard me," Ned repeated. "All of you get out of here."

None of them eager to start an action, the people began to back away. But they had an obscure sense of gratification. At least there was an opponent now. Someone who wasn't one of them. And this gave them a kind of secure feeling. The enemy was no longer formless and vague. The enemy had a front porch and a front yard and a car. And he had shouted threats at them.

43.   They started slowly back across the street forgetting for the moment what had started it all. Forgetting that there was no power, and no telephones. Forgetting even there had been a meteor overhead not twenty minutes earlier. It wasn't until much later, as a matter of fact, that anyone posed a certain question.

44.   Old man Van Horn had walked through his back yard over to Bennett Avenue. He'd never come back. Where was he? It was not one of the questions that passed through the minds of any of the thirty or forty people on Maple Street who sat on their front porches and watched the night come and felt the now menacing darkness close in on them.

45.   There were lanterns lit all along Maple Street by ten o'clock. Candles shone through living-room windows and cast flickering, unsteady shadows all along the street. Groups of people huddled on front lawns around their lanterns and a soft murmur of voices was carried over the Indian-summer night air. All eyes eventually were drawn to Ned Rosen's front porch.

He sat there on the railing, observing the little points of light spotted around in the darkness. He knew he was surrounded. He was an animal at bay.

46.   His wife came out on the porch and brought him a glass of lem-

onade. Her face was white and strained. Like her husband, Ann Rosen was a gentle person, unarmored by temper or any proclivity for outrage. She stood close to her husband now on the darkened porch feeling the suspicion that flowed from the people around lanterns, thinking to herself that these were people she had entertained in her house. These were women she talked to over clotheslines in the back yard; people who had been friends and neighbors only that morning. Oh dear God, could all this have happened in those few hours? It must be a nightmare, she thought. It had to be a nightmare that she could wake up from. It couldn't be anything else.

47. Across the street Mabel Farnsworth, Charlie's wife, shook her head and clucked at her husband who was drinking a can of beer. "It just doesn't seem right though, Charlie, keeping watch on them. Why he was right when he said he was one of our neighbors. I've known Ann Rosen ever since they moved in. We've been good friends."

48. Charlie Farnsworth turned to her disgustedly. "That don't prove a thing," he said. "Any guy who'd spend his time lookin' up at the sky early in the morning—well there's something wrong with that kind of person. There's something that ain't legitimate. Maybe under normal circumstances we could let it go by. But these aren't normal circumstances." He turned and pointed toward the street. "Look at that," he said. "Nothin' but candles and lanterns. Why it's like goin' back into the Dark Ages or something!"

49. He was right. Maple Street had changed with the night. The flickering lights had done something to its character. It looked odd and menacing and very different. Up and down the street, people noticed it. The change in Maple Street. It was the feeling one got after being away from home for many, many years and then returning. There was a vague familiarity about it, but it wasn't the same. It was different.

50. Ned Rosen and his wife heard footsteps coming toward their house. Ned got up from the railing and shouted out into the darkness.

"Whoever it is, just stay right where you are. I don't want any trouble, but if anybody sets foot on my porch, that's what they're going to get—trouble!" He saw that it was Steve Brand and his features relaxed.

"Ned," Steve began.

Ned Rosen cut him off. "I've already explained to you people, I don't sleep very well at night sometimes. I get up and I take a walk and I look up at the sky. I look at the stars."

51. Ann Rosen's voice shook as she stood alongside of him. "That's exactly what he does. Why this whole thing, it's—it's some kind of madness or something."

Steve Brand stood on the sidewalk and nodded grimly. "That's exactly what it is—some kind of madness."

Charlie Farnsworth's voice from the adjoining yard was spiteful. "You'd best watch who you're seen with, Steve. Until we get this all straightened out, you ain't exactly above suspicion yourself."

52. Steve whirled around to the outline of the fat figure that stood behind the lantern in the other yard. "Or you, either, Charlie," he shouted. "Or any of the rest of us!"

Mrs. Sharp's voice came from the darkness across the street. "What I'd like to know is—what are we going to do? Just stand around here all night?"

"There's nothing else we can do," Charlie Farnsworth said. He looked wisely over toward Ned Rosen's house. "One of em'll tip their hand. They *got* to."

53. It was Charlie's voice that did it for Steve Brand at this moment. The shrieking, pig squeal that came from the layers of fat and the idiotic sport shirt and the dull, dumb, blind prejudice of the man. "There's something *you* can do, Charlie," Steve called out to him. "You can go inside your house and keep your mouth shut!"

"You sound real anxious to have that happen, Steve," Charlie's voice answered him back from the little spot of light in the next yard. "I think we'd better keep our eye on you, too!"

54. Don Martin came up to Steve Brand, carrying a lantern. There was something hesitant in his manner, as if he were about to take a bit in his teeth, but wondered whether it would hurt. "I think everything might as well come out now," Don said. "I really do. I think everything should come out."

People came off porches, from front yards, to stand around in a group near Don who now turned directly toward Steve.

"Your wife's done plenty of talking, Steve, about how odd you are," he said.

Charlie Farnsworth trotted over. "Go ahead. Tell us what she said," he demanded excitedly.

55. Steve Brand knew this was the way it would happen. He was not really surprised but he still felt a hot anger rise up inside of him. "Go

ahead," he said. "What's my wife said? Let's get it *all* out." He peered around at the shadowy figures of the neighbors. "Let's pick out every peculiarity of every single man, woman and child on this street! Don't stop with me and Ned. How about a firing squad at dawn, so we can get rid of all the suspects! Make it easier for you!"

Don Martin's voice retreated fretfully. "There's no need getting so upset, Steve—" [56.]

"Go to blazes, Don," Steve said to him in a cold and dispassionate fury.

Needled, Don went on the offensive again but his tone held something plaintive and petulant. "It just so happens that, well, Agnes has talked about how there's plenty of nights you've spent hours in your basement working on some kind of radio or something. Well, none of us have ever seen that radio—"

"Go ahead, Steve," Charlie Farnsworth yelled at him. "What kind of a 'radio set' you workin' on? I never seen it. Neither has anyone else. Who do you talk to on that radio set? And who talks to you?" [57.]

Steve's eyes slowly traveled in an arc over the hidden faces and the shrouded forms of neighbors who were now accusers. "I'm surprised at you, Charlie," he said quietly. "I really am. How come you're so damn dense all of a sudden? Who do I talk to? I talk to monsters from outer space. I talk to three-headed green men who fly over here in what look like meteors."

Agnes Brand walked across the street to stand at her husband's elbow. She pulled at his arm with frightened intensity. "Steve! Steve! please," she said. "It's just a ham radio set," she tried to explain. "That's all. I bought him a book on it myself. It's just a ham radio set. A lot of people have them. I can show it to you. It's right down in the basement." [58.]

Steve pulled her hand off his arm. "You show them nothing," he said to her. "If they want to look inside our house, let them get a search warrant!"

Charlie's voice whined at him. "Look, buddy, you can't afford to—"

"Charlie," Steve shouted at him. "Don't tell me what I can afford. And stop telling me who's dangerous and who isn't. And who's safe and who's a menace!" He walked over to the edge of the road and saw that people backed away from him. "And you're with him— all of you," Steve bellowed at them. "You're standing there all set to [59.]

crucify—to find a scapegoat—desperate to point some kind of a finger at a neighbor!" There was intensity in his tone and on his face, accentuated by the flickering light of the lanterns and the candles. "Well look, friends, the only thing that's going to happen is that we'll eat each other up alive. Understand? *We are going to eat each other up alive!"*

60.   Charlie Farnsworth suddenly ran over to him and grabbed his arm. "That's not the *only* thing that can happen to us," he said in a frightened, hushed voice. "Look!"

"Oh, my God," Don Martin said.

Mrs. Sharp screamed. All eyes turned to look down the street where a figure suddenly materialized in the darkness and the sound of measured footsteps on concrete grew louder and louder as it walked toward them. Sally Bishop let out a stifled cry and grabbed Tommy's shoulder.

The child's voice screamed out, "It's the monster! It's the monster!"

61.   There was a frightened wail from another woman, and the residents of Maple Street stood transfixed with terror as something unknown came slowly down the street. Don Martin disappeared and came back out of his house a moment later carrying a shotgun. He pointed it toward the approaching form. Steve pulled it out of his hands.

"For God's sake, will somebody think a thought around here? Will you people wise up? What good would a shotgun do against—"

62.   A quaking, frightened Charlie Farnsworth grabbed the gun from Steve's hand. "No more talk, Steve," he said. "You're going to talk us into a grave! You'd let whoever's out there walk right over us, wouldn't yuh? Well, some of us won't!"

He swung the gun up and pulled the trigger. The noise was a shocking, shattering intrusion and it echoed and re-echoed through the night. A hundred yards away the figure collapsed like a piece of clothing blown off a line by the wind. From front porches and lawns people raced toward it.

63.   Steve was the first to reach him. He knelt down, turned him over and looked at his face. Then he looked up toward the semicircle of silent faces surveying him.

"All right, friends," he said quietly. "It happened. We got our first victim—Pete Van Horn!"

"Oh, my God," Don Martin said in a hushed voice. "He was just ^{64.} going over to the next block to see if the power was on—"

Mrs. Sharp's voice was that of injured justice. "You killed him, Charlie! You shot him dead!"

Charlie Farnsworth's face looked like a piece of uncooked dough, quivering and shaking in the light of the lantern he held.

"I didn't know who he was," he said. "I certainly didn't know ^{65.} who he was." Tears rolled down his fat cheeks. "He comes walking out of the dark—how am I supposed to know who he was?" He looked wildly around and then grabbed Steve's arm. Steve could explain things to people. "Steve," he screamed, "you know why I shot. How was I supposed to know he wasn't a monster or something?"

Steve looked at him and didn't say anything. Charlie grabbed ^{66.} Don.

"We're all scared of the same thing. I was just tryin' to protect my home, that's all. Look, all of you, that's all I was tryin' to do!" He tried to shut out the sight of Pete Van Horn who stared up at him with dead eyes and a shattered chest. "Please, please, please," Charlie Farnsworth sobbed, "I didn't know it was somebody we knew. I swear to God I didn't know—"

The lights went on in Charlie Farnsworth's house and shone ^{67.} brightly on the people of Maple Street. They looked suddenly naked. They blinked foolishly at the lights and their mouths gaped like fishes.

"Charlie," Mrs. Sharp said, like a judge pronouncing sentence, "how come you're the only one with lights on now?"

Ned Rosen nodded in agreement. "That's what I'd like to know," ^{68.} he said. Something inside tried to check him, but his anger made him go on. "How come, Charlie? You're quiet all of a sudden. You've got nothing to say out of that big, fat mouth of yours. Well, let's hear it, Charlie? Let's hear why you've got lights!"

Again the chorus of voices that punctuated the request and gave it legitimacy and a vote of support. "Why, Charlie?" the voices asked him. "How come you're the only one with lights?" The questions came out of the night to land against his fat wet cheeks. "You were so quick to tell us who we had to be careful of. Well maybe you had to kill, Charlie. Maybe Pete Van Horn, God rest his soul, was trying to tell us who there was among us we should watch out for."

Charlie's eyes were little pits of growing fear as he backed away ^{69.}

from people and found himself up against a bush in front of his house. "No," he said. "No, please." His chubby hands tried to speak for him. They waved around, pleading. The palms outstretched, begging for forgiveness and understanding. "Please—please, I swear to you—it isn't me! It really isn't me."

A stone hit him on the side of the face and drew blood. He screamed and clutched at his face as the people began to converge on him.

"No," he screamed. "No."

70.   Like a hippopotamus in a circus, he scrambled over the bush, tearing his clothes and scratching his face and arms. His wife tried to run toward him, somebody stuck a foot out and she tripped, sprawling head first on the sidewalk. Another stone whistled through the air and hit Charlie on the back of the head as he raced across his front yard toward his porch. A rock smashed at the porch light and sent glass cascading down on his head.

71.   "It isn't me," he screamed back at them as they came toward him across the front lawn. "It isn't me, but I know who it is," he said suddenly, without thought. Even as he said it, he realized it was the only possible thing to say.

People stopped, motionless as statues, and a voice called out from the darkness. "All right, Charlie, who is it?"

He was a grotesque, fat figure of a man who smiled now through the tears and the blood that cascaded down his face. "Well, I'm going to tell you," he said. "I am now going to tell you, because I know who it is. I really know who it is. It's . . ."

"Go ahead, Charlie," a voice commanded him. "Who's the monster?"

72.   Don Martin pushed his way to the front of the crowd. "All right, Charlie, now! Let's hear it!"

Charlie tried to think. He tried to come up with a name. A nightmare engulfed him. Fear whipped at the back of his brain. "It's the kid," he screamed. "That's who it is. It's the kid!"

Sally Bishop screamed and grabbed at Tommy, burying his face against her. "That's crazy," she said to the people who now stared at her. "That's crazy. He's a little boy."

73.   "But he knew," said Mrs. Sharp. "He was the only one who knew. He told us about it. Well, how did he know? How *could* he have known?"

Voices supported her. "How could he know?" "Who told him?" "Make the kid answer." A fever had taken hold now, a hot burning virus that twisted faces and forced out words and solidified the terror inside of each person on Maple Street.

Tommy broke away from his mother and started to run. A man 74. dove at him in a flying tackle and missed. Another man threw a stone wildly toward the darkness. They began to run after him down the street. Voices shouted through the night, women screamed. A small child's voice protested—a playmate of Tommy's, one tiny voice of sanity in the middle of a madness as men and women ran down the street, the sidewalks, the curbs, looking blindly for a twelve-year-old boy.

And then suddenly the lights went on in another house—a two-story, gray stucco house that belonged to Bob Weaver. A man screamed, "It isn't the kid. It's Bob Weaver's house!"

A porch light went on at Mrs. Sharp's house and Sally Bishop 75. screamed, "It isn't Bob Weaver's house. It's Mrs. Sharp's place."

"I tell you it's the kid," Charlie screamed.

The lights went on and off, on and off down the street. A power mower suddenly began to move all by itself lurching crazily across a front yard cutting an irregular path of grass until it smashed against the side of the house.

"It's Charlie," Don Martin screamed. "He's the one." And then he saw his own lights go on and off.

They ran this way and that way, over to one house and then 76. back across the street to another. A pane of glass smashed and there was the cry of a woman in pain. Lights on and off, on and off. Charlie Farnsworth went down on his knees as a piece of brick plowed a two-inch hole in the back of his skull. Mrs. Sharp lay on her back screaming, and felt the tearing jab of a woman's high heel in her mouth as someone stepped on her, racing across the street.

From a quarter of a mile away, on a hilltop, Maple Street looked 77. like this, a long tree-lined avenue full of lights going on and off and screaming people racing back and forth. Maple Street was a bedlam. It was an outdoor asylum for the insane. Windows were broken, street lights sent clusters of broken glass down on the heads of women and children. Power mowers started up and car engines and radios. Blaring music mixed with the screams and shouts and the anger.

^{78.}   Up on top of the hill two men, screened by the darkness, stood near the entrance to a spaceship and looked down on Maple Street.

"Understand the procedure now?" the first figure said. "Just stop a few of their machines and radios and telephones and lawn mowers. Throw them into darkness for a few hours and then watch the pattern unfold."

"And this pattern is always the same?" the second figure asked.

^{79.}   "With few variations," came the answer. "They pick the most dangerous enemy they can find and it's themselves. All we need do is sit back—and watch."

"Then I take it," figure two said, "this place, this Maple Street is not unique?"

Figure one shook his head and laughed. "By no means. Their world is full of Maple Streets and we'll go from one to the other and let them destroy themselves." He started up the incline toward the entrance of the spaceship. "One to the other," he said as the other figure followed him. "One to the other." There was just the echo of his voice as the two figures disappeared and a panel slid softly across the entrance. "One to the other," the echo said.

^{80.}   When the sun came up on the following morning Maple Street was silent. Most of the houses had been burned. There were a few bodies lying on the sidewalks and draped over porch railings. But the silence was total. There was simply no more life. At four o'clock that afternoon there was no more world, or at least not the kind of world that had greeted the morning. And by Wednesday afternoon of the following week, a new set of residents had moved into Maple Street. They were a handsome race of people. Their faces showed great character. Great character indeed. Great character and excellently shaped heads—two to each new resident!

DISCUSSION QUESTIONS

1. This could be called a science-fiction story. Do you find the people in it unrealistic?

2. Do you feel there are any people in the story who are naturally malicious? Are there decent, good-hearted people in the story, and if so, why and how are they pulled into the chaos?

3. Why is Brand, apparently a man experienced in confronting the

enemy in foreign lands, helpless before his closest friends in his own neighborhood?

4. Who are the monsters?

5. Why do the people in the story feel compelled to find a scapegoat (Ned Rosen, Tommy Bishop, Charlie Farnsworth)? Why is their search for one futile?

RHETORIC

1. Write a 350-word theme relating three things that would happen should there be a major electrical failure in your city.

2. Characterization can be handled either by "show" or "tell." For instance, in paragraph nine Serling tells us that Charlie Farnsworth is "fat and dumpy." But then he immediately *shows* us in the description of Charlie in a "loud Hawaiian sport shirt that featured hula girls with pineapple baskets on their heads." The image formed in our mind is of an equally loud, obnoxious figure. Locate other instances of such "show" or "tell" descriptions.

3. Comment on the details used in the introductory paragraph.

4. Serling, like most short-story writers, must present a character to a reader in a few sentences. Study his techniques and then in three brief paragraphs describe several of your classmates. Use sufficient details (see *Essay Development,* Chapter II, p. 14) so that we see them as individuals.

5. Create a science-fiction story related to events in your own neighborhood.

VOCABULARY

reflective (paragraph 1)	exhaust (35)
portable (5)	reluctance (39)
preoccupied (8)	idiosyncrasy (40)
conglomeration (10)	outrage (46)
perplexity (11)	proclivity (46)
squealed (16)	flickering (49)
derision (18)	menace (59)
optimism (19)	intrusion (62)
lapsed (25)	grotesque (71)
sobered (33)	bedlam (77)
sarcasm (34)	

The Magic White Suit

1.
     It was summer twilight in the city, and out front of the quiet-clicking poolhall three young Mexican-American men breathed the warm air and looked around at the world. Sometimes they talked and sometimes they said nothing at all, but watched the cars glide by like black panthers on the hot asphalt or saw trolleys loom up like thunderstorms, scatter lightning, and rumble away into silence.
     "Hey," sighed Martinez, at last. He was the youngest, the most sweetly sad of the three. "It's a swell night, huh? Swell."

2.
     As he observed the world it moved very close and then drifted away and then came close again. People, brushing by, were suddenly across the street. Buildings five miles away suddenly leaned over him. But most of the time everything—people, cars and buildings—stayed way out on the edge of the world and could not be touched. On this quiet warm summer evening, Martinez' face was cold.
     "Nights like this you wish—lots of things."

3.
     "Wishing," said the second man, Villanazul, a man who shouted books out loud in his room, but spoke only in whispers on the street, "is the useless pastime of the unemployed."
     "Unemployed?" cried Vamenos, the unshaven. "Listen to him! We got no jobs, no money!"
     "So," said Martinez, "we got no friends."

4.
     "True." Villanazul gazed off toward the green plaza where the palm trees swayed in the soft night wind. "Do you know what I wish? I wish to go into that plaza and speak among the businessmen who gather there nights to talk big talk. But dressed as I am, poor as I am, who would listen? So, Martinez, we have each other. The friendship of the poor is real friendship. We—"
     But now a handsome young Mexican with a fine thin mustache strolled by. And on each of his careless arms hung a laughing woman.

5.
     "Madre mia!" Martinez slapped his own brow. "How does one rate two friends?"
     "It's his nice new white suit." Vamenos chewed a black thumbnail. "He looks sharp."

Martinez leaned out to watch the three people moving away, and then at the tenement across the street, in one fourth-floor window of which, far above, a beautiful girl looked out, her dark hair faintly stirred by the wind. She had been there forever, which was to say, for six weeks. He had nodded, he had raised a hand, he had smiled, he had blinked rapidly; he had even bowed to her, on the street, in the hall when visiting friends, in the park, downtown. Even now, he put his hand up from his waist and moved his fingers. But all the lovely girl did was let the summer wind stir her dark hair. He did not exist. He was nothing.

"Madre mia!" He looked away and down the street where the man walked his two friends around a corner. "Oh, if just I had one suit, one! I wouldn't need money if I looked O.K." 6.

"I hesitate to suggest," said Villanazul, "that you see Gomez. But he's been talking some crazy talk for a month now, about clothes. I keep on saying I'll be in on it to make him go away. That Gomez."

"Friend," said a quiet voice.

"Gomez!" Everyone turned to stare.

Smiling strangely, Gomez pulled forth an endless thin yellow ribbon which fluttered and swirled on the summer air.

"Gomez," said Martinez, "what you doing with that tape measure?" 7.

Gomez beamed. "Measuring people's skeletons."

"Skeletons!"

"Hold on," Gomez squinted at Martinez. "Caramba! Where you been all my life! Let's try you!"

Martinez saw his arm seized and taped, his leg measured, his chest encircled.

"Hold still!" cried Gomez. "Arm—perfect. Leg—chest—*perfecto!* Now, quick, the height! There! Yes! Five-foot-five! You're in! Shake!" Pumping Martinez' hand he stopped suddenly. "Wait. You got—ten bucks?"

"I have!" Vamenos waved some grimy bills. "Gomez, measure me!"

"All I got left in the world is nine dollars and ninety-two cents." 8. Martinez searched his pockets. "That's enough for a new suit? Why?"

"Why? Because you got the right skeleton, that's why!"

"Senor Gomez, I don't hardly know you—"

"Know me? You're going to live with me! Come on!"

Gomez vanished into the poolroom. Martinez, escorted by the polite Villanazul, pushed by an eager Vamenos, found himself inside.

"Dominguez!" said Gomez.

Dominquez, at a wall telephone, winked at them. A woman's voice squeaked on the receiver.

"Manulo!" said Gomez.

9.   Manulo, a wine bottle tilted bubbling to his mouth, turned.

Gomez pointed at Martinez. "At last we found our fifth volunteer!"

Dominguez said, "I got a date, don't bother me—" and stopped. The receiver slipped from his fingers. His little black telephone book full of fine names and numbers went quickly back into his pocket. "Gomez, you—"

"Yes, yes! Your money, now! *Vamos!*"

The woman's voice sizzled on the dangling phone. Dominguez glanced at it uneasily.

Manulo considered the empty wine bottle in his hand and the liquor-store sign across the street.

Then, very reluctantly, both men laid ten dollars each on the green-velvet pool table.

Villanazul, amazed, did likewise, as did Gomez, nudging Martinez. Martinez counted out his wrinkled bills and change. Gomez flourished the money like a royal flush.

"Fifty bucks! The suit costs sixty! All we need is ten bucks!"

"Wait," said Martinez. "Gomez, are we talking about one suit? *Uno?*"

10.   "*Uno!*" Gomez raised a finger. "One wonderful white ice-cream summer suit! White, white as the August moon!"

"But who will own this one suit?"

"Men," said Gomez, "let's show him. Line up!"

Villanazul, Manulo, Dominguez and Gomez rushed to plant their backs against the poolroom wall.

"Martinez, you, too, the other end, line up! Now, Vamenos, lay that billiard cue across your heads!"

"Sure, Gomez; sure!"

The cue lay flat on all their heads, with no rise or fall, as Vamenos slid it, grinning, along.

"We're all the same height!" said Martinez.

"The same!" Everyone laughed.

"Sure!" Gomez said. "It took a month—four weeks, mind you— 11.
to find four guys the same size. But now, five of us, same shoulders, chests, waists, arms; and as for weight? Men!"

Manulo, Dominguez, Villanazul, Gomez and, at last, Martinez stepped onto the scales which flipped ink-stamped cards at them as Vamenos, still smiling, wildly fed pennies.

Heart pounding, Martinez read the cards.

"One hundred thirty-five pounds; one thirty-six; one thirty-three; one thirty-four; one thirty-seven. A miracle!"

"No," said Villanazul simply; "Gomez."

They all smiled upon that genius, who now circled them with his arms.

"Are we not fine?" he wondered. "All the same size, all the same dream—the suit. So each of us will look beautiful at least one night each week, eh?"

"I haven't looked beautiful in years," said Martinez. "The girls run away."

"They will run no more, they will freeze," said Gomez, "when they see you in the cool white summer ice-cream suit."

"Gomez," said Villanazul, "just let me ask one thing."

"Of course, *compadre.*"

"When we get this nice new white ice-cream summer suit, some 12.
night you're not going to put it on and walk down to the bus in it and go live in El Paso for a year in it, are you?"

"Villanazul, how can you say that?"

"My eye sees and my tongue moves," said Villanazul. "How about the Everybody Wins! Punchboard Lotteries you ran and kept running when nobody won? How about the United Chili Con Carne and Frijole Company you were going to organize and all that ever happened was the rent ran out on a two-by-four office?"

"The errors of a child now grown," said Gomez. "Enough! In 13.
this hot weather, someone may buy the special suit that is made just for us that stands waiting in the window of SHUMWAY'S SUNSHINE SUITS! We have fifty dollars. Now we need just one more skeleton!"

Martinez saw the men peer around the poolhall. He looked where they looked. He felt his eyes hurry past Vamenos, then come reluctantly back to examine his dirty shirt, his huge nicotined fingers.

"Me!" Vamenos burst out, at last. "My skeleton, measure it, it's great! Sure my hands are big, and my arms, from digging ditches! But—"

14.   Just then Martinez heard passing on the sidewalk outside, that same terrible man with his two girls, all laughing and yelling together. He saw anguish move like the shadow of a summer cloud on the faces of the other men in this poolroom.

Slowly, Vamenos stepped onto the scales and dropped his penny. Eyes closed, he breathed a prayer.

"Madre mia, please."

The machinery whirred, the card fell out. Vamenos opened his eyes.

"Look! One hundred thirty-five pounds! Another miracle!"

The men stared at his right hand and the card; at his left hand and a soiled ten-dollar bill.

Gomez swayed. Sweating, he licked his lips. Then his hand shot out, seized the money.

"The clothing store! The suit! Vamos!"

15.   Mr. Shumway, of SHUMWAY'S SUNSHINE SUITS, paused while adjusting a tie rack, aware of some subtle atmospheric change outside his establishment.

"Leo," he whispered to his assistant. "Look."

Outside, one man, Gomez, strolled by, looking in. Two men, Manulo and Dominguez, hurried by, staring in. Three men, Villanazul, Martinez, and Vamenos, jostling shoulders, did the same.

"Leo," Mr. Shumway swallowed. "Call the police!"

Suddenly, six men filled the doorway.

16.   Martinez, crushed among them, his stomach slightly upset, his face feeling feverish, smiled so wildly at Leo that Leo let go the telephone.

"Hey," breathed Martinez, eyes wide. "There's a great suit, over there!"

"No." Manulo touched a lapel. "This one!"

"There is only one suit in all the world!" said Gomez coldly, "Mr. Shumway, the ice-cream white, size thirty-four, was in your window just an hour ago! It's gone! You didn't—"

"Sell it?" Mr. Shumway exhaled. "No, no. In the dressing room. It's still on the dummy. This way, gents. Now which of you—"

"All for one, one for all!" Martinez heard himself say, and laughed wildly. "We'll all try it on!"

"All?" Mr. Shumway stared.

17.   *That's it,* thought Martinez, *look at our smiles, Now, look at the*

skeletons behind our smiles! Measure here, there; up, down; yes, do
you see?

Mr. Shumway saw. He nodded. He shrugged.

"All!" He jerked the curtain. "There! Buy it, and I'll throw in the dummy, free!"

Martinez peered quietly into the booth, his motion drawing the others to peer too. The suit was there. And it was white.

Martinez took a great trembling breath and exhaled, whispering, *"Ai, Ai, caramba!"*

"It puts out my eyes," murmured Gomez.

"Mr. Shumway." Martinez heard Leo hissing. "Ain't it dangerous, to sell it? I mean, what if everybody bought one suit for six people?"

"Leo," said Mr. Shumway, "you ever hear one single fifty-nine   18. dollar suit make so many people happy at the same time before?"

"Angel's wings," murmured Martinez. "The wings of white angels."

Martinez felt Mr. Shumway peering over his shoulder into the booth. The pale glow filled his eyes.

"You know something, Leo?" he said, in awe. "That's a suit!"

Gomez, shouting, whistling, ran up to the third-floor landing   19. and turned to wave on the others, who staggered, laughed, stopped and had to sit down on the steps below.

"Tonight!" cried Gomez. "Tonight you move in with me, eh? Save rent as well as clothes, eh? Sure! Martinez, you got the suit?"

"Have I?" Martinez lifted the white gift-wrapped box high. "From us to us! Ai-hah!"

"Vamenos, you got the dummy?"

"Here!"

Vamenos, chewing an old cigar, scattering sparks, slipped. The dummy, falling, toppled, turned over twice, and banged down the stairs.

"Vamenos! Dumb! Clumsy!"

They seized the dummy from him. Stricken, Vamenos looked as if he'd lost something.

Manulo snapped his fingers. "Hey, Vamenos, we got to celebrate! Go borrow some wine!"

Vamenos plunged downstairs in a whirl of sparks.   20.

The others moved into the room with the suit, leaving Martinez in the hall to study Gomez's face.

"Gomez, you look sick."

"I am," said Gomez. "For what have I done?" He nodded to the shadows in the room working about the dummy. "I pick Dominguez, a devil with the women. All right. I pick Manulo, who drinks, yes, but who sings as sweet as a girl, eh? O.K. Villanazul reads books. You, you wash behind your ears. But *then* what do I do? Can I wait? No! I got to buy that suit! So the last guy I pick is a clumsy slob who has the right to wear my suit—" He stopped, confused. "Who gets to wear our suit one night a week, fall down in it, or not come in out of the rain in it! Why, why, why did I do it!"

21.   "Gomez," whispered Villanazul from the room, "the suit is ready. Come, see if it looks as good using your light bulb."

Gomez and Martinez entered. And there on the dummy in the center of the room was the phosphorescent, the miraculously white-fired ghost with the incredible lapels, the precise stitching, the neat buttonholes. Standing with the white illumination of the suit upon his cheeks, Martinez suddenly felt he was in church. White! White! It was white as the whitest vanilla ice cream, as the bottled milk in tenement halls at dawn. White as a winter cloud all alone in the moon-lit sky late at night.

22.   "White," murmured Villanazul. "White as the snow on that mountain near our town in Mexico which is called the Sleeping Woman."

"Say that again," said Gomez.

Villanazul, proud yet humble, was glad to repeat his tribute: "White as the snow on the mountain called—"

"I'm back!"

Shocked, the men whirled to see Vamenos in the door, wine bottles in each hand.

"A party! Here! Now tell us, who wears the suit first tonight? Me?"

"It's too late!" said Gomez.

"Late! It's only nine-fifteen!"

"Late?" said everyone, bristling. "Late?"

Gomez edged away from these men who glared from him to the suit to the open window.

23.   Outside and below, it was, after all, thought Martinez, a fine Saturday night in a summer month, and through the calm darkness

the women drifted like flowers on a quiet stream. The men made a mournful sound.

"Gomez, a suggestion." Villanazul licked his pencil and drew a chart on a pad. "You wear the suit from nine-thirty to ten, Manulo till ten-thirty, Dominguez till eleven, myself till eleven-thirty, Martinez till midnight, and——"

"Why me last?" demanded Vamenos, scowling.

Martinez thought quickly and smiled. "After midnight is the best time, friend."

"Hey," said Vamenos, "That's right. I never thought of that. O.K."

Gomez sighed. "All right. A half hour each. But from now on, 24. remember, we each wear the suit just one night a week. Sundays we draw straws for who wears the suit the extra night."

"Me!" laughed Vamenos. "I'm lucky!"

Gomez held onto Martinez, tight.

"Gomez," urged Martinez, "you first. Dress."

Gomez could not tear his eyes from that disreputable Vamenos. At last, impulsively, he yanked his shirt off over his head. "Ai-yeah!" he howled. "Ai-yeee!"

Whisper, rustle—the clean shirt. 25.

"Ah!"

How clean the new clothes felt, thought Martinez, holding the coat ready. How clean they sounded; how clean they smelled!

Whisper—the pants, the tie; rustle—the suspenders. Whisper. Now Martinez let loose the coat, which fell in place on flexing shoulders.

"Olé!"

Gomez turned like a matador in his wondrous suit-of-lights.

"Olé, Gomez; olé!"

Gomez bowed and went out the door.

Martinez fixed his eyes on his watch. At ten sharp he heard 26. someone wandering about in the hall as if he had forgotten where to go. Martinez pulled the door open and looked out. Gomez was there, heading for nowhere.

He looks sick, thought Martinez. *No; stunned, shook up, surprised, many things.*

"Gomez! This is the place!"

Gomez turned around and found his way through the door.

"Oh, friends, friends," he said. "Friends, what an experience! This suit! This suit!"

"Tell us, Gomez!" said Martinez.

"I can't; how can I say it!" He gazed at the heavens, arms spread, palms up.

"Tell us, Gomez!"

27.   "I have no words, no words. You must see, yourself! Yes, you must see." And here he lapsed into silence, shaking his head until at last he remembered they all stood watching him. "Who's next? Manulo?"

Manulo, stripped to his shorts, leaped forward.

"Ready!"

All laughed, shouted, whistled.

Manulo, ready, went out the door. He was gone twenty-nine minutes and thirty seconds. He came back holding to doorknobs, touching the wall, feeling his own elbows, putting the flat of his hand to his face.

"Oh, let me tell you," he said. *"Compadres,* I went to the bar, eh, to have a drink? But no, I did not go in the bar, do you hear? I did not drink. For as I walked I began to laugh and sing. Why, why? I listened to myself and asked this. Because. The suit made me feel better than wine ever did. The suit made me drunk, drunk! So I went to the *Guadalajara Refriteria* instead and played the guitar and sang four songs, very high! The suit, ah, the suit!"

28.   Dominguez, next to be dressed, moved out through the world, came back from the world.

The black telephone book! thought Martinez. *He had it in his hands when he left! Now he returns, hands empty! What? What?*

"On the street," said Dominguez, seeing it all again, eyes wide, "on the street I walked, a woman cried, 'Dominguez, is that you?' Another said, 'Dominguez? No. Quetzalcoatl, the Great White God come from the East,' do you hear? And suddenly I didn't want to go with six women or eight, no. One, I thought. One! And to this one, who knows what I would say? 'Be mine!' Or 'Marry me!' *Caramba!* This suit is dangerous! But I did not care! I live, I live! Gomez, did it happen this way with you?"

29.   Gomez, still dazed by the events of the evening, shook his head. "No, no talk. It's too much. Later. Villanazul?"

Villanazul moved shyly forward.

Villanazul went shyly out.

Villanazul came shyly home.

"Picture it," he said, not looking at them, looking at the floor, talking to the floor. "The Green Plaza, a group of elderly businessmen gathered under the stars and they are talking, nodding, talking. Now one of them whispers. All turn to stare. They move aside, they make a channel through which a white-hot light burns its way as through ice. At the center of the great light is this person. I take a deep breath. My stomach is jelly. My voice is very small, but it grows louder. And what do I say? I say, 'Friends. Do you know Carlyle's *Sartor Resartus?* In that book we find *his* Philosophy of Suits.' "

And at last it was time for Martinez to let the suit float him out to haunt the darkness. 30.

Four times he walked around the block. Four times he paused beneath the tenement porches, looking up at the window where the light was lit, a shadow moved, the beautiful girl was there, not there, away and gone, and on the fifth time, there she was on the porch above, driven out by the summer heat, taking the cooler air. She glanced down. She made a gesture.

At first he thought she was waving to him. He felt like a white explosion that had riveted her attention. But she was not waving. Her hand gestured, and the next moment a pair of framed glasses sat upon her nose. She gazed at him. 31.

Ah, ah, he thought, *so that's it! So! Even the blind may see this suit!* He smiled up at her. He did not have to wave. And at last, she smiled back. She did not have to wave either. Then, because he did not know what else to do, and he could not get rid of this smile that had fastened itself to his cheeks, he hurried, almost ran around the corner, feeling her stare after him.

When he looked back, she had taken off her glasses and gazed now with the look of the nearsighted at what, at most, must be a moving blob of light in the great darkness here. Then, for good measure he went around the block again, through a city so suddenly beautiful he wanted to yell, then laugh, then yell again. 32.

Returning, he drifted, oblivious, eyes half-closed, and seeing him in the door the others saw not Martinez, but themselves, come home. In that moment, they sensed that something had happened to them all.

"You're late!" cried Vamenos, but stopped. The spell could not be broken.

"Somebody tell me," said Martinez. "Who am I?"

He moved in a slow circle through the room.

33.   Yes, he thought, yes, it was the suit; yes, it had to do with the suit and them all together in that store on this fine Saturday night and then here, laughing and feeling more drunk without drinking, as Manulo said himself, as the night ran and each slipped on the pants and held, toppling, to the others and, balanced, let the feeling get bigger and warmer and finer as each man departed and the next took his place in the suit until now here stood Martinez all splendid and white as one who gives orders and the world grows quiet and moves aside.

"Martinez, we borrowed three mirrors while you were gone. Look!"

34.   The mirrors, set up as in the store, angled to reflect three Martinezes and the echoes and memories of those who had occupied the suit with him and known the bright world inside this thread and cloth. Now, in the shimmering mirror, Martinez saw the enormity of this thing they were living together, and his eyes grew wet. The others blinked. Martinez touched the mirrors. They shifted. He saw a thousand, a million white-armored Martinezes march off into eternity, reflected, re-reflected forever, indomitable, and unending.

35.   He held the white coat out on the air. In a trance, the others did not at first recognize the dirty hand that reached to take the coat. Then:

"Vamenos!"

"Pig!"

"You didn't wash!" cried Gomez. "Or even shave, while you waited! *Compadres,* the bath!"

"The bath!" said everyone.

"No!" Vamenos flailed. "The night air! I'm dead!"

They hustled him, yelling, out and down the hall.

36.   Now here stood Vamenos, unbelievable in white suit, beard shaved, hair combed, nails scrubbed.

His friends scowled darkly at him. For was it not true, thought Martinez, that when Vamenos passed by, avalanches itched on mountain tops. If he walked under windows, people spat, dumped garbage or worse. Tonight now, this night, he would stroll beneath ten thousand wide-opened windows, near balconies, past alleys. Suddenly the world absolutely sizzled with flies. And here was Vamenos, a fresh-frosted cake.

"You sure look keen in that suit, Vamenos," said Manulo sadly.   37.

"Thanks." Vamenos twitched, trying to make his skeleton comfortable where all their skeletons had so recently been. In a small voice, Vamenos said, "Can I go now?"

"Villanazul!" said Gomez. "Copy down these rules."

Villanazul licked his pencil.

"First," said Gomez, "don't fall down in that suit, Vamenos!"

"I won't."

"Don't lean against buildings in that suit."

"No buildings."

"Don't walk under trees with birds in them in that suit. Don't smoke. Don't drink—"

"Please," said Vamenos, "can I sit down in this suit?"   38.

"When in doubt, take the pants off, fold them over a chair."

"Wish me luck," said Vamenos.

"Go with God, Vamenos."

He went out. He shut the door. There was a ripping sound.

"Vamenos!" cried Martinez. He whipped open the door.

Vamenos stood with two halves of a handkerchief torn in his hands, laughing.

"R-r-rip! Look at your faces! R-r-rip!" He tore the cloth again. "Oh, oh, your faces, your faces! Ha!"

Roaring, Vamenos slammed the door, leaving them stunned and alone.

Gomez put both hands on top of his head and turned away.   39. "Stone me. Kill me. I have sold our souls to a demon!"

Villanazul dug in his pockets, took out a silver coin and studied it for a long while.

"Here is my last fifty cents. Who else will help me buy back Vamenos' share of the suit?"

"It's no use." Manulo showed them ten cents. "We got only enough to buy the lapels and the buttonholes."

Gomez, at the open window, suddenly leaned out and yelled, "Vamenos! No!"

Below on the street, Vamenos, shocked, blew out a match, and   40.

threw away an old cigar butt he had found somewhere. He made a strange gesture to all the men in the window above, then waved airily and sauntered on.

Somehow, the five men could not move away from the window. They were crushed together there.

"I bet he eats a hamburger in that suit," mused Villanazul. "I'm thinking of the mustard."

"Don't!" cried Gomez. "No, no!"

Manulo was suddenly at the door. "I need a drink, bad."

"Manulo, there's wine here, that bottle, on the floor."

Manulo went out and shut the door.

A moment later, Villanazul stretched with great exaggeration and strolled about the room.

"I think I'll walk down to the plaza, friends."

He was not gone a minute when Dominguez turned the doorknob.

"Dominguez," said Gomez.

"Yes?"

41.   "If you see Vamenos, by accident," said Gomez, "warn him away from Mickey Murillo's Red Rooster Cafe. They got fights not only *on* TV but out front of the TV too."

"He wouldn't go into Murillo's," said Dominguez. "That suit means too much to Vamenos. He wouldn't do anything to hurt it."

"He'd shoot his mother first," said Martinez.

"Sure he would."

Martinez and Gomez, alone, listened to Dominguez' footsteps hurry away down the stairs. They circled the undressed window dummy.

42.   For a long while, biting his lips, Gomez stood at the window, looking out. He touched his shirt pocket twice, pulled his hand away, and then at last pulled something from the pocket. Without looking at it, he handed it to Martinez.

"Martinez, take this."

"What is it?"

Martinez looked at the piece of folded pink paper with print on it, with names and numbers. His eyes widened.

"A ticket on the bus to El Paso, three weeks from now!"

Gomez nodded. He couldn't look at Martinez. He stared out into the summer night.

"Turn it in. Get the money," he said. "Buy us a nice white panama hat and a pale blue tie to go with the white ice-cream suit, Martinez. Do that."

Mickey Murillo's Red Rooster Cafe and Cocktail Lounge was   43. squashed between two big brick buildings and, being narrow, had to be deep. Outside, serpents of red and sulphur-green neon fizzed and snapped. Inside, dim shapes loomed and swam away to lose themselves in a swarming night sea.

Martinez, on tiptoe, peeked through a flaked place on the red-painted front window. He felt a presence on his left, heard breathing on his right. He glanced in both directions.

"Manulo! Villanazul!"

"I decided I wasn't thirsty," said Manulo. "So I took a walk."

"I was just on my way to the plaza," said Villanazul, "and de-   44. cided to go the long way around."

As if by agreement the three men shut up now and turned together to peer on tiptoe through various flaked spots on the window.

A moment later, all three felt a new very warm presence behind them and heard still faster breathing.

"Is our white suit in there?" asked Gomez' voice.

"Gomez!" said everyone, surprised. "Hi!"

"Yes!" cried Dominguez, having just arrived to find his own peephole. "There's the suit! And, praise God, Vamenos is still in it!"

"I can't see!" Gomez squinted, shielding his eyes. "What's he doing?"

Martinez peered. Yes! There, way back in the shadows, was a   45. big chunk of snow and the idiot smile of Vamenos winking above it, wreathed in smoke.

"He's smoking!" said Martinez.

"He's drinking!" said Dominguez.

"He's eating a taco!" reported Villanazul.

"A juicy taco," added Manulo.

"No," said Gomez. "No, no, no."

"Ruby Escuadrillo's with him!"

"Let me see that!" Gomez pushed Martinez aside.

Yes, there was Ruby! Two hundred pounds of glittering sequins and tight black satin on the hoof, her scarlet fingernails clutching

Vamenos' shoulder. Her cowlike face, floured with powder, greasy with lipstick, hung over him!

46.   "That hippo!" said Dominguez. "She's crushing the shoulder pads. Look, she's going to sit on his lap!"

"No, no; not with all that powder and lipstick!" said Gomez. "Manulo, inside! Grab that drink! Villanazul, the cigar, the taco! Dominguez, date Ruby Escuadrillo, get her away. *Vamos,* men!"

The three vanished, leaving Gomez and Martinez to stare, gasping, through the peephole.

"Manulo, he's got the drink; he's drinking it!"

"*Olé!* There's Villanazul, he's got the cigar; he's eating the taco!"

"Hey, Dominguez, he's got Ruby! What a brave one!"

A shadow bulked through Murillo's front door, traveling fast.

"Gomez!" Martinez clutched Gomez' arm. "That was Ruby Escuadrillo's boy friend, Toro Ruiz. If he finds her with Vamenos, the ice-cream suit will be covered with blood, covered with blood——"

47.   "Don't make me nervous," said Gomez. "Quickly!"

Both ran. Inside, they reached Vamenos just as Toro Ruiz grabbed about two feet of the lapels of that wonderful ice-cream suit.

"Let go of Vamenos!" said Martinez.

"Let go of the suit!" corrected Gomez.

Toro Ruiz, tap-dancing Vamenos, leered at these intruders.

Villanazul stepped up shyly. Villanazul smiled. "Don't hit him. Hit me."

Toro Ruiz hit Villanazul on the nose.

Villanazul, holding his nose, tears stinging his eyes, wandered off.

Gomez grabbed one of Toro Ruiz's arms, Martinez the other.

"Drop him, let go, *coyote, vaca!*"

48.   Toro Ruiz twisted the ice-cream-suit material until all six men screamed in mortal agony. Grunting, sweating, Toro Ruiz dislodged as many as climbed on. He was winding up to hit Vamenos when Villanazul wandered back, eyes streaming.

"Don't hit him. Hit me!"

As Toro Ruiz hit Villanazul on the nose, a chair crashed on Toro's head. A moment later Toro was ruins at their feet.

"*Compadres,* this way!"

They ran Vamenos outside and set him down, where he freed himself of their hands with injured dignity.

"O.K., O.K. My time ain't up. I still got two minutes and—ten seconds."

"What!" said everybody.

"Vamenos," said Gomez, "you let a Guadalajara cow climb on you, you pick fights, you smoke, you drink, you eat tacos, and now you have the nerve to say your time ain't up?"   49.

"I got two minutes and one second left!"

"Hey, Vamenos, you sure look sharp!" Distantly, a woman's voice called from across the street.

Vamenos smiled and buttoned his coat. "It's Ramona Alvarez! Ramona, wait!" Vamenos stepped off the curb.

"Vamenos," pleaded Gomez, "what can you do in one minute and"—he checked his watch—"forty seconds."

"Watch! Hey, Ramona!" Vamenos loped.

"Vamenos, look out!"

Vamenos, surprised, whirled, saw a car, heard the shriek of brakes.

"No," said all five men on the sidewalk.

Martinez heard the impact and flinched. His head moved up. Vamenos looked like white laundry, he thought, flying through the air. His head came down.

"I don't want to live," said Gomez quietly. "Kill me, someone."   50.

Then, shuffling, Martinez looked down and told his feet to walk, stagger, follow one after the other. He collided with other men. Now they were trying to run. They ran at last and somehow crossed a street like a deep river through which they could only wade, to look down at Vamenos.

"Vamenos!" said Martinez. "You're alive!"

Strewn on his back, mouth open, eyes squeezed tight, tight, Vamenos motioned his head back and forth, back and forth, moaning.

"Tell me, tell me; oh, tell me, tell me."

"Tell you what, Vamenos?"

Vamenos clenched his fists, ground his teeth. "The suit, what have I done to the suit, the suit, the suit!"

The men crouched lower.

"Vamenos, it's—Why, it's O.K.!"

"You lie!" said Vamenos. "It's torn, it must be, it must be, it's torn, all around, underneath?"

51.   "No." Martinez knelt and touched here and there. "Vamenos, all around, underneath of it, it's O.K.!"

Vamenos opened his eyes to let the tears run free at last. "A miracle," he sobbed. "Praise the saints!" He quieted at last. "The car?"

"Hit and run." Gomez suddenly remembered and glared at the empty street. "It's good he didn't stop. We'd have—"

Everyone listened. Distantly, a siren wailed.

"Someone phoned for an ambulance."

"Quick!" said Vamenos, eyes rolling. "Set me up! Take off our coat!"

"Vamenos—"

52.   "Shut up, idiots!" cried Vamenos. "The coat, that's it! Now, the pants; the pants, quick, quick, *peons!* Those doctors! You seen movies? They rip the pants with razors to get them off! They don't care! They're maniacs! Ah, quick, quick!"

The siren screamed. The men, panicking, all handled Vamenos at once.

"Right leg, easy; hurry, cows! Good! Left leg, now; left, you hear! There, easy, easy! Quick! Martinez, your pants, take them off!"

"What?" Martinez froze.

The siren shrieked.

"Fool!" wailed Vamenos. "All is lost! Your pants! Give me!"

Martinez jerked at his belt buckle.

"Close in, make a circle!"

Dark pants, light pants, flourished on the air.

"Quick, here come the maniacs with the razors! Right leg on, left leg, there!"

"The zipper, cows, zip my zipper!" babbled Vamenos.

The siren died.

53.   *"Madre mia,* yes, just in time! They arrive." Vamenos lay back down and shut his eyes. *"Gracias."*

Martinez turned, nonchalantly buckling on the white pants as the interns brushed past.

"Broken leg," said one intern as they moved Vamenos onto a stretcher.

"Compadres," said Vamenos, "don't be mad with me."

Gomez snorted. "Who's mad?"

In the ambulance, head tilted back, looking out at them upside down, Vamenos faltered.

"Compadres, when—when I come from the hospital, am I still in the bunch? You won't kick me out? Look, I'll give up smoking, keep away from Murillo's, swear off women—"

"Vamenos," said Martinez gently, "don't promise nothing." 54.

Vamenos, upside down, eyes brimming wet, saw Martinez there, all white now against the stars.

"Oh, Martinez, you sure look great in that suit. *Compadres,* don't he look beautiful?"

Villanazul climbed in beside Vamenos. The door slammed. The four remaining men watched the ambulance drive away. Then, surrounded by his friends, inside the white suit, Martinez was carefully escorted back to the curb.

In the tenement, Martinez got out the cleaning fluid and the 55. others stood around, telling him how to clean the suit and, later, how not to have the iron too hot and how to work the lapels and the crease and all. When the suit was cleaned and pressed so it looked like a fresh gardenia just opened, they fitted it to the dummy.

"Two o'clock," murmured Villanazul. "I hope Vamenos sleeps well. When I left him, he looked good."

Manulo cleared his throat. "Nobody else is going out with that suit tonight, huh?"

The others glared at him.

Manulo flushed. "I mean—it's late. We're tired. Maybe no one 56. will use the suit for forty-eight hours, huh? Give it a rest. Sure. Well. Where do we sleep?"

The night being still hot and the room unbearable, they carried the suit on its dummy out and down the hall. They brought with them also some pillows and blankets. They climbed the stairs toward the roof of the tenement. There, thought Martinez, was the cooler wind, and sleep.

On the way, they passed a dozen doors that stood open, people still perspiring and awake, playing cards, drinking pop, fanning themselves with movie magazines.

I wonder, thought Martinez, *I wonder if —yes!*

On the fourth floor, a certain door stood open. The beautiful girl looked up as the five men passed. She wore glasses and when she saw Martinez she snatched them off and hid them under her book.

57.   The others went on, not knowing they had lost Martinez, who seemed stuck fast in the open door.

For a long moment he could say nothing. Then he said: "José Martinez."

And she said: "Celia Obregon."

And then both said nothing.

He heard the men moving up on the tenement roof. He moved to follow.

She said, quickly, "I saw you tonight!"

He came back. "The suit," he said.

"The suit," she said, and paused. "But not the suit."

"Eh?" he said.

She lifted the book to show the glasses lying in her lap. She touched the glasses.

58.   "I do not see well. You would think I would wear my glasses, but no. I walk around for years now, hiding them, seeing nothing. But tonight, even without the glasses, I see. A great whiteness passes below in the dark. So white! And I put on my glasses quickly!"

"The suit, as I said," said Martinez.

"The suit for a little moment, yes; but there is another whiteness above the suit."

"Another?"

"Your teeth! Oh, such white teeth, and so many!"

Martinez put his hand over his mouth.

"So happy, Mr. Martinez," she said. "I have not often seen such a happy face and such a smile."

"Ah," he said, not able to look at her, his face flushing now.

"So, you see," she said quietly, "the suit caught my eye, yes, the whiteness filled the night, below. But the teeth were much whiter. Now, I have forgotten the suit."

59.   Martinez flushed again. She, too, was overcome with what she had said. She looked at her hands and at the door above his head.

"May I—" he said, at last.

"May you—"

"May I call for you," he asked, "when next the suit is mine to wear?"

"You do not need the suit," she said.

"But—"

"If it were just the suit," she said, "anyone would be fine in it.

But no, I watched. I saw many men in that suit, all different, this night. So again I say, you do not need to wait for the suit."

"Madre mia, madre mia!" he cried happily. And then, quieter, **60** "I will need the suit for a little while. A month, six months, a year, I am uncertain. I am fearful of many things. I am young. The suit changes me, makes me strong."

"That is as it should be," she said.

"Good night, Miss—"

"Celia Obregon."

"Celia Obregon," he said, and was gone from the door.

The others were waiting on the roof of the tenement. A cooler night wind was blowing here, up in the sky.

Martinez stood alone by the white suit, smoothing the lapels, talking half to himself.

"Ai, caramba, what a night! Seems ten years since seven o'clock, **61.** when it all started and I had no friends. Two in the morning, I got all kinds of friends." He paused and thought. *Celia Obregon, Celia Obregon.* "All kinds of friends," he went on. "I got a room, I got clothes. You tell me. You know what?" He looked around at the men lying on the rooftop, surrounding the dummy and himself. "It's funny. When I wear this suit, I know I will win at pool, like Gomez. A woman will look at me like Dominguez. I will be able to sing like Manulo, sweetly. I will talk fine politics like Villanazul. I'm strong as Vamenos. So? So, tonight, I am more than Martinez. I am Gomez, Manulo, Dominguez, Villanazul, Vamenos. I am everyone. Ai. Ai." He stood a moment longer by this suit which could save all the ways they sat or stood or walked. This suit which could move fast and nervous like Gomez or slow and thoughtfully like Villanazul or drift like Dominguez who never touched the ground, who always found a wind to take him somewhere. This suit which belonged to them, but which also owned them all. This suit that was what? A parade.

"Martinez," said Gomez. "You going to sleep?" **62.**

"Sure. I'm just thinking."

"What?"

"If we ever get rich," said Martinez softly, "it'll be kind of sad. Then we'll all have suits. And there won't be no more nights like to-night. It'll break up the old gang. It'll never be the same, after that."

The men lay thinking of what had just been said.

Gomez nodded gently. "Yeah. It'll never be the same, after that."

Martinez lay down on his blanket. In darkness, with the others, he faced the middle of the roof and the dummy, which was the center of their lives.

63.   And their eyes were bright, shining, and good to see in the dark as the neon lights from nearby buildings flicked on, flicked off, flicked on, flicked off, revealing and then vanishing, revealing and then vanishing, their wonderful white vanilla-ice-cream summer suit.

DISCUSSION QUESTIONS

1. What does the suit mean originally to each man?
2. In light of these original attitudes toward the suit, what do you think is the meaning of Martinez's statement near the conclusion of the story: "It's funny. When I wear this suit, I know I will win at pool, like Gomez. A woman will look at me like Dominguez. I will be able to sing like Manulo, sweetly. I will talk fine politics like Villanazul. I'm strong as Vamenos. So? So, tonight, I am more than Martinez. I am Gomez, Manulo, Dominguez, Villanazul, Vamenos. I am everyone."
3. Celia tells Martinez that he does not need the suit. Is she correct?
4. What is the source of the happiness gained by the men at the end of the story?

RHETORIC

1. A simile is a comparison between two dissimilar things, a comparison introduced by *like* or *as*. What effect does Bradbury achieve by using similes at the end of the first paragraph? Discuss the use of the similes in sections fourteen, twenty-one, twenty-two, twenty-three, and fifty-five.
2. Using the details in the story and any additions you want to make, write a comparison-contrast theme on two of the suit's owners. See *Essay Development,* Chapter IV, p. 19.
3. The beginning of section forty-three illustrates in an abbreviated manner one way to achieve spatial unity in a paragraph. Here Bradbury describes the Red Rooster Cafe from the outside first and then moves inside. Attempt a similar but more lengthy description of a particular

area or building in your own neighborhood or campus. Visit it and then try to give your reader a verbal picture, working first from the outside and then moving inside.

4. Using examples from the story itself, defend or attack in a 200-word paragraph the statement that "clothes make the man."

VOCABULARY

tenement (paragraph 5)
tilted (9)
peer (13)
reluctantly (13)
phosphorescent (21)
bristling (22)
glared (22)
scowling (23)
disreputable (24)
impulsively (24)
riveted (31)

nearsighted (32)
oblivious (32)
blob (32)
indomitable (34)
avalanches (36)
sizzled (36)
squashed (43)
clutched (46)
shriek (49)
nonchalantly (53)
flicked (63)

pictures and poems

A.

Courtesy of Austin Scott

B.

Courtesy of Judith Belasco

Courtesy of Judith Belasco

C.

D.

Courtesy of United Press International, Inc.

Harlem

What happens to a dream deferred?

Does it dry up
like a raisin in the sun?
Or fester like a sore—
And then run?   5
Does it stink like rotten meat?
Or crust and sugar over—
like a syrupy sweet?

Maybe it just sags
like a heavy load.   10

Or does it explode?

"Harlem" from Langston Hughes, *The Panther and the Lash* (New York: Alfred A. Knopf, Inc., 1951). Copyright © 1951 by Langston Hughes. Reprinted by permission of the publisher.

Ex-Basketball Player

Pearl Avenue runs past the high-school lot,
Bends with the trolley tracks, and stops, cut off
Before it has a chance to go two blocks,
At Colonel McComsky Plaza. Berth's Garage
Is on the corner facing west, and there,   5
Most days, you'll find Flick Webb, who helps Berth out.

Flick stands tall among the idiot pumps—
Five on a side, the old bubble-head style,
Their rubber elbows hanging loose and low.
One's nostrils are two S's, and his eyes   10
An E and O. And one is squat, without
A head at all—more of a football type.

Once Flick played for the high-school team, the Wizards.
He was good: in fact, the best. In '46
He bucketed three hundred ninety points,   15
A county record still. The ball loved Flick.
I saw him rack up thirty-eight or forty
In one home game. His hands were like wild birds.

"Ex-Basketball Player" from John Updike, *The Carpentered Hen and Other Tame Creatures* (New York: Harper & Row, Publishers, 1957). Copyright © 1957 by John Updike. Reprinted by permission of the publisher.

He never learned a trade, he just sells gas,
Checks oil, and changes flats. Once in a while, 20
As a gag, he dribbles an inner tube,
But most of us remember anyway.
His hands are fine and nervous on the lug wrench.
It makes no difference to the lug wrench, though.

Off work, he hangs around Mae's Luncheonette. 25
Grease-grey and kind of coiled, he plays pinball,
Sips lemon cokes, and smokes those thin cigars;
Flick seldom speaks to Mae, just sits and nods
Beyond her face toward bright applauding tiers
Of Necco Wafers, Nibs, and Juju Beads. 30

DISCUSSION QUESTIONS

1. In a theme, compare "Harlem" with some of the questions and predictions in King's "Letter."
2. What is the effect of the similes in Hughes' poem—a raisin, a sore, rotten meat, syrup sweet, heavy load? Would similes with different connotations have altered the meaning of the poem or made it less effective?
3. Do you consider Flick Webb a failure? Does the speaker consider Flick a failure?
4. Is Flick's memory of his past glories enough for him? Is he happy with them?
5. Why did Updike feel it necessary to use specific details in the poem? Since we do not know where Mae's Luncheonette is wouldn't it have been simpler to say "a corner lunchroom"? What difference does it make that his drink is a *lemon* coke?

Richard Cory

Whenever Richard Cory went down town,
We people on the pavement looked at him;
He was a gentleman from sole to crown,
Clean favored, and imperially slim.

And he was always quietly arrayed, 5
And he was always human when he talked;
But still he fluttered pulses when he said,
"Good-morning," and he glittered when he walked.

"Richard Cory" from Edwin Arlington Robinson, *The Children of the Night* (1897). Reprinted by permission of Charles Scribner's Sons.

And he was rich—yes, richer than a king—
And admirably schooled in every grace: 10
In fine, we thought that he was everything
To make us wish that we were in his place.

So on we worked, and waited for the light,
And went without the meat, and cursed the bread;
And Richard Cory, one calm summer night,   15
Went home and put a bullet through his head.

DISCUSSION QUESTIONS

1. Why did Richard Cory kill himself?
2. What is the attitude of the people toward Richard Cory? How do we see this in the language or diction of the poem?
3. One might say that the poem shows that "money can't buy happiness." Do you feel that this does justice to the total experience of the poem?
4. Irony is basically a discrepancy between what is and what appears to be. The most obvious irony in the poem is its surprise ending. Is this ending merely cheap and theatrical, or does it imply deeper ironies?

The War Against the Trees

The man who sold his lawn to standard oil
Joked with his neighbors come to watch the show
While the bulldozers, drunk with gasoline,
Tested the virtue of the soil
Under the branchy sky   5
By overthrowing first the privet-row.

Forsythia-forays and hydrangea-raids
Were but preliminaries to a war
Against the great-grandfathers of the town,
So freshly lopped and maimed.   10
They struck and struck again,
And with each elm a century went down.

All day the hireling engines charged the trees,
Subverting them by hacking underground
In grub-dominions, where dark summer's mole   15
Rampages through his halls,

"The War Against the Trees" from Stanley Kunitz, *Selected Poems 1928–1958* (Boston: Atlantic-Little, Brown and Co., 1958), p. 68. Copyright © 1957 by Stanley Kunitz. Reprinted by permission of the publisher. Originally appeared in *The Nation*.

Till a northern seizure shook
Those crowns, forcing the giants to their knees.

I saw the ghosts of children at their games
Racing beyond their childhood in the shade,   20
And while the green world turned its death-foxed page
And a red wagon wheeled,
I watched them disappear
Into the suburbs of their grievous age.

Ripped from the craters much too big for hearts   25
The club-roots bared their amputated coils,
Raw gorgons matted blind, whose pocks and scars
Cried Moon! on a corner lot
One witness-moment caught
In the rear-view mirrors of the passing cars.   30

DISCUSSION QUESTIONS

1. A metaphor is a comparison between two dissimilar things that yet makes sense. For example, Shakespeare's comparison of the trees in the fall to "Bare ruined choirs where late the sweet birds sang" is both imaginative and perceptive. The tree limbs without leaves and the singing birds do appear like empty choir lofts. Does Kunitz use any metaphors in his poem?
2. Paper D in the *Student Papers* section, p. 256, argues that the destruction of the trees is necessary for social progress. Do you agree?
3. Is Kunitz more concerned about the actual destruction or the reaction of the people toward it?
4. Is Kunitz on the side of progress or the trees? Defend your answer by analyzing the words he uses in the poem.

Theme for English B

The instructor said,

Go home and write
a page tonight.
And let that page come out of you—
Then, it will be true.   5

I wonder if it's that simple?

I am twenty-two, colored, born in Winston-Salem.
I went to school there, then Durham, then here
to this college on the hill above Harlem.
I am the only colored student in my class.   10
The steps from the hill lead down into Harlem,
through a park, then I cross St. Nicholas,
Eighth Avenue, Seventh, and I come to the Y,
the Harlem Branch Y, where I take the elevator
up to my room, sit down, and write this page: 15

It's not easy to know what is true for you or me
at twenty-two, my age. But I guess I'm what
I feel and see and hear, Harlem, I hear you:
hear you, hear me—we two—you, me, talk on this page.
(I hear New York, too.) Me—who?   20
Well, I like to eat, sleep, drink, and be in love.
I like to work, read, learn, and understand life.
I like a pipe for a Christmas present,
or records—Bessie, bop, or Bach.
I guess being colored doesn't make me *not* like   25
the same things other folks like who are other races.
So will my page be colored that I write?
Being me, it will not be white.
But it will be
a part of you, instructor.   30
You are white—
yet a part of me, as I am a part of you.
That's American.
Sometimes perhaps you don't want to be a part of me.
Nor do I often want to be a part of you.   35
But we are, that's true!
As I learn from you,
I guess you learn from me—
although you're older—and white—
and somewhat more free.   40

This is my page for English B.

Hokku Poems

In the falling snow
A laughing boy holds out his palms
Until they are white

The crow flew so fast
That he left his lonely caw
Behind in the fields

Make up your mind snail!
You are half inside your house
And halfway out!

The spring lingers on
In the scent of a damp log
Rotting in the sun

Japanese Haiku

Since my house burned down,
I now own a better view
of the rising moon.

—MASAHIDE

If things were better
for me, flies, I'd invite you
to share my supper.

—ISSA

What a pretty kite
The beggar's children fly high
above their hovel!

—ISSA

Asleep in the sun
on the temple's silent bronze
bell, a butterfly . . .

—BUSON

Well! Hello down there,
friend snail! When did you arrive
in such a hurry?

—ISSA

Cricket Songs: Japanese Haiku, trans. Harry Behn (New York: Harcourt, Brace & World, Inc., 1964). Copyright © 1964 by Harry Behn. Reprinted by permission of the publisher.

One dream all heroes
find to be true . . . cool green grass
on forgotten tombs

—BASHO

A mountain village
deep in snow . . . under the drifts
a sound of water.

—SHIKI

the hero

Frederick Douglass (1817–1895): Fighter
for Freedom

1.   [During the middle of the nineteenth century an American Negro became very famous in Europe.] He had crossed the ocean three times, once fleeing America for his life. But he did not remain abroad. He always came home to battle for the freedom of his people. His name was Frederick Douglass. His father was white but, nevertheless, Frederick was born a slave. His grandmother cared for him, and he never remembered seeing his mother more than a half dozen times in his life. The last time he saw her, she had walked twelve miles after dusk to hold him on her knees until he went to sleep. Then she had to walk twelve miles back to a distant plantation before sunrise to be at work in the fields.

2.   When Frederick was born in the backwoods of Maryland, his name was not Douglass. It was Bailey. About the time when he was shedding his first teeth the boy was taken from his grandmother and, with a dozen other slave children, put into the care of a mean old hag on the plantation who whipped them often and frequently sent them to sleep on a dirt floor without their suppers. Frederick was ragged, ne-

glected, and sometimes so hungry that he would wait at the kitchen door of the mansion house for the serving girls to shake the bones and crumbs from his master's table cloth. Then he would scramble with the dogs to pick up what fell into the yard. Fortunately, however, while still a young lad, he was sent to work for his master's relatives in Baltimore as errand boy and servant to that family's little son. Seeing that he was an apt boy, his new mistress taught him his A-B-C's. But her husband soon stopped her, saying, "If you teach him how to read, he'll want to know how to write, and this accomplished, he'll be running away with himself." However, white playmates in the streets sometimes lent him their bluebacked spellers and helped him to learn the words. When he was thirteen, with fifty cents earned from shining shoes, he bought a copy of *The Columbian Orator,* which included the speeches of William Pitt and other great men. This was his only book so he read it over and over. Many of the speeches were about liberty and freedom—as applied to white people, of course. But young Frederick took them to heart. "I wish myself a beast, a bird, anything rather than slave," he said.

His whole life eventually became a dedication to freedom. There [3.] was an old song he must have heard about "hard trials and deep tribulations." Such trials young Fred knew well. Meanwhile, he found comfort in religion under the guidance of a kindly old Negro named Lawson who could not read very well. Young Frederick taught Lawson "the letter" of the Bible; Lawson in turn taught Frederick "the spirit." Lawson strengthened his hope for freedom by assuring him, "If you want liberty, ask the Lord for it *in faith,* and He will give it to you." Frederick had begun to discover, too, that there were white people in America who did not believe in bondage. These were called *Abolitionists.* The Baltimore papers were always condemning them roundly as anarchists in league with the devil. But Frederick Douglass thought to himself that whatever the Abolitionists might be, they were not unfriendly to the slave, nor sympathetic to the slaveholder.

The more Frederick read the Bible and the newspaper, the more [4.] he began to realize that learning opened the way to achievement. As his master had warned, Frederick soon began to want to learn to write. In secret, at night in the loft where he slept, with a flour barrel for a table, his copy books being the Bible and a hymnal, the teenage boy began to teach himself. When no one was at home, he sometimes borrowed his white master's pen and ink. In time he learned to write. When he was sent to work for another branch of the family in a small town, he found a Sunday school held there in the home of a free Negro. Frederick was asked to be one of the instructors. But on his second Sunday in this Sabbath school, a white mob rushed in armed with sticks and stones and drove everybody away. Young Fred was warned that if he kept on teaching Sunday school, he would be filled with shot. In the small community this sixteen-year-old slave who could read and write had gotten the reputation of being a "dangerous Negro," putting thoughts into other Negroes' heads. Shortly his apprehensive master sent him away to a "Negro breaker" to be made a better slave—that is, to be tamed, humbled, taught to be contented with slavery—in other words, "to be broken."

5. The man's name was Covey. His plantation was a sort of reformatory work-farm on a sandy, desolate point of Chesapeake Bay. Covey specialized in taking unruly young slaves for a year and "cutting them down to size," so that their masters would have no more trouble with them. Three days after Frederick arrived there, Covey gave him a team of untamed oxen and sent him to the woods for a load of logs. The boy had never driven oxen before, but he dared not object to the job. The oxen ran away, overturned the wagon, and smashed a gate. For this the sixteen year old lad had his clothes torn from him by the "slave-breaker," and was flogged on his bare skin with ox-goads. As he described it many years later in his autobiography, under Covey's "heavy blows blood flowed freely, and wales were left on my back as large as my little finger. The sores from this flogging continued for weeks, for they were kept open by the rough and coarse cloth which I wore for shirting . . . during the first six months I was there I was whipped, either with sticks or cow-skins, every week. Aching bones and a sore back were my constant companions." The scars which Covey put on Frederick's shoulders never went away.

6. Work from before dawn until long after sundown was a part of Covey's system. One day Frederick fainted in the broiling sun of the treading-yard where the wheat was being separated from the straws. He was dizzy. His head ached violently. He was deathly ill. When Covey commanded him to rise, he could not. The slaver gave him a series of savage kicks which finally brought him to his feet. Frederick fell down again, whereupon Covey took a hickory slab and struck

him in the head, leaving him bleeding beside the fence. That night Frederick in despair dragged himself seven miles through the woods to his own master's house to beg that he be taken away from the slave-breaker. But his master did no such thing. Instead, he accused the boy of trying to avoid work and sent him back the next day to finish out his year with Covey. Then it was that Frederick made up his mind to defend himself and never to let anyone mistreat him so again. He returned to the plantation but, it being the Lord's Day, Covey waited until Monday morning to flog him. To the slaver's surprise and chagrin, the tall young Negro had resolved to fight it out, man to man. Instead of submitting to a whipping, he flung the slave-breaker on the ground each time he came near. Covey finally gave up. Frederick was not whipped again as long as he was there. But Covey almost worked him to death.

"I was a changed being after that fight." Douglass wrote in his *Life and Times*. "I was *nothing* before; I was a *man* now." On Christmas Day, 1834, his year with the slave-breaker was up. But his spirit, far from being broken, had been strengthened. His hatred of the cruelties of slavery intensified. And his determination to be free grew ever stronger. When the boy was transferred to a new master, even though conditions were much more pleasant, he began to plan a break for freedom. Frederick persuaded five other slaves to run away with him. On the eve of their departure, someone betrayed them. Frederick was bound and dragged off to jail. When he was released, he was not wanted on that plantation any more. (He was a "dangerous Negro.") So he was sent back to Baltimore and put to work in a shipyard where he learned the calker's trade. But the white workers objected to Negroes working with them. One day a number of them ganged up on Frederick (who was certainly there through no fault of his own) and beat him almost to death. In fact, he was beaten so badly that his master, for fear of losing a valuable slave, did not send him back to the shipyards again. Instead, he allowed Frederick to hire himself out, providing that every Saturday night he turned *all* his wages in to his master. Sometimes he might let Frederick keep a quarter for himself. Eventually, Frederick managed to save enough secretly to pay his fare to New York. Though it might mean his life if he were captured, Frederick decided to dare to try to escape from slavery again. Disguised as a sailor, and with borrowed seaman's papers, he leaped on a train just as it was leaving Baltimore. A day later, he reached New York. He was twenty-one years old when he set foot on free soil. A dream had at last come true. *He belonged to himself.*

8.   A new world had opened for him. "I felt as one might feel upon escape from a den of hungry lions," he wrote in his first letter to a friend. But soon his money was gone. In the big city nobody paid any attention to him. He was afraid to approach anyone, since he did not know whom to trust for fear he might be returned to slave territory. As he later described his condition, "I was without a home, without acquaintance, without money, without credit, without work, and without any definite knowledge as to what course to take or where to look for succor. In such an extremity, a man has something beside his new-born freedom of which to think. While wandering about the streets of New York, and lodging at least one night among the barrels on one of the wharves, I was indeed free—free from slavery—but free from food and shelter as well."

9.   A sailor who lived near the docks took him in, gave him a place to sleep, and put him in touch with a committee whose work it was to help escaped slaves. While in hiding in New York, Frederick was married to a girl with whom he had fallen in love in Baltimore and who followed him to the big city. Together they set out for Massachusetts on the deck of a steamer, for Negro passengers were not allowed in the cabins. In New Bedford he found employment on the wharves. There he dropped his slave name, Bailey, and took the name of one of the characters in *The Lady of the Lake*—Douglass. From then on he was known as Frederick Douglass, a name shortly to be in headlines around the world. For the young freeman was not satisfied just to be free himself. He became an Abolitionist.

10.   In 1841, Douglass made his first talk at an Anti-Slavery Society meeting in Nantucket. There, groping for words, since he had never faced an audience before, he told the story of his childhood, his bondage, and his escape. People were deeply moved. William Lloyd Garrison, who followed Douglass as a speaker, cried, "Is he a man or a thing?" And proceeded to point out how, in spite of slave-owners treating Frederick as a *thing,* free people could see that here was a man, worthy of being treated as a man.

11.   Douglass was then twenty-four years old, six feet tall, with hair like a lion, and very handsome. The more speeches he made, the more effective he became. Soon he was persuaded to quit his work on

the docks and become an orator for the cause of freedom. In 1845 he made his first trip to England to tell sympathizers there about the plight of America's slave millions. When he returned he began to publish a paper in Rochester, called *The North Star*. From then on, for fifty years, Douglass was a great public figure. He spoke on platforms with many of the distinguished men and women of his times— Wendell Phillips, Harriet Beacher Stowe, Charles Sumner, and Lucretia Mott. He published his life story. He defied the Fugitive Slave Law of 1850 and sheltered runaways in his home. Mobs attacked his meetings. He was sometimes stoned. After John Brown's famous raid on Harper's Ferry, in which he had no part, the newspapers and the slave-owners sought to implicate him. Douglass had to flee for his life to Canada, whence he made his second trip to England. When the War between the States broke out, he was back in this country, counselling with President Lincoln and recruiting troops for the Union Army—in which his own sons served. More than two hundred thousand Negroes fought in this War for freedom and the preservation of the Union. Many were inspired to do so by the brilliant speeches of Frederick Douglass.

When the War was over, Douglass became one of the leaders of the Republican Party. He was made a United States Marshall. Later he was appointed the Recorder of Deeds for the District of Columbia. And in 1889 he was confirmed as United States Minister to the Republic of Haiti. Active not just as a leader of the Negro people, at the first convention for women's suffrage Douglass was the *only* man of any color to stand up on the floor and defend the right of women to the ballot equally with men. "Right is of no sex," he stated in the first issue of *The North Star*. He was active, too, in the national temperance organizations and many other movements for social betterment. After Emancipation, Douglass demanded no special privileges for Negroes. For them he wanted simply the same freedom of action he felt *every* citizen should have. In a famous speech called, *What the Black Man Wants,* he said, "The American people have always been anxious to know what to do with us. I have had but one answer from the beginning. Do nothing with us! . . . If the Negro cannot stand on his own legs, let him fall. All I ask is, give him a *chance* to stand on his own legs! Let him alone! If you see him on his way to school, let him alone—don't disturb him. If you see him going to the dinner table at a hotel, let him go! If you see him going to the ballot box, let

12.

him alone—don't disturb him! If you see him going into a workshop, just let him alone."

13.   The only school from which Douglass was ever graduated, as he often repeated, was the school of slavery. His diploma was the scars upon his back. But he had about him a wit and wisdom that many a better educated person did not possess. His speeches moved thousands to action. As a writer he left behind him his *Life and Times,* an autobiography that is an American classic. His simple but effective use of words, tinged sometimes with wry humor, is illustrated in the final paragraph of a letter he wrote to his former master on the tenth anniversary of his escape to freedom. In this letter he listed all the wrongs this man had done him, but closed by stating:

> There is no roof under which you would be more safe than mine, and there is nothing in my house which you might need for your comfort, which I would not readily grant. Indeed, I should esteem it a privilege to set you an example as to how mankind ought to treat each other.
>
> I am your fellow man, but not your slave,
>
> Frederick Douglass.

DISCUSSION QUESTIONS

1. What is your definition of the word "hero"? Would Frederick Douglass fit that definition?
2. Part of the American Dream is the idea that no matter who you are or where you come from you can, with hard work and determination, become a success. Is this concept applicable to Douglass?
3. In what sense can this story be related to the quotation from Malcolm X in the Preface? Are these two figures similar in any way? From what you know of Malcolm X, do you think he would have approved of Douglass' political views?
4. What do Douglass' desires to learn to read and write have to do with the question of freedom?

RHETORIC

1. How does Langston Hughes order and develop the basic facts about Douglass' life?

2. Read over *Mechanics of Style,* Chapter II, p. 223, on phrases and clauses. Then discuss how Hughes uses dependent constructions in paragraph two to achieve variety of sentence structure. Construct a punctuation diagram of this paragraph similar to those done in Chapter VII of *Mechanics of Style,* p. 235.
3. How effective is the concluding paragraph of the essay?
4. Write a paragraph on the single most impressive fact you learned while reading this piece.
5. Research the background of a friend or relative by interviewing them and taking notes. Then, using the chronological structure of Hughes' essay, write a brief biography.
6. Is a large city or small town a more conducive setting for harmonious race relations? In a theme of 400 words, give three reasons for your choice of either one.

VOCABULARY

shedding (paragraph 2)	resolved (6)
hag (2)	intensified (7)
scramble (2)	succor (8)
unruly (5)	plight (11)
flogged (5)	implicate (11)

Inaugural Address

We observe today not a victory of party but a celebration of freedom, symbolizing an end as well as a beginning, signifying renewal as well as change. For I have sworn before you and Almighty God the same solemn oath our forebears prescribed nearly a century and three-quarters ago. 1.

The world is very different now. For man holds in his mortal hands the power to abolish all forms of human life. And yet the same revolutionary belief for which our forebears fought is still at issue around the globe, the belief that the rights of man come not from the generosity of the state but from the hand of God. 2.

We dare not forget today that we are the heirs of that first revo- 3.

John F. Kennedy, *Inaugural Address.* Delivered at the Capitol in Washington, D.C., January 20, 1961.

lution. Let the word go forth from this time and place, to friend and foe alike, that the torch has been passed to a new generation of Americans, born in this century, tempered by war, disciplined by a hard and bitter peace, proud of our ancient heritage, and unwilling to witness or permit the slow undoing of those human rights to which this nation has always been committed, and to which we are committed today at home and around the world.

4.   Let every nation know, whether it wishes us well or ill, that we shall pay any price, bear any burden, meet any hardship, support any friend, oppose any foe to assure the survival and the success of liberty.

5.   This much we pledge—and more.

6.   To those old allies whose cultural and spiritual origins we share, we pledge the loyalty of faithful friends. United, there is little we cannot do in a host of cooperative ventures. Divided, there is little we can do, for we dare not meet a powerful challenge at odds and split asunder.

7.   To those new states whom we welcome to the ranks of the free, we pledge our word that one form of colonial control shall not have passed away merely to be replaced by a far more iron tyranny. We shall not always expect to find them supporting our view. But we shall always hope to find them strongly supporting their own freedom, and to remember that, in the past, those who foolishly sought power by riding the back of the tiger ended up inside.

8.   To those peoples in the huts and villages of half the globe struggling to break the bonds of mass misery, we pledge our best efforts to help them help themselves, for whatever period is required, not because the Communists may be doing it, not because we seek their votes, but because it is right. If a free society cannot help the many who are poor, it cannot save the few who are rich.

9.   To our sister republics south of our border, we offer a special pledge: to convert our good words into good deeds, in a new alliance for progress, to assist free men and free governments in casting off the chains of poverty. But this peaceful revolution of hope cannot become the prey of hostile powers. Let all our neighbors know that we shall join with them to oppose aggression or subversion anywhere in the Americas. And let every other power know that this hemisphere intends to remain the master of its own house.

10.   To that world assembly of sovereign states, the United Nations,

our last best hope in an age where the instruments of war have far outpaced the instruments of peace, we renew our pledge of support; to prevent it from becoming merely a forum for invective, to strengthen its shield of the new and the weak, and to enlarge the area in which its writ may run.

Finally, to those nations who would make themselves our adversary, we offer not a pledge but a request: that both sides begin anew the quest for peace, before the dark powers of destruction unleashed by science engulf all humanity in planned or accidental self-destruction. [11.]

We dare not tempt them with weakness. For only when our arms are sufficient beyond doubt can we be certain beyond doubt that they will never be employed. [12.]

But neither can two great and powerful groups of nations take comfort from our present course—both sides overburdened by the cost of modern weapons, both rightly alarmed by the steady spread of the deadly atom, yet both racing to alter that uncertain balance of terror that stays the hand of mankind's final war. [13.]

So let us begin anew, remembering on both sides that civility is not a sign of weakness, and sincerity is always subject to proof. Let us never negotiate out of fear, but let us never fear to negotiate. [14.]

Let both sides explore what problems unite us instead of belaboring those problems which divide us. [15.]

Let both sides, for the first time, formulate serious and precise proposals for the inspection and control of arms, and bring the absolute power to destroy other nations under the absolute control of all nations. [16.]

Let both sides seek to invoke the wonders of science instead of its terrors. Together let us explore the stars, conquer the deserts, eradicate disease, tap the ocean depths and encourage the arts and commerce. [17.]

Let both sides unite to heed in all corners of the earth the command of Isaiah to "undo the heavy burdens . . . [and] let the oppressed go free." [18.]

And if a beachhead of cooperation may push back the jungle of suspicion, let both sides join in creating a new endeavor, not a new balance of power, but a new world of law, where the strong are just and the weak secure and the peace preserved. [19.]

All this will not be finished in the first one hundred days. Nor [20.]

will it be finished in the first one thousand days, nor in the life of this Administration, nor even perhaps in our lifetime on this planet. But let us begin.

21.   In your hands, my fellow citizens, more than mine, will rest the final success or failure of our course. Since this country was founded, each generation of Americans has been summoned to give testimony to its national loyalty. The graves of young Americans who answered the call to service surround the globe.

22.   Now the trumpet summons us again—not as a call to bear arms, though arms we need; not as a call to battle, though embattled we are; but a call to bear the burden of a long twilight struggle, year in and year out, "rejoicing in hope, patient in tribulation," a struggle against the common enemies of man: tyranny, poverty, disease and war itself.

23.   Can we forge against these enemies a grand and global alliance, North and South, East and West, that can assure a more fruitful life for all mankind? Will you join in that historic effort?

24.   In the long history of the world, only a few generations have been granted the role of defending freedom in its hour of maximum danger. I do not shrink from this responsibility; I welcome it. I do not believe that any of us would exchange places with any other people or any other generation. The energy, the faith, the devotion which we bring to this endeavor will light our country and all who serve it, and the glow from that fire can truly light the world.

25.   And so, my fellow Americans, ask not what your country can do for you; ask what you can do for your country.

26.   My fellow citizens of the world, ask not what America will do for you, but what together we can do for the freedom of man.

27.   Finally, whether you are citizens of America or citizens of the world, ask of us here the same high standards of strength and sacrifice which we ask of you. With a good conscience our only sure reward, with history the final judge of our deeds, let us go forth to lead the land we love, asking His blessing and His help, but knowing that here on earth God's work must truly be our own.

DISCUSSION QUESTIONS

1. To what extent have the plans and hopes in this address been fulfilled?
2. Some men argue that history results from inevitable events about which we can do nothing. Others argue that *men* influence these events

and thus make things happen. Which statement would you support?

3. Does the fact that Kennedy never had to struggle for money diminish his stature in any way? Did he have any other struggles?

RHETORIC

1. To be effective a sentence need not be long and filled with big words. Discuss Kennedy's use of the simple sentence in paragraphs five and twenty.

2. The major characteristic of Kennedy's address is its use of parallel structure (see *Mechanics of Style,* Chapter V, p. 231). How does Kennedy use this technique to structure his address?

3. Write a theme agreeing or disagreeing with *Student Paper* K, p. 260.

4. Assume that you had to compose such an address for the next presidential inauguration. Write a theme listing the major intentions of your administration.

5. Do you feel that Kennedy's death greatly affected the fulfillment of the ideas in this address? If so, develop a theme on this subject using concrete examples.

VOCABULARY

renewal (paragraph 1)	engulf (11)
subversion (9)	civility (14)
invective (10)	negotiate (14)
writ (10)	eradicate (17)
adversary (11)	tribulation (22)

Hub Fans Bid Kid Adieu

Fenway Park, in Boston, is a lyric little bandbox of a ballpark. Everything is painted green and seems in curiously sharp focus, like the inside of an old-fashioned peeping-type Easter egg. It was built in 1912 and rebuilt in 1934, and offers, as do most Boston artifacts, a compromise between Man's Euclidean determinations and Nature's

1.

"Hub Fans Bid Kid Adieu" from John Updike, *Assorted Prose* (New York: Alfred A. Knopf, Inc., 1965), pp. 127–47. Copyright © 1960 by John Updike. Reprinted by permission of the publisher. Originally appeared in *The New Yorker.*

beguiling irregularities. Its right field is one of the deepest in the American League, while its left field is the shortest; the high left-field wall, three hundred and fifteen feet from home plate along the foul line, virtually thrusts its surface at right-handed hitters. On the afternoon of Wednesday, September 28th, 1960, as I took a seat behind third base, a uniformed groundkeeper was treading the top of this wall, picking batting-practice home runs out of the screen, like a mushroom gatherer seen in Wordsworthian perspective on the verge of a cliff. The day was overcast, chill, and uninspirational. The Boston team was the worst in twenty-seven seasons. A jangling medley of incompetent youth and aging competence, the Red Sox were finishing in seventh place only because the Kansas City Athletics had locked them out of the cellar. They were scheduled to play the Baltimore Orioles, a much nimbler blend of May and December, who had been dumped from pennant contention a week before by the insatiable Yankees. I, and 10,453 others, had shown up primarily because this was the Red Sox's last home game of the season, and therefore the last time in all eternity that their regular left fielder, known to the headlines as TED, KID, SPLINTER, THUMPER, TW, and, most cloyingly, MISTER WONDERFUL, would play in Boston. "WHAT WILL WE DO WITHOUT TED? HUB FANS ASK" ran the headline on a newspaper being read by a bulb-nosed cigar smoker a few rows away. Williams' retirement had been announced, doubted (he had been threatening retirement for years), confirmed by Tom Yawkey, the Red Sox owner, and at last widely accepted as the sad but probable truth. He was forty-two and had redeemed his abysmal season of 1959 with a—considering his advanced age—fine one. He had been giving away his gloves and bats and had grudgingly consented to a sentimental ceremony today. This was not necessarily his last game; the Red Sox were scheduled to travel to New York and wind up the season with three games there.

2.   I arrived early. The Orioles were hitting fungos on the field. The day before, they had spitefully smothered the Red Sox, 17–4, and neither their faces nor their drab gray visiting-team uniforms seemed very gracious. I wondered who had invited them to the party. Between our heads and the lowering clouds a frenzied organ was thundering through, with an appositeness perhaps accidental, "You *maaaade* me love you, I didn't wanna do it, I didn't wanna do it. . . ."

The affair between Boston and Ted Williams was no mere sum-   3.
mer romance; it was a marriage composed of spats, mutual disap-
pointments, and, toward the end, a mellowing hoard of shared
memories. It fell into three stages, which may be termed Youth,
Maturity, and Age; or Thesis, Antithesis, and Synthesis; or Jason,
Achilles, and Nestor.

First, there was the by now legendary epoch[1] when the young   4.
bridegroom came out of the West and announced "All I want out
of life is that when I walk down the street folks will say 'There goes
the greatest hitter who ever lived.' " The dowagers of local journalism
attempted to give elementary deportment lessons to this child who

[1] This piece was written with no research materials save an outdated record
book and the Boston newspapers of the day; and Williams' early career preceded the dawning of my *Schlagballewusstsein* (Baseball-consciousness). Also
for reasons of perspective was my account of his beginnings skimped. Williams first attracted the notice of a major-league scout—Bill Essick of the
Yankees—when he was a fifteen-year-old pitcher with the San Diego American
Legion Post team. As a pitcher-outfielder for San Diego's Herbert Hoover
High School, Williams recorded averages of .586 and .403. Essick balked at
signing Williams for the $1,000 his mother asked; he was signed instead, for
$150 a month, by the local Pacific Coast League franchise, the newly created
San Diego Padres. In his two seasons with this team, Williams hit merely .271
and .291, but his style and slugging (23 home runs the second year) caught
the eye of, among others, Casey Stengel, then with the Boston Braves, and
Eddie Collins, the Red Sox general manager. Collins bought him for the
Padres for $25,000 in cash and $25,000 in players. Williams was then nineteen. Collins' fond confidence in the boy's potential matched Williams' own.
Williams reported to the Red Sox training camp in Sarasota in 1938 and,
after showing more volubility than skill, was shipped down to the Minneapolis
Millers, the top Sox farm team. It should be said, perhaps, that the parent
club was equipped with an excellent, if mature, outfield, mostly purchased
from Connie Mack's dismantled A's. Upon leaving Sarasota, Williams is supposed to have told the regular outfield of Joe Vosmik, Doc Cramer, and Ben
Chapman that he would be back and would make more money than the three
of them put together. At Minneapolis he hit .366, batted in 142 runs, scored
130, and hit 43 home runs. He also loafed in the field, jabbered at the fans,
and smashed a water cooler with his fist. In 1939 he came north with the Red
Sox. On the way, in Atlanta, he dropped a foul fly, accidentally kicked it
away in trying to pick it up, picked it up, and threw it out of the park. It would
be nice if, his first time up in Fenway Park, he had hit a home run. Actually,
in his first Massachusetts appearance, the first inning of an exhibition game
against Holy Cross at Worcester, he *did* hit a home run, a grand slam. The
Red Sox season opened in Yankee Stadium. Facing Red Ruffing, Williams
struck out and, the next time up, doubled for his first major-league hit. In the
Fenway Park opener, against Philadelphia, he had a single in five trips. His
first home run came on April 23, in that same series with the A's. Williams
was then twenty, and played *right* field. In his rookie season he hit .327; in
1940, .344.

spake as a god, and to their horror were themselves rebuked. Thus
began the long exchange of backbiting, bat-flipping, booing, and
spitting that has distinguished Williams' public relations.[2] The spitting
incidents of 1957 and 1958 and the similar dockside courtesies that
Williams has now and then extended to the grandstand should be
judged against this background: the left-field stands at Fenway for
twenty years have held a large number of customers who have bought
their way in primarily for the privilege of showering abuse on Williams. Greatness necessarily attracts debunkers, but in Williams' case
the hostility has been systematic and unappeasable. His basic offense
against the fans has been to wish that they weren't there. Seeking a
perfectionist's vacuum, he has quixotically desired to sever the game
from the ground of paid spectatorship and publicity that supports it.
Hence his refusal to tip his cap[3] to the crowd or turn the other cheek
to newsmen. It has been a costly theory—it has probably cost him,
among other evidences of good will, two Most Valuable Player
awards, which are voted by reporters[4]—but he has held to it. While

[2] See *Ted Williams,* by Ed Linn (Sport Magazine Library), Chapter 6, "Williams vs. the Press." It is Linn's suggestion that Williams walked into a circulation war among the seven Boston newspapers, who in their competitive zeal
headlined incidents that the New York papers, say, would have minimized,
just as they minimized the less genial side of the moody and aloof DiMaggio
and smoothed Babe Ruth into a folk hero. It is also Linn's thought, and an
interesting one, that Williams thrived on even adverse publicity, and needed a
hostile press to elicit, contrariwise, his defiant best. The statistics (especially
of the 1958 season, when he snapped a slump by spitting in all directions, and
inadvertently conked an elderly female fan with a tossed bat) seem to cor-
roborate this. Certainly Williams could have had a truce for the asking, and
his industrious perpetuation of the war, down to his last day in uniform, implies its usefulness to him. The actual and intimate anatomy of the matter
resides in locker rooms and hotel corridors fading from memory. When my
admiring account was printed, I received a letter from a sports reporter who
hated Williams with a bitter and explicit immediacy. And even Linn's hagiol-
ogy permits some glimpses of Williams' locker-room manners that are not
pleasant.

[3] But he did tip his cap, high off his head, in at least his first season, as cartoons
from that period verify. He also was extravagantly cordial to taxi-drivers and
stray children. See Linn, Chapter 4, "The Kid Comes to Boston": "There has
never been a ballplayer—anywhere, anytime—more popular than Ted Williams
in his first season in Boston." To this epoch belong Williams' prankish use of
the Fenway scoreboard lights for rifle practice, his celebrated expressed preference for the life of a fireman, and his determined designation of himself as
"The Kid."

[4] In 1947 Joe DiMaggio and in 1957 Mickey Mantle, with seasons inferior to
Williams', won the MVP award because sportswriters, who vote on ballots with
ten places, had vengefully placed Williams ninth, tenth, or nowhere at all. The
1941 award to Joe DiMaggio, even though this was Williams' .406 year, is

his critics, oral and literary, remained beyond the reach of his discipline, the opposing pitchers were accessible, and he spanked them
to the tune of .406 in 1941.[5] He slumped to .356 in 1942 and went
off to war.

In 1946, Williams returned from three years as a Marine pilot to
the second of his baseball avatars, that of Achilles, the hero of in-
comparable prowess and beauty who nevertheless was to be found
sulking in his tent while the Trojans (mostly Yankees) fought through
to the ships. Yawkey, a timber and mining maharajah, had surrounded his central jewel with many gems of slightly lesser water,
such as Bobby Doerr, Dom DiMaggio, Rudy York, Birdie Tebbetts,
and Johnny Pesky. Throughout the late forties, the Red Sox were the
best paper team in baseball, yet they had little three-dimensional to
show for it, and if this was a tragedy, Williams was Hamlet. A succinct
review of the indictment—and a fair sample of appreciative sports-
page prose—appeared the very day of Williams' valedictory, in a
column by Huck Finnegan in the Boston *American* (no sentimental-
ist, Huck):

> Williams' career, in contrast [to Babe Ruth's], has been a series of
> failures except for his averages. He flopped in the only World Series
> he ever played in (1946) when he batted only .200. He flopped in
> the playoff game with Cleveland in 1948. He flopped in the final
> game of the 1949 season with the pennant hinging on the outcome
> (Yanks 5, Sox 3). He flopped in 1950 when he returned to the lineup
> after a two-month absence and ruined the morale of a club that
> seemed pennant-bound under Steve O'Neill. It has always been Wil-
> liams' records first, the team second, and the Sox non-winning record
> is proof enough of that.

---

more understandable, since this was also *annus miraculorum* when DiMaggio
hit safely in 56 consecutive games.

[5] The sweet saga of this beautiful decimal must be sung once more. Williams,
after hitting above .400 all season, had cooled to .39955 with one doubleheader left to play, in Philadelphia. Joe Cronin, then managing the Red Sox,
offered to bench him to safeguard his average, which was exactly .400 when
rounded to the third decimal place. Williams said (I forget where I read this)
that he did not want to become the .400 hitter with just his toenails over the
line. He played the first game and singled, homered, singled, and singled. With
less to gain than to lose, he elected to play the second game and got two more
hits, including a double that dented a loudspeaker horn on the top of the
right-field wall, giving him six-for-eight on the day and a season's average that,
in the forty years between Rogers Hornsby's .403 (1925) and the present,
stands as unique.

6.   There are answers to all this, of course. The fatal weakness of the great Sox slugging teams was not-quite-good-enough pitching rather than Williams' failure to hit a home run every time he came to bat. Again, Williams' depressing effect on his teammates has never been proved. Despite ample coaching to the contrary, most insisted that they *liked* him. He has been generous with advice to any player who asked for it. In an increasingly combative baseball atmosphere, he continued to duck beanballs docilely. With umpires he was gracious to a fault. This courtesy itself annoyed his critics, whom there was no pleasing. And against the ten crucial games (the seven World Series games with the St. Louis Cardinals, the 1948 playoff with the Cleveland Indians, and the two-game series with the Yankees at the end of the 1949 season, when one victory would have given the Red Sox the pennant) that make up the Achilles' heel of Williams' record, a mass of statistics can be set showing that day in and day out he was no slouch in the clutch.[6] The correspondence columns of the Boston papers now and then suffer a sharp flurry of arithmetic on this score; indeed, for Williams to have distributed all his hits so they did nobody else any good would constitute a feat of placement unparalleled in the annals of selfishness.

7.   Whatever residue of truth remains of the Finnegan charge those of us who love Williams must transmute as best we can, in our own personal crucibles. My personal memories of Williams began when I was a boy in Pennsylvania, with two last-place teams in Philadelphia to keep me company. For me, "W'ms, lf" was a figment of the box scores who always seemed to be going 3-for-5. He radiated, from afar, the hard blue glow of high purpose. I remember listening over the radio to the All-Star Game of 1946, in which Williams hit two singles and two home runs, the second one off a Rip Sewell "blooper" pitch; it was like hitting a balloon out of the park. I remember watching one of his home runs from the bleachers of Shibe Park; it went over the first baseman's head and rose methodically along a straight line and was still rising when it cleared the fence. The trajectory seemed qualitatively different from anything anyone else might hit. For me, Williams is the classic ballplayer of the game

---

[6] For example: In 1948, the Sox came from behind to tie the Indians by winning three straight; in those games Williams went two for two, two for two; and two for four. In 1949, the Sox overtook the Yankees by winning nine in a row; in that streak, Williams won four games with home runs.

on a hot August weekday, before a small crowd, when the only
thing at stake is the tissue-thin difference between a thing done well
and a thing done ill. Baseball is a game of the long season, of relent-
less and gradual averaging-out. Irrelevance—since the reference point
of most individual contests is remote and statistical—always threatens
its interest, which can be maintained not only by the occasional hero-
ics that sportswriters feed upon but by players who always *care;* who
care, that is to say, about themselves and their art. Insofar as the
clutch hitter is not a sportswriter's myth, he is a vulgarity, like a
writer who writes only for money. It may be that, compared to such
managers' dreams as the manifestly classy Joe DiMaggio and the always helpful Stan Musial, Williams was an icy star. But of all team
sports, baseball, with its graceful intermittences of action, its immense
and tranquil field sparsely settled with poised men in white, its dispassionate mathematics, seems to me best suited to accommodate, and
be ornamented by, a loner. It is an essentially lonely game. No other
player visible to my generation concentrated within himself so much
of the sport's poignance, so assiduously refined his natural skills, so
constantly brought to the plate that intensity of competence that
crowds the throat with joy.

By the time I went to college, near Boston, the lesser stars Yaw-   8.
key had assembled around Williams had faded, and his rigorous pride
of craftsmanship had become itself a kind of heroism. This brittle
and temperamental player had developed an unexpected quality of
persistence. He was always coming back—back from Korea, back
from a broken collarbone, a shattered elbow, a bruised heel, back
from drastic bouts of flu and ptomaine poisoning. Hardly a season
went by without some enfeebling mishap, yet he always came back,
and always looked like himself. The delicate mechanism of timing and
power seemed sealed, shockproof, in some case deep within his
frame.[7] In addition to injuries, there was a heavily publicized divorce,

---

[7] Two reasons for his durability may be adduced. A non-smoker, non-drinker,
   habitual walker, and year-round outdoorsman, Williams spared his body the
   vicissitudes of the seasonal athlete. And his hitting was in large part a mental
   process; the amount of cerebration he devoted to such details as pitchers' patterns, prevailing winds, and the muscular mechanics of swinging a bat would
   seem ridiculous, if it had not paid off. His intellectuality, as it were, perhaps
   explains the quickness with which he adjusted, after the war, to the changed
   conditions—the night games, the addition of the slider to the standard pitching
   repertoire, the new cry for the long ball. His reaction to the Williams Shift,
   then, cannot be dismissed as unconsidered.

and the usual storms with the press, and the Williams Shift—the maneuver, custom-built by Lou Boudreau of the Cleveland Indians, whereby three infielders were concentrated on the right side of the infield.[8] Williams could easily have learned to punch singles through the vacancy on his left and fattened his average hugely. This was what Ty Cobb, the Einstein of average, told him to do. But the game had changed since Cobb; Williams believed that his value to the club and to the league was as a slugger, so he went on pulling the ball, trying to blast it through three men, and paid the price of perhaps fifteen points of lifetime average. Like Ruth before him, he bought the occasional home run at the cost of many directed singles—a calculated sacrifice certainly not, in the case of a hitter as average-minded as Williams, entirely selfish.

9.   After a prime so harassed and hobbled, Williams was granted by the relenting fates a golden twilight. He became at the end of his career perhaps the best *old* hitter of the century. The dividing line falls between the 1956 and 1957 seasons. In September of the first year, he and Mickey Mantle were contending for the batting championship. Both were hitting around .350, and there was no one else near them. The season ended with a three-game series between the Yankees and the Sox, and, living in New York then, I went up to the Stadium. Williams was slightly shy of the four hundred at-bats needed to qualify; the fear was expressed that the Yankee pitchers would walk him to protect Mantle. Instead, they pitched to him. It was wise. He looked terrible at the plate, tired and discouraged and unconvincing. He never looked very good to me in the Stadium.[9] The final outcome in 1956 was Mantle .353, Williams .345.

10.   The next year, I moved from New York to New England, and it made all the difference. For in September of 1957, in the same situa-

---

[8] Invented, or perpetrated (as a joke?) by Boudreau on July 14, 1946, between games of a doubleheader. In the first game of the doubleheader, Williams had hit three homers and batted in eight runs. The shift was not used when men were on base and, had Williams bunted or hit late against it immediately, it might not have spread, in all its variations, throughout the league. The Cardinals used it in the lamented World Series of that year. Toward the end, in 1959 and 1960, rather sadly, it had faded from use, or degenerated to the mere clockwise twitching of the infield customary against pull hitters.

[9] Shortly after his retirement, Williams, in *Life,* wrote gloomily of the Stadium, "There's the bigness of it. There are those high stands and all those people smoking—and, of course, the shadows. . . . It takes at least one series to get accustomed to the Stadium and even then you're not sure." Yet his lifetime batting average there is .340, only four points under his median average.

tion, the story was reversed. Mantle finally hit .365; it was the best season of his career. But Williams, though sick and old, had run away from him. A bout of flu had laid him low in September. He emerged from his cave in the Hotel Somerset haggard but irresistible; he hit four successive pinch-hit home runs. "I feel terrible," he confessed, "but every time I take a swing at the ball it goes out of the park." He ended the season with thirty-eight home runs and an average of .388, the highest in either league since his own .406, and, coming from a decrepit man of thirty-nine, an even more supernal figure. With eight or so of the "leg hits" that a younger man would have beaten out, it would have been .400. And the next year, Williams, who in 1949 and 1953 had lost batting championships by decimal whiskers to George Kell and Mickey Vernon, sneaked in behind his teammate Pete Runnels and filched his sixth title, a bargain at .328.

In 1959, it seemed all over. The dinosaur thrashed around in the .200 swamp for the first half of the season, and was even benched ("rested," Manager Mike Higgins tactfully said). Old foes like the late Bill Cunningham began to offer batting tips. Cunningham thought Williams was jiggling his elbows;[10] in truth, Williams' neck was so stiff he could hardly turn his head to look at the pitcher. When he swung, it looked like a Calder mobile with one thread cut; it reminded you that since 1954 Williams' shoulders had been wired together. A solicitous pall settled over the sports pages. In the two decades since Williams had come to Boston, his status had imperceptibly shifted from that of a naughty prodigy to that of a municipal monument. As his shadow in the record books lengthened, the Red Sox teams around him declined, and the entire American League seemed to be losing life and color to the National. The inconsistency of the new superstars—Mantle, Colavito, and Kaline—served to make Williams appear all the more singular. And off the field, his private philanthropy —in particular, his zealous chairmanship of the Jimmy Fund, a charity for children with cancer—gave him a civic presence matched

11.

---

[10] It was Cunningham who, when Williams first appeared in a Red Sox uniform at the 1938 spring training camp, wrote with melodious prescience: "The Sox seem to think Williams is just cocky enough and gabby enough to make a great and colorful outfielder, possibly the Babe Herman type. Me? I don't like the way he stands at the plate. He bends his front knee inward and moves his foot just before he takes a swing. That's exactly what I do just before I drive a golf ball and knowing what happens to the golf balls I drive, I don't believe this kid will ever hit half a singer midget's weight in a bathing suit."

only by that of Richard Cardinal Cushing. In religion, Williams appears to be a humanist, and a selective one at that, but he and the abrasive-voiced Cardinal, when their good works intersect and they appear in the public eye together, make a handsome pair of seraphim.

12.   Humiliated by his '59 season, Williams determined, once more, to come back. I, as a specimen Williams partisan, was both glad and fearful. All baseball fans believe in miracles; the question is, how *many* do you believe in? He looked like a ghost in spring training. Manager Jurges warned us ahead of time that if Williams didn't come through, he would be benched, just like anybody else. As it turned out, it was Jurges who was benched. Williams entered the 1960 season needing eight home runs to have a lifetime total of 500; after one time at bat in Washington, he needed seven. For a stretch, he was hitting a home run every second game that he played. He passed Lou Gehrig's lifetime total, and finished with 521, thirteen behind Jimmy Foxx, who alone stands between Williams and Babe Ruth's unapproachable 714. The summer was a statistician's picnic. His two-thousandth walk came and went, his eighteen-hundredth run batted in, his sixteenth All-Star Game. At one point, he hit a home run off a pitcher, Don Lee, off whose father, Thornton Lee, he had hit a home run a generation before. The only comparable season for a forty-two-year-old man was Ty Cobb's in 1928. Cobb batted .323 and hit one homer. Williams batted .316 but hit twenty-nine homers.

13.   In sum, though generally conceded to be the greatest hitter of his era, he did not establish himself as "the greatest hitter who ever lived." Cobb, for average, and Ruth, for power, remain supreme. Cobb, Rogers Hornsby, Joe Jackson, and Lefty O'Doul, among players since 1900, have higher lifetime averages than Williams' .344. Unlike Foxx, Gehrig, Hack Wilson, Hank Greenberg, and Ralph Kiner, Williams never came close to matching Babe Ruth's season home-run total of sixty.[11] In the list of major-league batting records, not one is held by Williams. He is second in walks drawn, third in home runs, fifth in lifetime average, sixth in runs batted in, eighth in runs scored and in total bases, fourteenth in doubles, and thirtieth in hits.[12] But if we allow him merely average seasons for the four-plus

[11] Written before Roger Maris's fluky, phenomenal sixty-one.

[12] Again, as of 1960. Since then, Musial may have surpassed him in some statistical areas.

seasons he lost to two wars, and add another season for the months he lost to injuries, we get a man who in all the power totals would be second, and not a very distant second, to Ruth. And if we further allow that these years would have been not merely average but prime years, if we allow for all the months when Williams was playing in sub-par condition, if we permit his early and later years in baseball to be some sort of index of what the middle years could have been, if we give him a right-field fence that is not, like Fenway's, one of the most distant in the league, and if—the least excusable "if"—we imagine him condescending to outsmart the Williams Shift, we can defensibly assemble, like a colossus induced from the sizeable fragments that do remain, a statistical figure not incommensurate with his grandiose ambition. From the statistics that are on the books, a good case can be made that in the *combination* of power and average Williams is first; nobody else ranks so high in both categories. Finally, there is the witness of the eyes; men whose memories go back to Shoeless Joe Jackson—another unlucky natural—rank him and Williams together as the best-looking hitters they have seen. It was for our last look that ten thousand of us had come.

    Two girls, one of them with pert buckteeth and eyes as black as vest buttons, the other with white skin and flesh-colored hair, like an underdeveloped photograph of a redhead, came and sat on my right. On my other side was one of those frowning chestless young-old men who can frequently be seen, often wearing sailor hats, attending ball games alone. He did not open his program but instead tapped it, rolled up, on his knee as he gave the game his disconsolate attention. A young lady, with freckles and a depressed, dainty nose that by an optical illusion seemed to thrust her lips forward for a kiss, sauntered down into the box seat right behind the roof of the Oriole dugout. She wore a blue coat with a Northeastern University emblem sewed to it. The girls beside me took it into their heads that this was Williams' daughter. She looked too old to me, and why would she be sitting behind the visitors' dugout? On the other hand, from the way she sat there, staring at the sky and French-inhaling, she clearly was *some-body*. Other fans came and eclipsed her from view. The crowd looked less like a weekday ball park crowd than like the folks you might find in Yellowstone National Park, or emerging from automobiles at the top of scenic Mount Mansfield. There were a lot of competitively well-dressed couples of tourist age, and not a few babes in arms. A row of five seats in front of me was abruptly filled with a woman and four children, the youngest of them two years old, if that. Someday, presumably, he could tell his grandchildren that he saw Williams play. Along with these tots and second-honeymooners, there were Harvard freshmen, giving off that peculiar nervous glow created when a sufficient quantity of insouciance is saturated with enough insecurity; thick-necked Army officers with brass on their shoulders and steel in their stares; pepperings of priests; perfumed bouquets of Roxbury Fabian fans; shiny salesmen from Albany and Fall River; and those gray, hoarse men—taxi drivers, slaughterers, and bartenders—who will continue to click through the turnstiles long after everyone else has deserted to television and tramporamas. Behind me, two young male voices blossomed, cracking a joke about God's five proofs that Thomas Aquinas exists—typical Boston College levity.

15.   The batting cage was trundled away. The Orioles fluttered to the sidelines. Diagonally across the field, by the Red Sox dugout, a cluster of men in overcoats were festering like maggots. I could see a splinter of white uniform, and Williams' head, held at a self-deprecating and evasive tilt. Williams' conversational stance is that of a six-foot-three-inch man under a six-foot ceiling. He moved away to the patter of flash bulbs, and began playing catch with a young Negro outfielder named Willie Tasby. His arm, never very powerful, had grown lax with the years, and his throwing motion was a kind of muscular drawl. To catch the ball, he flicked his glove hand onto his left shoulder (he batted left but threw right, as every schoolboy ought to know) and let the ball plop into it comically. This catch session with Tasby was the only time all afternoon I saw him grin.

16.   A tight little flock of human sparrows who, from the lambent and pampered pink of their faces, could only have been Boston politicians moved toward the plate. The loudspeakers mammothly coughed as someone huffed on the microphone. The ceremonies began. Curt Gowdy, the Red Sox radio and television announcer, who sounds like everybody's brother-in-law, delivered a brief sermon, taking the two words "pride" and "champion" as his text. It began. "Twenty-one years ago, a skinny kid from San Diego, California . . ." and ended, "I don't think we'll ever see another like him." Robert Tibolt, chairman of the board of the Greater Boston Chamber of Commerce, presented Williams with a big Paul Revere silver bowl. Harry Carlson,

a member of the sports committee of the Boston Chamber, gave him a plaque, whose inscription he did not read in its entirety, out of deference to Williams' distaste for this sort of fuss. Mayor Collins, seated in a wheelchair, presented the Jimmy Fund with a thousand-dollar check.

Then the occasion himself stooped to the microphone, and his [17.] voice sounded, after the others, very Californian; it seemed to be coming, excellently amplified, from a great distance, adolescently young and as smooth as a butternut. His thanks for the gifts had not died from our ears before he glided, as if helplessly, into "In spite of all the terrible things that have been said about me by the knights of the keyboard up there. . . ." He glanced up at the press row suspended behind home plate. The crowd tittered, appalled. A frightful vision flashed upon me, of the press gallery pelting Williams with erasers, of Williams clambering up the foul screen to slug journalists, of a riot, of Mayor Collins being crushed. ". . . And they *were* terrible things," Williams insisted, with level melancholy, into the mike. "I'd like to forget them, but I can't." He paused, swallowed his memories, and went on, "I want to say that my years in Boston have been the greatest thing in my life." The crowd, like an immense sail going limp in a change of wind, sighed with relief. Taking all the parts himself, Williams then acted out a vivacious little morality drama in which an imaginary tempter came to him at the beginning of his career and said, "Ted, you can play anywhere you like." Leaping nimbly into the role of his younger self (who in biographical actuality had yearned to be a Yankee), Williams gallantly chose Boston over all the other cities, and told us that Tom Yawkey was the greatest owner in baseball and we were the greatest fans. We applauded ourselves lustily. The umpire came out and dusted the plate. The voice of doom announced over the loudspeakers that after Williams' retirement his uniform number, 9, would be permanently retired—the first time the Red Sox had so honored a player. We cheered. The national anthem was played. We cheered. The game began.

Williams was third in the batting order, so he came up in the [18.] bottom of the first inning, and Steve Barber, a young pitcher born two months before Williams began playing in the major leagues, offered him four pitches, at all of which he disdained to swing, since none of them were within the strike zone. This demonstrated simultaneously that Williams' eyes were razor-sharp and that Barber's control wasn't. Shortly, the bases were full, with Williams on second. "Oh, I hope he gets held up at third! That would be wonderful," the girl beside me moaned, and, sure enough, the man at bat walked and Williams was delivered into our foreground. He struck the pose of Donatello's David, the third-base bag being Goliath's head. Fiddling with his cap, swapping small talk with the Oriole third basemen (who seemed delighted to have him drop in), swinging his arms with a sort of prancing nervousness, he looked fine—flexible, hard, and not unbecomingly substantial through the middle. The long neck, the small head, the knickers whose cuffs were worn down near his ankles —all these clichés of sports cartoon iconography were rendered in the flesh.

19.   With each pitch, Williams danced down the baseline, waving his arms and stirring dust, ponderous but menacing, like an attacking goose. It occurred to about a dozen humorists at once to shout "Steal home! Go, go!" Williams' speed afoot was never legendary. Lou Clinton, a young Sox outfielder, hit a fairly deep fly to center field. Williams tagged up and ran home. As he slid across the plate, the ball, thrown with unusual heft by Jackie Brandt, the Oriole center fielder, hit him on the back.

20.   "Boy, he was really loafing, wasn't he?" one of the collegiate voices behind me said.

21.   "It's cold," the other voice explained. "He doesn't play well when it's cold. He likes heat. He's a hedonist."

22.   The run that Williams scored was the second and last of the inning. Gus Triandos, of the Orioles, quickly evened the score by plunking a home run over the handy left-field wall. Williams, who had had this wall at his back for twenty years,[13] played the ball flawlessly. He didn't budge. He just stood still, in the center of the little patch of grass that his patient footsteps had worn brown, and, limp with lack of interest, watched the ball pass overhead. It was not a very interesting game. Mike Higgins, the Red Sox manager, with nothing to lose, had restricted his major-league players to the left-field line— along with Williams, Frank Malzone, a first-rate third baseman,

---

[13] In his second season (1940) he was switched to left field, to protect his eyes from the right-field sun.

played the game—and had peopled the rest of the terrain with unpre-
dictable youngsters fresh, or not so fresh, off the farms. Other than
Williams' recurrent appearances at the plate, the *maladresse* of the Sox
infield was the sole focus of suspense; the second baseman turned
every grounder into a juggling act, while the shortstop did a breath-
taking impersonation of an open window. With this sort of assistance,
the Orioles wheedled their way into a 4–2 lead. They had early replaced Barber with another young pitcher, Jack Fisher. Fortunately
(as it turned out), Fisher is no cutie; he is willing to burn the ball
through the strike zone, and inning after inning this tactic punctured
Higgins' string of test balloons.

23. Whenever Williams appeared at the plate—pounding the dirt
from his cleats, gouging a pit in the batter's box with his left foot,
wringing resin out of the bat handle with his vehement grip, switching
the stick at the pitcher with an electric ferocity—it was like having a
familiar Leonardo appear in a shuffle of *Saturday Evening Post*
covers. This man, you realized—and here, perhaps, was the difference, greater than the difference in gifts—really desired to hit the ball.
In the third inning, he hoisted a high fly to deep center. In the fifth,
we thought he had it; he smacked the ball hard and high into the heart
of his power zone, but the deep right field in Fenway and the heavy
air and a casual east wind defeated him. The ball died. Al Pilarcik
leaned his back against the big "380" painted on the right-field wall
and caught it. On another day, in another park, it would have been
gone. (After the game, Williams said, "I didn't think I could hit one
any harder than that. The conditions weren't good.")

24. The afternoon grew so glowering that in the sixth inning the arc
lights were turned on—always a wan sight in the day-time, like the
burning headlights of a funeral procession. Aided by the gloom,
Fisher was slicing through the Sox rookies, and Williams did not come
to bat in the seventh. He was second up in the eighth. This was almost
certainly his last time to come to the plate in Fenway Park, and instead of merely cheering, as we had at his three previous appearances,
we stood, all of us, and applauded. I had never before heard pure
applause in a ballpark. No calling, no whistling, just an ocean of
handclaps, minute after minute, burst after burst, crowding and running together in continuous succession like the pushes of surf at the
edge of the sand. It was a sombre and considered tumult. There was

not a boo in it. It seemed to renew itself out of a shifting set of memories as the Kid, the Marine, the veteran of feuds and failures and injuries, the friend of children, and the enduring old pro evolved down the bright tunnel of twenty-two summers toward this moment. At last, the umpire signalled for Fisher to pitch; with the other players, he had been frozen in position. Only Williams had moved during the ovation, switching his bat impatiently, ignoring everything except his cherished task. Fisher wound up, and the applause sank into a hush.

25.   Understand that we were a crowd of rational people. We knew that a home run cannot be produced at will; the right pitch must be perfectly met and luck must ride with the ball. Three innings before, we had seen a brave effort fail. The air was soggy, the season was exhausted. Nevertheless, there will always lurk, around the corner in a pocket of our knowledge of the odds, an indefensible hope, and this was one of the times, which you now and then find in sports, when a density of expectation hangs in the air and plucks an event out of the future.

26.   Fisher, after his unsettling wait, was low with the first pitch. He put the second one over, and Williams swung mightily and missed. The crowd grunted, seeing that classic swing, so long and smooth and quick, exposed. Fisher threw the third time, Williams swung again, and there it was. The ball climbed on a diagonal line into the vast volume of air over center field. From my angle, behind third base, the ball seemed less an object in flight than the tip of a towering, motionless construct, like the Eiffel Tower or the Tappan Zee Bridge. It was in the books while it was still in the sky. Brandt ran back to the deepest corner of the outfield grass, the ball descended beyond his reach and struck in the crotch where the bullpen met the wall, bounced chunkily, and vanished.

27.   Like a feather caught in a vortex, Williams ran around the square of bases at the center of our beseeching screaming. He ran as he always ran out home runs—hurriedly, unsmiling, head down, as if our praise were a storm of rain to get out of. He didn't tip his cap. Though we thumped, wept, and chanted "We want Ted" for minutes after he hid in the dugout, he did not come back. Our noise for some seconds passed beyond excitement into a kind of immense open anguish, a wailing, a cry to be saved. But immortality is nontransferable. The papers said that the other players, and even the umpires on

the field, begged him to come out and acknowledge us in some way, but he refused. Gods do not answer letters.

Every true story has an anticlimax. The men on the field refused 28. to disappear, as would have seemed decent, in the smoke of Williams' miracle. Fisher continued to pitch, and escaped further harm. At the end of the inning, Higgins sent Williams out to his left-field position, then instantly replaced him with Carrol Hardy, so we had a long last look at Williams as he ran out there and then back, his uniform jogging, his eyes steadfast on the ground. It was nice, and we were grateful, but it left a funny taste.

One of the scholasticists behind me said, "Let's go. We've seen 29. everything. I don't want to spoil it." This seemed a sound aesthetic decision. Williams' last word had been so exquisitely chosen, such a perfect fusion of expectation, intention, and execution, that already it felt a little unreal in my head, and I wanted to get out before the castle collapsed. But the game, though played by clumsy midgets under the feeble glow of the arc lights, began to tug at my attention, and I loitered in the runway until it was over. Williams' homer had, quite incidentally, made the score 4–3. In the bottom of the ninth inning, with one out, Marlin Coughtry, the secondbase juggler, singled. Vic Wertz, pinch-hitting, doubled off the left-field wall, Coughtry advancing to third. Pumpsie Green walked, to load the bases. Willie Tasby hit a double-play ball to the third baseman, but in making the pivot throw Billy Klaus, an ex-Red Sox infielder, reverted to form and threw the ball past the first baseman and into the Red Sox dugout. The Sox won, 5–4. On the car radio as I drove home I heard that Williams, his own man to the end, had decided not to accompany the team to New York. He had met the little death that awaits athletes. He had quit.

DISCUSSION QUESTIONS

1. Updike seems to feel that Williams has certain ideas about which he cares deeply. Is this necessary in a hero?
2. What are those ideas? Do they have anything in common with Kennedy's?
3. Both Williams and Kennedy have contempt for mediocrity. Does this

indicate conceit on their part? Is there a difference between pride and conceit?

4. Some claim that Williams, being a mere sports figure, can in no sense be called a hero. Would you agree?

5. What motivates people to make heroes out of sports figures? Why do people need heroes at all?

RHETORIC

1. What is the purpose of the final sentence in paragraph thirteen?

2. Updike makes liberal use of concrete details in the essay. Indicate where Updike uses these details for their argumentative rather than for their interest value (see *Essay Development,* Chapters II and III, pp. 14 and 17, for a discussion of details and examples). For instance, what is his reaction to Huck Finnegan's attack on Williams in paragraph five?

3. Write a 400-word theme on your favorite figure in sports. List the major qualities that you admire in him.

4. Who are the figures mentioned in paragraph three and why does Updike allude to them? (Research in such books as Edith Hamilton's *Mythology* should prove helpful.)

5. Notice the time structure used by Updike. The description of Williams' final game frames the recounting in paragraphs three through thirteen of his entire career. Yet Updike also structures these paragraphs (three through thirteen) around a central organizing sentence. Which one is it?

6. Why is the title so difficult to pronounce?

VOCABULARY

medley (paragraph 1)	reversed (10)	maggots (15)
nimbler (1)	decrepit (10)	pampered (16)
insatiable (1)	pall (11)	mammothly (16)
hoard (3)	prodigy (11)	vivacious (17)
debunkers (4)	abrasive (11)	flexible (18)
vacuum (4)	partisan (12)	hedonist (21)
accessible (4)	conceded (13)	vehement (23)
docilely (6)	condescending (13)	density (25)
figment (7)	eclipsed (14)	grunted (26)
persistence (8)	saturated (14)	vortex (27)
harassed (9)	festering (15)	anticlimax (28)

The Culture Hero of the Sixties

"History," President Kennedy said, "is the final judge of our deeds." When the conversation dies around the dinner tables in a thousand villages and towns, it is fascinating to bring up the subject of the current decade. What verdict will history have on our poor efforts in this confusing age? Will we be remembered as the generation in which man's enlightenment was put into full harness for the good of humanity, or will we simply be remembered as inhabitants of the period in which God died? Will we be remembered as the forebears of a Great Society, or merely as the generation which shrank from its responsibility of defending freedom in its hour of maximum danger?

The nineteen-sixties signaled the coming of a new age. The post-war period was over and man was reaching beyond his planet into the mysterious realms of space. There was a young president in Washington and government was fun, even entertaining. "They" (the enigmatic powers which do everything that ever gets done) gave a Nobel Peace Prize to Martin Luther King. A jolly old Pope in Rome was able to awaken a new interest in religion, and church leaders from all over the world congregated in the Eternal City in a humane effort to tidy up Christianity so God would not be able to see the mess from His death bed. On a couple of occasions "they" steered the national course close to the brink of nuclear war (just to see what would happen), but nobody worried about it very much. "After all," Bob Hope said, "we had a president who was young enough to get drafted." It was an age, indeed, when the world hearkened to a noble cry to "get moving again," and Americans watched with approval and did all they could do, short of actually getting involved.

As in all ages, the nineteen-sixties awakened in American hearts the desire to crown a national hero who would symbolize with breath-taking simplicity the frustrating complexities of the age. President Kennedy was the foremost candidate in many hearts, but he was found to be the antithesis rather than the symbol of the decade. He was young and handsome, stylish and cultured, intelligent and forceful, rich and established, and eternally victorious—a perfect composite, in fact, of all the virtues the generation lacked. But while Americans

"The Culture Hero of the Sixties," by Philip E. Jenks. Reprinted by permission of the author.

—© 1952 United Feature Syndicate.

were loving President Kennedy for being everything they could not be, the true hero of the sixties was reaching maturity in a world of newsprint and india ink. His name was Charlie Brown.

4.   Charlie Brown was born at the tip of a pen wielded by cartoonist Charlie Schultz. By Schultz's own description, Charlie Brown is the neurotic product of society. Charlie Brown is a "nobody," and by virtue of that very act he becomes everybody. In an age when heroes are idolized, Charlie Brown is the classical anti-hero. A Schultz cartoon finds two of Charlie Brown's young friends discussing a recent episode in his life. "I've got to hand it to Charlie Brown," says one. "He was being chased by five fourth graders on the playground today. Suddenly he stopped running and organized a discussion group."

5.   In an age demanding decisiveness and singleness of purpose, Charlie Brown is wishy-washy. His great ambition in life is to meet and talk with the little red-haired girl who sits across the playground from him during the school lunch hour. A hundred times he decides to "just get right up" and talk with her, and a hundred times he fails to leave the security of his bench. When the little red-haired girl walks within whispering distance of Charlie Brown he summons great moral courage and ties his peanut butter sandwich into a knot.

6.   In an age in which the victors are acclaimed by the multitudes, Charlie Brown is the eternal loser. With admirable persistence he

struggles to get his kite into the air—to send it skyward, free as a bird, in the pursuit of its own destinies. A faithful reader of Schultz, however, well knows that the kite is doomed to end its journey in the merciless branches of the nearest "kite-eating" tree. One is convinced that if Charlie Brown were to attempt to fly his kite in the most barren of deserts, the kite would shortly find its way to the only tree for miles around.

7. In an age in which one must be charismatic and popular in order to gain approval, Charlie Brown must walk a lonely road, unliked and unwanted. If, on Valentine's Day, his mailbox were to overflow with Valentine cards, every card would be addressed not to him, but to his faithful dog Snoopy. Society requires much strength, and Charlie Brown is weak. He fails to adjust.

8. Why does America love Charlie Brown? Why does America identify with him? An indication of his appeal may lie in the fact that although America idolizes a victor, she fosters a greater admiration for the loser. America's great folk heroes are not the unbeatable General Grants, but the General Custers who demonstrate great talent for snatching defeat from the jaws of victory. President Kennedy noticed that his popularity in the polls rose sharply immediately after his admission of responsibility for the Bay of Pigs disaster. "My God," he exclaimed, "it's as bad as Eisenhower! The worse I do, the more popular I get!"

9. The average reader of Schultz cartoons can also find in Charlie Brown's poor endeavors a reminder of his own childhood. Charlie Brown's failure to meet and talk with the little red-haired girl reminds the reader of his own personal dreams that were never fulfilled. Charlie Brown is the embodiment of the great times that never were.

10. Every man who roots for Charlie Brown roots for himself. Because he is not a "winner," he demonstrates most poignantly the in-born desire of all men to win. Because he is unpopular, he is a vivid example of man's need to be popular. Those who love Charlie Brown love him not for what he is, but for what he could be. Those who can identify with his inability to adjust to society are confident that in the end—somehow, somewhere—Charlie Brown will eventually "make it." In some glorious moment in the future, Charlie Brown *will* get his kite high in the air. Someday Charlie Brown *will* meet and talk with and (who knows?) eventually marry the little red-haired girl. And someday Charlie Brown's mailbox will overflow with greeting cards from all his many fans.

11.   When that day comes, Charlie Brown's appeal to the people will be over. When Charlie Brown finally "makes it" (as we all know he will), he will join the ranks of Flash Gordon and Barney Google and Smilin' Jack and all the other forgotten heroes of yesterday's comics. In the meantime, Charlie Brown's appeal lies in the fact that there is nothing so admired or so closely followed in today's society than the detailed, blow-by-blow account of the Great All-American Failure Story.

12.   Keep at it, Charlie Brown!

DISCUSSION QUESTIONS

1. This essay suggests that Charlie Brown, insofar as he resembles the majority of the people, should justly be called the culture hero of the decade. Do you agree with its argument?

2. Must a majority of the people respect and admire a person before he can be considered a hero?

3. Do the people most admired in an age reflect its essential mood and character? If this is the case, characterize our present age in terms of the people most respected in our country and the people we have elected to rule us.

RHETORIC

1. Write a paragraph similar in development to paragraph eight. Use your own example to support the topic sentence (in this case, sentence three in the paragraph).

2. What is the tone of this essay?

3. Discuss the organization of paragraphs five through seven. What are the topic sentences in these paragraphs?

4. Write a theme in which you give an abstract statement of the qualifications of a hero in the first paragraph, and then, in the rest of the paper, discuss a living person or persons who meet these qualifications.

5. Write a punctuation diagram (see *Mechanics of Style,* Chapter VII, p. 235) of paragraph three. How many kinds of sentences are there? Is any parallelism used?

VOCABULARY

verdict (paragraph 1)
enlightenment (1)
harness (1)
congregated (2)
humane (2)
antithesis (3)
neurotic (4)

idolized (4)
summons (5)
persistence (6)
charismatic (7)
embodiment (9)
poignantly (10)
vivid (10)

urban living: problems and solutions

The Cities: Waging a Battle for Survival

1. The green and white police helicopter clattered through the night over the most awesome cityscape on earth. Inside the chopper's plastic bubble cockpit, Mayor John V. Lindsay gazed fixedly down on the great city he has tried to govern for more than three years. He talked hopefully of a turn in the tide against crime in the streets and garbage on the sidewalks, of soothing the smoldering despair of the black slums and mollifying the growing anger of the white middle class, of salvaging the school system and humanizing the welfare treadmill. Suddenly, the helicopter was over the East River, and the twinkling lights of the city's bridges gleamed below like necklaces on black velvet. "I lit up those bridges," said the mayor of New York, savoring the stunning panorama.

2. There was both poignance and irony in the moment. For despite his unflagging energy and his unquestioned commitment, John Lindsay and the city he loves are in a battle for survival. From the sky on a

"The Cities: Waging a Battle for Survival," *Newsweek,* LXXIII (March 17, 1969), 40–42. Copyright © Newsweek, Inc. (March, 1969). Reprinted by permission of the publisher.

clear winter's night, New York still sparkles in majesty as the fabled Baghdad-on-the-Hudson. But the drear light of workaday reality paints a far different picture. Behind their bold skylines, New York and America's other great urban centers are gripped in an agonizing crisis of confidence so profound that it prompts wise men to wring their hands and sends cowards running for cover.

3. The cities are truly America's last frontier, and life in the urban wilds has never seemed more precarious—or more preposterous. (Just last week in Pontiac, Mich., police clubbed and tear-gassed an unruly crowd besieging City Hall—most of them firemen demanding a raise.) Choking in air so polluted that it filters out a quarter of the sun's light; stifled by traffic jams; plagued by strikes that cripple essential services; victimized by muggers who fill the streets with fear, America's cities daily appear to confirm Thomas Jefferson's sour conviction that they would be "penitential to the morals, the health and the liberties of man."

4. Trouble has been brewing in the cities for a long time. "Ever since World War II," says Lindsay, "the urban explosion has gotten worse and worse. Somehow people assumed that the American city would work by itself—that it would provide police protection and run the school and build housing. People *assumed* it would happen, and it didn't—and no one paid any attention."

5. If sheer attention could cure the sick cities, their salvation would be close at hand. Increasingly, Americans have been turning inward in the growing realization that the country's future is inextricably entwined in the fate of its great urban centers. City problems are being diagnosed in stupefying detail by squadrons of earnest academics, analyzed by banks of computers, brainstormed by urban planners, hashed out in countless public hearings and self-conscious "confrontations" around America. Working through John Gardner's Urban Coalition, businessmen in 39 cities are having the novel (and sobering) experience of grappling with the stubborn realities of ghetto unemployment and welfare dependency.

**The Problems of the City Will Be on the
Front Burner in This Administration**

6. Washington has its eye on urban America, too. "I want you to understand," President Nixon recently told a group of mayors, "that

problems of the city will be on the front burner in this Administration." In his understated way, Mr. Nixon is trying to make good on his pledge. He has enticed the nation's most controversial cities expert, Democratic intellectual Daniel P. (Pat) Moynihan, from Cambridge and ensconced him in motel-modern splendor in the White House basement as head of the new Council for Urban Affairs—on paper, at least, the equivalent of the global National Security Council. The plight of the cities is the top order of business for such key Cabinet members as Robert Finch of HEW and George Romney of HUD. Last week, the new President's urban strategy began to come clear . . . —a cautious, underfunded, yet systematic approach to the tangle of slum employment, housing, crime and other city woes. Tax incentives, "black capitalism" and other campaign talking points are getting only token emphasis, but the Republicans are moving toward equalizing welfare payments around the U.S.

7. For all their stress on tidiness, however, the new Nixon men know that the initial prescription for urban ills is more money. "Cities are broke," says John J. Gunther, executive director of the U.S. Conference of Mayors. The cry is echoed daily in City Halls from Portland, Ore., to Portland, Maine. "We have a $1 billion economic blueprint," says Newark Mayor Hugh Addonizio, "but where are we going to get the $1 billion?" Fully half of Boston's taxable real estate is held by churches, schools and other tax-exempt institutions—symptomatic of the financial squeeze strangling the cities. "It's just gotten beyond us," admits Frederick O'R. Hayes, budget director of New York City, where the million-plus welfare rolls hold more people than the entire population of Baltimore and will cost an incredible $1.7 billion next year.

8. A quantum leap in Federal expenditures for the cities is unlikely to come under a Republican Administration, and is certainly out of the question until the Vietnam war is phased out. Even then, the prospect is dubious. "We have," says Finch, who is likely to be the most influential Cabinet member on domestic policy, "to de-escalate the notion that progress in Vietnam will turn on the faucet."

9. The drip-drip-drip of the Federal and state faucets has for years been an exquisite water torture for the men charged with running American cities. But the savviest of them are well aware that even if the flow suddenly turned into a torrent, the cities would still be in serious difficulties. For the bleak experience of the past few years has

produced a deep streak of pessimism in many of the best men on the urban frontier. Most believe that such technological problems as air pollution and traffic flow are receptive to strictly financial solution; an all-out anti-pollution effort might cost $5 billion a year, about what the nation is now spending on the space program. But the larger social and psychic enigmas are something else again.

"Maybe What's Happening in the Cities Is the Natural Order, and Can't Be Changed"

10.
   Can the suburban "white noose" around the cities, for example, be broken by genuine integration in housing? Is there any real way to end the cycle of welfare dependency? Will better-paid, better-trained, more mobile police cut the spiraling crime rate? Do decentralization and community control really promise better education for city dwellers? In the last analysis, is big-city life still worth living?

11.
   Whatever the abrasions and frustrations of city life, it still clearly has its rewards for many Americans. . . . Especially in the South and the West, people are continuing to flock to the cities. Last week the population clock on Atlanta's Peachtree Street proudly raised its count to 1,300,000, and one local booster enthused: "Atlanta is a city where time is still young." Milwaukeeans are justly proud of their fresh-swept streets, neatly manicured parks—and relatively low crime rate. But the bigger, older cities are losing population, especially child-rearing, middle-class whites, who carry much of the tax burden. And, as a Census Bureau expert reported a fortnight ago, the flight to the suburbs has more than doubled (to a rate of nearly 500,000 a year) since 1966.

12.
   As their problems pile up, some of America's last frontiersmen have lost much of the hopeful spark that spurred them on during the early 1960's. Highly prized mayors, including Atlanta's Ivan Allen and Arthur Naftalin of Minneapolis, are stepping down—and even Lindsay won't say for sure that he will run again (although last week he set aides to work on his campaign). The bright young men who surround Detroit's Mayor Jerome Cavanagh have begun to droop. "Maybe," says one over a doleful drink, "what's happening in the cities is the natural order of things, and there is nothing anyone can realistically do to change it." In New York, John Doar, once a star of Robert Kennedy's Justice Department and now head of the Board of

Education (more than 1 million pupils, $1.5 billion annual budget) has turned uncommonly introspective. "I don't know whether it's my own failings," he muses, "or the failings of the system." Talk of "the system," "the machinery," "the power structure" is very modish these days—both on the part of urban experts and among lesser folk who just don't like what's going on.

"The Next Step Is the Titanic Scene: To Hell with Everybody, I Want Mine"

But can all the frustrations and anxieties fairly be placed at the door of unseen bureaucracies and hidden power brokers? "The serious problems of the cities are largely insoluble now and will be for the foreseeable future," insists one of the nations's most astute urbanists, Prof. Edward Banfield of Harvard. Few would go quite that far. But everyone agrees that the cities are at once the victims and the perpetrators of a larger crisis in America—a clutch of racial, economic, technological and generational frictions—that has strained the social fabric to a new and dangerous degree. "The millionaire who owns a plant and pours soot into the air does so because he doesn't know who you are and doesn't feel he has to act as if it matters to him," Moynihan has observed. "He doesn't have a sense of community. He's no different from the half-crazy kid snatching purses in the ghetto." 13.

The lack of feeling of community—whether in sterile suburban split-level developments or on the gritty sidewalks of a megalopolis— is at the heart of the urban malaise. Striding around his office in Boston's spanking new $23 million City Hall, freshman Mayor Kevin White talks of the corrosive impatience of the urban citizenry—the strikes by police and firemen, the clamorous demonstrations by welfare mothers. "The next step," White fears, "is the Titanic lifeboats scene —every man for himself. Everybody tries to get theirs to survive, saying, 'To hell with everybody else, I want mine. There's no guarantee that if I wait it'll come along.' " 14.

Five riotous summers finally made the nation aware that its black minority wanted a fair share of the American pie—and perhaps a compensatory extra slice. Now, a disturbing new element has been added to the urban crisis: the increasing discontent of blue-collar and middle-class whites. The stinging bite of the new backlash is being felt at the polls. "The middle-class guy sitting in his house just doesn't think he's getting enough for his tax dollars," says Bob Finch. The 15.

result is a widespread refusal by urban and suburban whites to pay for big-city improvements. Badly needed transportation bond issues have gone down to defeat in Los Angeles and Atlanta, to cite two recent cases, and San Francisco's ambitious $1.2 billion Bay Area Rapid Transit System remains unfinished because neither the state legislature nor local taxpayers are willing to fork over another $150 million.

16.   The white rebellion runs deeper than economics. At its core lies deep-seated resentment over the social problems springing from the great Negro migration to the cities that reached floodtide during World War II. The latest figures indicate that the exodus from the South has dwindled substantially, but the population explosion within the ghettos goes on unabated. Washington, Newark and Gary, Ind., now have more blacks than whites. Unless current patterns change, eleven more cities (including Chicago, Philadelphia and Detroit) will have Negro majorities by 1984.

17.   Working-class whites who must share their inner-city neighborhoods with unwelcome blacks feel themselves under the most pressure. More affluent whites—sheltered though they may be in the suburbs or in downtown high-rises—grow more vocal on the subject everyday. Chicago's Anthony Downs, a consultant on Lyndon Johnson's riot-commission report, says with finality: "The white surburban middle-class American is tired of race."

18.   Tired of race white America may be, but the problem—like all the other factors in the urban mix—is likely to get worse before it gets better. "There is a great error in the minds of whites," says Downs, "that since we have been talking about solving problems we've actually been getting it done. And the sudden quiet in the ghetto only underscores that feeling. There's been a tremendous substitution of rhetoric for fact—like black capitalism, which is a myth. There is an attitude of hope because people have been discussing these questions, but no bread has appeared on the table—and that's dynamite."

"They Won't Get Far with the Cities—
They Ought to Try the Model Suburb"

19.   The question is not so much how to defuse the urban powder keg—no one presumes to suggest an inclusive answer to that—but where to begin. Harvard's tough-minded Prof. James Q. Wilson all but

dismisses reform of welfare ("It's literally hopeless") and suggests his own top priorities: "Crime and schools, because of my conception of what a city is—a collection of neighborhoods. The central institution in the neighborhood is the school, and the central quality of neighborhood life is the level of public order. We've got to deal with these two first because that's the way people perceive urban problems."

Urban historian Richard Wade of the University of Chicago believes the Nixon Administration should look beyond the cities to the new world of the suburbs. "The Republicans do have a chance, with their constituency, to make a model *suburb,*" he says. "They won't get far with the cities anyway, so rather than try to redeem the past, they ought to try to process the future." [20]

Wade has a point. Although more than 70 per cent of the nation's population is technically "urban," the majority lives in smallish cities and in the suburbs. Futurists project a coming America in which most people live in one of several megalopolises, including "Boswash"—the urban network stretching from Beacon Hill to the Potomac. By 2001, the U.S. population will probably have grown by something like 100 million—most of it "urban." Logically enough, some observers—including Vice President Spiro T. Agnew—believe that the best answer would be the creation of wholly new towns, planned communities that theoretically would factor out most of the problems that plague the metropolises today. [21]

"Rather Than Try to Redeem the Past, They Ought to Process the Future"

"New Towns" have taken root overseas—most notably in Great Britain and Finland—but the American experience so far has been spotty. One ambitious U.S. example—Reston, Va.—found the early financial going difficult, a knotty problem recent Federal legislation is not likely to solve overnight. Significantly perhaps, one of America's biggest corporations, General Electric, abandoned the idea of developing new communities last month. After three years of study in more than 30 locations, GE finally junked the venture as unprofitable. [22]

So, for the foreseeable future at least, the urban drama is certain to be played on more familiar terrain. And that means that the men in America's bankrupt City Halls are going to have to risk their political lives—and sometimes their necks—in daily combat on the firing line. [23]

The price of activism can be painfully high. In New York, infuriated citizens have taken to heckling John Lindsay publicly over everything from racial tensions in the schools to slow snow removal. LINDSAY MUST GO buttons are in circulation, and disgruntled Republican conservatives are gathering their forces to try to dump him in the spring primary. After just sixteen months in office, Cleveland's new black mayor, Carl Stokes, fatalistically counts the days until he expects repudiation at the polls.

24.   Yet, even with the odds stacked so dramatically against the cities and their leaders, neither the politicians nor the people can shrink from the challenge. For better or worse much of the nation's destiny is being forged each day on the tense streets of Chicago, the crumbling stoops of the Baltimore slums, and the clogged freeways of Los Angeles. There can be no turning back from America's last frontier.

DISCUSSION QUESTIONS

1. Do you feel that conditions have changed at all since the writing of this article?
2. People in the suburbs, beyond the jurisdiction of the cities, perhaps are like the man in Frost's "Mending Wall" who claims that "good fences make good neighbors." In the light of this article, do you feel this is the case?
3. Could you answer a suburbanite who claims: "Why should I concern myself about the city's problems? I have enough of my own."
4. What does *Newsweek* mean when it says: "For better or worse much of the nation's destiny is being forged each day on the tense streets of Chicago, the crumbling stoops of the Baltimore slums, and clogged freeways of Los Angeles. There can be no turning back from America's last frontier."

RHETORIC

1. Write a five-paragraph theme on three major urban problems. Model your organization on the paper in *Essay Development,* Chapter VII, pp. 32–33, which develops the same topic.
2. You probably noticed that in producing this article, the *Newsweek* staff obviously interviewed a number of people and did a great deal of research. Think of any issue relevant to your neighborhood or

school (trash collection services, the worth of the student newspaper, favorite television programs, the best teacher on campus, etc.). Explore the topic by library research and by interviews with neighbors, friends, local officials. Draw your material together into a logical, organized theme modeled on *Newsweek*'s essay.

3. Underline the topic sentences in the following paragraphs: seven, twelve, sixteen. How are the paragraphs developed?

4. How many examples of parallel structure are there in the first five paragraphs?

5. How does the writer handle the transition from the ideas in paragraph nine to those in paragraph ten? From fifteen to sixteen? From seventeen to eighteen? Can you generalize from these examples on one way of handling transitions from one paragraph to another?

VOCABULARY

awesome (paragraph 1)	doleful (12)
salvaging (1)	bureaucracies (13)
unflagging (2)	astute (13)
precarious (3)	sterile (14)
entwined (5)	exodus (16)
stubborn (5)	affluent (17)
controversial (6)	myth (18)
tangle (6)	perceive (19)
initial (7)	theoretically (21)
torture (9)	bankrupt (23)
psychic (9)	infuriated (23)
enigmas (9)	shrink (24)
mobile (10)	clogged (24)
spurred (12)	

The Slums of New York

The tenant house is the offspring of municipal neglect as well as   1.
of its primary causes, over population and destitution. As a city grows
in commerce, and demands new localities for traffic and manufacture,
the store and workshop encroach upon the dwelling house and dispos-
sesses its occupants. At first the habitations of citizens are removed

"The Slums of New York," *Report of the Select Committee Appointed to Examine into the Condition of Tenant Houses in New-York and Brooklyn* (Assembly Document 205; March 9, 1857).

to a limited distance, because, with an industrious population, time is money, and neighborhood of residence and business secures both economy and convenience. The merchant and master, then, find it for their interest to dwell in the vicinity of their active operations; and so, likewise, do the mechanic, laborer, and all dependent on business life. It is at this stage of a community's growth that proper regulations and restrictions, looking to the ultimate well-being of the city, are of paramount necessity; and herein the authorities of former years were unmindful of future public good, precisely as we, in our day and generation, are pertinaciously regardless of our posterity's welfare. Had the evils which now appall us, been prevented or checked in their earlier manifestation, by wise and simple laws, the city of New-York would now exhibit more gratifying bills of health, more general social comfort and prosperity, and less, far less expenditure for the support of pauperism and of crime.

2. But legislation interposed not in its proper season, and hence the system of tenant-house leasing was soon begotten of the wants of poverty. As our wharves became crowded with warehouses, and encompassed with bustle and noise, the wealthier citizens, who peopled old "Knickerbocker" mansions near the bay, transferred their residence to streets beyond the din; compensating for remoteness from their counting houses, by the advantages of increased quiet and luxury. Their habitations then passed into the hands, on the one side, of boarding house keepers, on the other, of real estate agents; and here, in its beginning, the tenant house became a real blessing to that class of industrious poor whose small earnings limited their expenses and whose employment in workshops, stores, or about the wharves and thoroughfares, rendered a near residence of much importance. At this period, rents were moderate, and a mechanic with family could hire two or more comfortable and even commodious apartments, in a house once occupied by wealthy people, for less than half what he is now obliged to pay for narrow and unhealthy quarters. This state of tenantry comfort did not, however, continue long; for the rapid march of improvement speedily enhanced the value of property in the lower wards of the city, and as this took place, rents rose, and accommodations decreased in the same proportion. At first the better class of tenants submitted to retain their single floors, or two and three rooms, at the onerous rates, but this rendered them poorer,

and those who were able to do so, followed the example of former proprietors, and emigrated to the upper wards. The spacious dwelling houses fell before improvements, or languished for a season, as tenant houses of the type which is now the prevailing evil of our city; that is to say, their large rooms were partitioned into several smaller ones, (without regard to proper light or ventilation), the rates of rent being lower in proportion to space or height from the street; and they soon became filled, from cellar to garret, with a class of tenantry living from hand to mouth, loose in morals, improvident in habits, degraded or squalid as beggary itself. This, in its primary aspects, was the tenant-house system, which has repeated itself, in every phase, as it followed the track of population from ward to ward, until it now becomes a distinguishing feature of our social existence, the parent of constant disorders, and the nursery of increasing vices.

It was soon perceived, by astute owners or agents of property, [3.] that a greater percentage of profit would be realized by the conversion of houses and block into barracks, and dividing their space into the smallest proportions capable of containing human life within four walls. The fact had become apparent to speculation that, in a climate subject to inclement change, as in the meridian of New-York, it is necessary, even for the poorest people, to dwell within doors and be sheltered by a roof, humble though it may be; so speculation immediately proceeded to provide walls and roof. Blocks were rented of real-estate owners, or purchased on time, or taken in charge at a percentage, and held for underletting to applicants with no ready money and precarious means of livelihood. To such unfortunates it was not difficult to dictate terms or furnish habitations, for to them the mere sufferance of tenancy might appear like benevolence on the part of house-owners. To this class, then, entire blocks of buildings, worn out in other service, were let in hundreds of sub-divided apartments, and rates of rent were established, as well as seasons and modes of payment, which, while affording the wretched tenantry some sort of shelter within their scanty means, secured at the same time prompt payment of weekly dues, and an aggregate of profit from the whole barracks (risks and losses taken into account) of twice or thrice the amount which a legitimate lease of the building to one occupant would bring, if granted for business purposes at the usual rate of real-estate interest.

4.   As no care-taking of premises could be expected from the majority of this class of tenants, collected, or rather herded together thus indiscriminately, the charges for occupancy by the month or week were fixed at a rate which not only covered all risks, and secured exorbitant interest on investment, but left wide margin for damage and abuse, allowing the buildings to decay or fall to pieces as rapidly as constant occupancy would permit. It is true that stipulations were usually made to secure the property from wanton or wilful demolition by tenants, and provisos to guard against accumulation of filth or insure precautions against accidents by fire, were generally indicated in the terms of contract, but no stringent regulations on the part of landlords, no provisions for the maintenance of health, and no convenience for securing neatness, cleanliness, ventilation or general order and comfort in the establishment, were ever dreamed of in connection with the tenant-house system, as it spread its localities from year to year. It sufficed that conservation of property in the aggregate, and a particular supervision of the rent, remained as distinguished characteristics of landlord or agent, while on the other hand reckless slovenliness, discontent, privation and ignorance among the tenants were left to work out their invariable results, in the gradual destruction of doors, shutters, windows, fences, ceilings, floors, until the entire premises reached the level of tenant-house dilapidation, containing, but sheltering not, the miserable hordes that crowded beneath mouldering, water-rotted roofs, or burrowed among the rats of clammy cellars.

5.   In this stage of tenancy, the evils of a system which crowds hundreds of human beings into quarters, inferior in comfort and accommodation to the pens of our cattle, appear in flagrant distinctness. . . . Poverty, as we have seen it in New York, is wedded to despair, and its offspring is vengeance. It is a shape that sickens the heart with disgust, and chills the blood with horror. Do you think this strong language? Do you intimate that you have been here a score of years and have never been disgusted or horrified by anything of the sort? Do you say that you have never spied it from your window or met it in the street? Talk not of this, doubters, till you have sought out its real habitations and have yourself crossed its threshold. It is to be seen in its real aspect at home, and no where else; and if you have not looked for it there, your doubts are foolishness. We sat down for

the purpose of detailing some of our own personal observations of household wretchedness in the fourth and sixth wards of this city, but our taste revolts and our pen shrinks for the narration. We could tell of one room, twelve feet by twelve, in which were five resident families comprising twenty persons, of both sexes, and all ages, with only two beds, without partition or screen, or chair or table; and all dependent for their support upon the sale of chips gleaned from the streets, at four cents a basket; of another department, still smaller and still more destitute, inhabited by a man, a woman, two girls and a boy, who were supported by permitting the room to be used as a rendezvous by abandoned women of the street; of another, an attic room, seven feet by five, containing scarcely an article of furniture but a bed, on which lay a fine looking man in a raging fever, without medicine, drink or suitable food, his toil-worn wife engaged in cleaning the dirt from the floor, and his little child asleep on a bundle of rags in the corner; of another of the same dimensions, in which we found, seated on low boxes, around a candle, placed on a keg, a woman and her eldest daughter, (the latter a girl of fifteen, and, as we were told a prostitute,) sewing on shirts, for the making of which they were paid four cents apiece, and even at that price, out of which they had to support two small children, they could not get a supply of work; of another room, about as large, occupied by a street rag picker and his family, the income of whose industry was about eight dollars per month; of another apartment, scarce larger, (into which we were drawn by the screams of a wife beaten by her drunken husband,) containing no article of furniture whatever; of another, warmed only by a tin pail of lighter charcoal, placed in the centre of the floor, over which a blind man bent, endeavoring to warm himself, while three or four men and women were quarreling around him, and in one corner lay the body of a woman who had died the day before of disease, her orphan children sleeping near on a pile of rags; of another room, from which a short time before, twenty persons, sick with fever, had been taken to the hospital to die. But why extend the catalogue? or why attempt to convey to the imagination by words, the hideous squalor and deadly effluvia; the dim, undrained courts oozing with pollution; the dark, narrow stairways, decayed with age, reeking with filth, overrun with vermin; the rotted floors, ceilings begrimed, and often too low to permit you to stand upright; the windows stuffed with rags?

or why try to portray the gaunt, shivering forms and wild ghastly faces, in these black and beetling abodes, wherein, from cellar to garret,

> All life dies, death lives, and nature breeds
> Perverse, all monstrous, all prodigious things,
> Abominable, unutterable! . . .

Re-Constructed Tenant-Houses

6.   These consist mainly of a series of contiguous buildings, of a combination of apartments adapted or re-constructed for tenant purposes within the walls of some large house or public-building. Of this class (proceeding from the lower point of New York city) we came, firstly, to one of inferior dimensions, but with its full proportion of wretchedness, the entrance of which is at 16 Washington-street, in the first ward. This is a three-story building, (owned by an Irish woman residing in Pearl-street;) accessible through a narrow door and steep stairway, ascending over a stable wherein an express company's horses are kept. The dilapidation of this entire building is extreme; its rickety floors shook under the tread, and portions of the wall, black and mildewed, were continually breaking off, whilst nearly every vestige of mortar had disappeared from some of the rooms, leaving only smoke-discolored lathing, through which thick moisture was constantly oozing. A poor woman who occupied an apartment on the second floor complained that this last discomfort was incessant. "The ould ceiling," she said, "is ould as meself, and its full uv the *dhrop* it is," i.e. it was soaked with water that entered through the broken roof whenever it rained; indeed, the committee were assured, (and from appearances the fact could not be doubted,) that in wet weather the upper floors of this ruinous habitation were completely flooded, and the poor occupants were obliged to move their drenched beds from spot to spot as the dropping became too troublesome to permit sleep. In the rear of this building was another of the same height (three stories), and with a ground floor of one hundred feet in length to sixteen deep, connecting with the street by two narrow alleys. The decay and dilapidation of the premises was only equalled by the filth of the inhabitants. The number of tenants in both houses was reported as seventy, all Irish. In the front section the rent varied from

$2 to $6 per month; in the rear from $6 to $8; rooms dark, narrow and ill ventilated. The price for an apartment, with two small closets, answering for bed-rooms, was $7 per month. The lessee of the premises, who underlet, and was responsible to the proprietor, informed the committee that he paid $1,456 per annum, including taxes. In one of the rooms of the front house, an apartment six by ten feet in area, a widow lived with five children. At 97 Washington-street the Committee visited an old building, three stories high, 18 by 30 feet in area, very much out of repair and extremely filthy. In a cellar beneath rooms were "to let." The first floor was used by the lessee as a sailors' lodging-house, the accommodation of which consisted of bunks, arranged one above another like a ship's lockers. The upper floors were occupied by Irish families, to the height of the garret, which was reached by a kind of ladder. Under the broken and leaky roof three families were crouching, one of which (a woman and child) paid three dollars per month for a portion of the miserable garret; the woman had been obliged to sell her bedstead to meet the rent, and slept with her baby on the floor. The total rent collected from tenants in this house (18 by 30 feet, and three stories) was $90 per month.

At 46 Trinity-place (third ward), in rear of Trinity church, and overlooked by the stained windows of that beautiful edifice, was a tenant-house, which had been altered from a school building; in this house there were fourteen families—in all seventy-six persons—each tenement comprising a room 12 by 14 feet in area, with two bed-rooms, or rather closets, where neither light nor air penetrated. Some of the families inhabiting these premises kept lodgers at one shilling per night. One widow woman had nine men boarding with her, dwelling in the one dining-room and two bed-rooms. In this range of tenements, rear of Trinity Church, epidemics have originated on two distinct occasions—the yellow fever, several years since, and, more recently, the cholera. Filth and want of ventilation are enough to infect the very walls with disease. [7.]

At No. 51, Worth street, (fifth ward) the Committee inspected a building in the last stages of decay, though two or three wretched families still clung to it. The rear rooms of this ruin, even with the ground, appear to be abandoned to general filth and excrements. Such a nuisance must sicken a whole neighborhood with its noisomeness. [8.]

In Mulberry street, near the "Five Points," (sixth ward) the [9.]

Committee examined a large tenant house, in a very dilapidated condition. It had been reconstructed, through its interior, from an old wooden church, once used by the Baptists, and adapted to occupancy in the most careless manner. The sewer connection, serving for the premises, was a four inch pipe, wholly inadequate to the necessary uses of such a conduit. In this establishment there were 85 apartments, containing more than 100 families, and comprising 310 persons. In the basement, entered by shattered steps, the depth below the street level was measured by the Committee, and ascertained to be five feet, two inches. In these vaults, families were dwelling, and paying $3 per month, for their damp and sickly quarters. On the fifth floor of this structure $4.50 per month was paid for apartments. The entire fabric is cased and cramped, and the walls, floors and roofing of such inflammable materials that, in case of fire in any portion, it would be impossible to arrest its spread. Should such a calamity take place at night, it is more than probable that scores of the unfortunate inmates would perish ere they could find egress through the narrow doors and passages. Yet, in this building, bad as it is, the main entrances are wider than in most of the re-constructed, or even specially-built tenant-houses, one of the latter of which has been erected on the front lots.

10.   At No. 17 Baxter-street, the Committee penetrated through an alley-passage, where the black mud was two inches deep, to a rear entrance under the building; the basement rooms, with floor five and a half feet below the street-level, was occupied as a dance-house and bar-room, the former 27 feet by 16, the latter 13 by 16, for which $13 per month was paid; two beds for lodgers were in the dance-room. The class of basement or cellar lodgers accommodated in such places pay from six-pence to a shilling per night; average number of lodgers to one bed is three, and no distinction is made between male and female. On the upper floors of this tenant-house, twelve families, comprising seventy-five persons, dwelt in twelve apartments; walls damp, rooms dark, passages filthy, and with no sort of ventilation. Rear of these premises was a collection of sheds built of rough boards, each containing four dark rooms, rent $3 per month, inhabited by poor people who subsisted by the sale of spearmint, which they grew in boxes on the roof, and disposed of to hotels and bar-rooms, a fact which suggested that certain fashionable beverages in vogue might be traced back for their constituents to the malaria and filth of the Five

Point tenant-houses. The average rent of rooms in this locality, where are many houses of the same description, is $4 per month.

At the rear of 37½ Baxter-street (ground said to be the lowest in the city) apartments were entered six feet beneath the street level, ceilings barely six feet in height, renting at $4 per month, and on the second story of the house a rear room, with two dark closets, rented for $5 per month, and a front room at $6.50, the latter to a family consisting of an old dame of sixty and two daughters, who supported themselves by picking curled hair sixteen hours per day, the three earning five dollars per week.   11.

At 39 Baxter-street, a rear building, the Committee found fif-teen persons living in one room, the height of which, from floor to ceiling, was seven feet, and the floor 15 feet by 14, rent $6 per month. To reach these premises it was necessary to pass through an alley, the largest portion of which was but two feet, the narrowest nineteen inches. In case of fires escape to the street would be a miracle. In the vicinity of this habitation were many other forlorn and squalid houses, let in the same way, at the average price of $7 per month.   12.

DISCUSSION QUESTIONS

1. Many people lived in these apartments in order to be close to their work. Is this still the case? If not, why not?
2. Why didn't the people living in these tenements make an effort to fix them up and thus improve their living conditions?
3. This essay concentrates on a serious problem of urban living. Is it related to any others?
4. Does the fact that this report was written in 1857 indicate that poverty is an accepted fact of the human condition and can *never* be eliminated?

RHETORIC

1. What is the purpose of the rhetorical questions in paragraph five? Why does the author include the examples that follow these questions?
2. Using this essay as a guide, investigate and describe your own apartment or home or that of a friend. Evaluate the rooms in terms of

space, ventilation, privacy, etc. Then organize your researches into a well-constructed theme which moves the reader clearly from one end of the house to the other, or from top to bottom.

3. What prevents the long sentence at the end of paragraph four from falling apart into a confusing jumble of words?

4. Notice that the topic sentence in paragraph six defines what is meant by a reconstructed tenant house; the paragraph then elaborates on this definition. Similarly, present a general definition in your topic sentence of some familiar item (automobile, wagon, television, bicycle, etc.), and then continue to develop its uses.

VOCABULARY

offspring (paragraph 1)	flagrant (5)
ultimate (1)	vermin (5)
appall (1)	accessible (6)
remoteness (2)	epidemics (7)
moderate (2)	nuisance (8)
onerous (2)	comprising (10)
indiscriminately (4)	vogue (10)
dilapidation (4)	vicinity (12)
inferior (5)	forlorn (12)

A Contemporary City

1.
   Proceeding in the manner of the investigator in his laboratory, I have avoided all special cases, and all that may be accidental, and I have assumed an ideal site to begin with. My object was not to overcome the existing state of things, but *by constructing a theoretically water-tight formula to arrive at the fundamental principles of modern town planning*. Such fundamental principles, if they are genuine, can serve as the skeleton of any system of modern town planning; being as it were the *rules* according to which development will take place. We shall then be in a position to take a special case, no matter what: whether it be Paris, London, Berlin, New York or some small town. Then, as a result of what we have learnt, we can take control and decide in what direction the forthcoming battle is to be waged. For

"A Contemporary City" from Le Corbusier, *The City of Tomorrow*, trans. Frederick Etchells (New York: Payson & Clarke, 1928), pp. 165–76. Reprinted by permission of Mme. Héléna Strassova, 4 Rue Git-Le-Coeur, Paris.

the desire to rebuild any great city in a modern way is to engage in a formidable battle. Can you imagine people engaging in a battle without knowing their objectives? Yet that is exactly what is happening. The authorities are compelled to do something, so they give the police white sleeves or set them on horseback, they invent sound signals and light signals, they propose to put bridges over streets or moving pavements under the streets; more garden cities are suggested, or it is decided to suppress the tramways, and so on. And these decisions are reached in a sort of frantic haste in order, as it were, to hold a wild beast at bay. That BEAST is the great city. It is infinitely more powerful than all these devices. And it is just beginning to wake. What will to-morrow bring forth to cope with it?

We must have some rule of conduct.[1]   2.

We must have fundamental principles for modern town plan-   3.
ning.

Site.   A level site is the ideal site. In all those places where   4.
traffic becomes over-intensified the level site gives a chance of a normal solution to the problem. Where there is less traffic, differences in level matter less.

The river flows far away from the city. The river is a kind of   5.
liquid railway, a goods station and a sorting house. In a decent house the servants' stairs do not go through the drawing-room—even if the maid is charming (or if the little boats delight the loiterer leaning on a bridge).

Population.   This consists of the citizens proper; of suburban   6.
dwellers; and of those of a mixed kind.

a. Citizens are of the city: those who work and live in it.

b. Suburban dwellers are those who work in the outer industrial zone and who do not come into the city: they live in garden cities.

---

[1] New suggestions shower on us. Their inventors and those who believe in them have their little thrill. It is so easy for them to believe in them. But what if they are based on grave errors? How are we to distinguish between what is reasonable and an over-poetical dream? The leading newspapers accept everything with enthusiasm. One of them said, "The cities of to-morrow must be built on new virgin soil." But no, this is not true! We must go to the old cities, all our inquiries confirm it. One of our leading papers supports the suggestion made by one of our greatest and most reasonable architects, who for once gives us bad counsel in proposing to erect round about Paris a ring of skyscrapers. The idea is romantic enough, but it cannot be defended. The skyscrapers must be built *in the centre* and not on the periphery.

c. The mixed sort are those who work in the business parts of the city but bring up their families in garden cities.

7.   To classify these divisions (and so make possible the transmutation of these recognized types) is to attack the most important problem in town planning, for such a classification would define the areas to be allotted to these three sections and the delimitation of their boundaries. This would enable us to formulate and resolve the following problems:

1. The *City,* as a business and residential centre.
2. The *Industrial City* in relation to the *Garden Cities* (*i.e.* the question of transport).
3. The *Garden Cities* and the *daily transport* of the workers.

8.   Our first requirement will be an organ that is compact, rapid, lively and concentrated: this is the City with its well-organized centre. Our second requirement will be another organ, supple, extensive and elastic; this is *the Garden City* on the periphery.

9.   Lying between these two organs, we must *require the legal establishment* of that absolute necessity, a protective zone which allows of extension, *a reserved zone* of woods and fields, a fresh-air reserve.

10.   **Density of Population.** The more dense the population of a city is the less are the distances that have to be covered. The moral, therefore, is that we must *increase the density of the centres of our cities, where business affairs are carried on.*

11.   **Lungs.** Work in our modern world becomes more intensified day by day, and its demands affect our nervous system in a way that grows more and more dangerous. Modern toil demands quiet and fresh air, not stale air.

12.   The towns of to-day can only increase in density at the expense of the open spaces which are the lungs of a city.

13.   We must *increase the open spaces and diminish the distances to be covered.* Therefore the centre of the city must be constructed *vertically.*

14.   The city's residential quarters must no longer be built along "corridor-streets," full of noise and dust and deprived of light.

15.   It is a simple matter to build urban dwellings away from the streets, without small internal courtyards and with the windows

looking on to large parks; and this whether our housing schemes are of the type with "set-backs" or built on the "cellular" principle.

The Street. The street of to-day is still the old bare ground 16. which has been paved over, and under which a few tube railways have been run.

The modern street in the true sense of the word is a new type 17. of organism, a sort of stretched-out workshop, a home for many complicated and delicate organs, such as gas, water and electric mains. It is contrary to all economy, to all security, and to all sense to bury these important service mains. They ought to be accessible throughout their length. The various storeys of this stretched-out workshop will each have their own particular functions. If this type of street, which I have called a "workshop," is to be realized, it becomes as much a matter of *construction* as are the houses with which it is customary to flank it, and the bridges which carry it over valleys and across rivers.

The modern street should be a masterpiece of civil engineering 18. and no longer a job for navvies.

The "corridor-street" should be tolerated no longer, for it 19. poisons the houses that border it and leads to the construction of small internal courts or "wells."

Traffic. Traffic can be classified more easily than other things. 20.

To-day traffic is not classified—it is like dynamite flung at haz- 21. ard into the street, killing pedestrians. Even so, *traffic does not fulfill its function.* This sacrifice of the pedestrian leads nowhere.

If we classify traffic we get: 22.

a. Heavy goods traffic.

b. Lighter goods traffic, *i.e.* vans, etc., which make short journeys in all directions.

c. Fast traffic, which covers a large section of the town.

Three kinds of roads are needed, and in superimposed storeys: 23.

a. Below-ground[2] there would be the street for heavy traffic. This

---

[2] I say "below-ground," but it would be more exact to say at what we call *basement level,* for if my town, built on concrete piles, were realized (see *Towards a New Architecture,* Chap. IV), this "basement" would no longer be buried under the earth.

storey of the houses would consist merely of concrete piles, and between them large open spaces which would form a sort of clearing-house where heavy goods traffic could load and unload.

b. At the ground floor level of the buildings there would be the complicated and delicate network of the ordinary streets taking traffic in every desired direction.

c. Running north and south, and east and west, and forming the two great axes of the city, there would be great *arterial roads for fast one-way traffic* built on immense reinforced concrete bridges 120 to 180 yards in width and approached every half-mile or so by subsidiary roads from ground level. These arterial roads could therefore be joined at any given point, so that even at the highest speeds the town can be traversed and the suburbs reached without having to negotiate any cross-roads. . . .

24.   This triple system of superimposed levels answers every need of motor traffic (lorries, private cars, taxis, 'buses) because it provides for rapid and *mobile* transit.

25.   Traffic running on fixed rails is only justified if it is in the form of a convoy carrying an immense load; it then becomes a sort of extension of the underground system or of trains dealing with suburban traffic. *The tramway has no right to exist in the heart of the modern city.*

26.   If the city thus consists of plots about 400 yards square, this will give us sections of about 40 acres in area, and the density of population will vary from 50,000 down to 6,000, according as the "lots" are developed for business or for residential purposes. The natural thing, therefore, would be to continue to apply our unit of distance as it exists in the Paris tubes to-day (namely, 400 yards) and to put a station in the middle of each plot.

27.   Following the two great axes of the city, two "storeys" below the arterial roads for fast traffic, would run the tubes leading to the four furthest points of the garden city suburbs, and linking up with the metropolitan network. . . . At a still lower level, and again following these two main axes, would run the one-way loop systems for suburban traffic, and below these again the four great main lines serving the provinces and running north, south, east and west. These main lines would end at the Central Station, or better still might be connected up by a loop system.

28.   **The Station.** There is only one station. The only place for the

station is in the centre of the city. It is the natural place for it, and there is no reason for putting it anywhere else. The railway station is the hub of the wheel.

The station would be an essentially subterranean building. Its roof, which would be two storeys above the natural ground level of the city, would form the aerodrome for aero-taxis. This aerodrome (linked up with the main aerodrome in the protected zone) must be in close contact with the tubes, the surburban lines, the main lines, the main arteries and the administrative services connected with all these. . . . 29.

The Plan of the City

The basic principles we must follow are these: 30.

1. We must de-congest the centres of our cities.
2. We must augment their density.
3. We must increase the means for getting about.
4. We must increase parks and open spaces.

At the very centre we have the STATION with its landing stage for aero-taxis. 31.

Running north and south, and east and west, we have the MAIN ARTERIES for fast traffic, forming elevated roadways 120 feet wide. 32.

At the base of the sky-scrapers and all round them we have a great open space 2,400 yards by 1,500 yards, giving an area of 3,600,000 square yards, and occupied by gardens, parks and avenues. In these parks, at the foot of and round the sky-scrapers, would be the restaurants and cafés, the luxury shops, housed in buildings with receding terraces: here too would be the theatres, halls and so on; and here the parking places or garage shelters. 33.

The sky-scrapers are designed purely for business purposes. 34.

On the left we have the great public buildings, the museums, the municipal and administrative offices. Still further on the left we have the "Park" (which is available for further logical development of the heart of the city). 35

On the right, and traversed by one of the arms of the main arterial roads, we have the warehouses, and the industrial quarters with their goods stations. 36.

Le Corbusier and Jeanneret,
Voisin Plan for Rebuilding Paris (model) 1925.
Photograph courtesy The Museum of Modern
Art, New York.

37. All round the city is the *protected zone* of woods and green fields.

38. Further beyond are the *garden cities,* forming a wide encircling band.

39. Then, right in the midst of all these, we have the *Central Station,* made up of the following elements:

    a. The landing-platform; forming an aerodrome of 200,000 square yards in area.

    b. The entresol or mezzanine; at this level are the raised tracks for fast motor traffic: the only crossing being gyratory.

    c. The ground floor where are the entrance halls and booking offices for the tubes, suburban, main line and air traffic.

    d. The "basement": here are the tubes which serve the city and the main arteries.

    e. The "sub-basement": here are the suburban lines running on a one-way loop.

    f. The "sub-sub-basement": here are the main lines (going north, south, east and west).

The City.   Here we have twenty-four sky-scrapers capable each of housing 10,000 to 50,000 employees; this is the business and hotel section, etc., and accounts for 400,000 to 600,000 inhabitants.

The residential blocks, of the two main types already mentioned, account for a further 600,000 inhabitants.

The garden cities give us a further 2,000,000 inhabitants, or more.

In the great central open space are the cafés, restaurants, luxury shops, halls of various kinds, a magnificent forum descending by stages down to the immense parks surrounding it, the whole arrangement providing a spectacle of order and vitality.

Density of Population.

a. The sky-scraper: 1,200 inhabitants to the acre.

b. The residential blocks with set-backs: 120 inhabitants to the acre. These are the luxury dwellings.

c. The residential blocks on the "cellular" system, with a similar number of inhabitants.

This great density gives us our necessary shortening of dis- tances and ensures rapid intercommunication.

Note—The average density to the acre of Paris in the heart of the town is 146, and of London 63; and of the over-crowded quarters of Paris 213, and of London 169.

Open Spaces.   Of the area (a), 95 per cent of the ground is open (squares, restaurants, theatres).

Of the area (b), 85 per cent of the ground is open (gardens, sports grounds).

Of the area (c), 48 per cent of the ground is open (gardens, sports grounds).

Educational and Civic Centres, Universities, Museums of Art **and Industry, Public Services, County Hall.**   The "Jardin anglais." (The city can extend here, if necessary.)

Sports grounds: Motor racing track, Racecourse, Stadium, Swimming baths, etc.

The Protected Zone (which will be the property of the city), **with its Aerodrome.**   A zone in which all building would be prohibited; reserved for the growth of the city as laid down by the municipality: it would consist of woods, fields, and sports grounds. The

forming of a "protected zone" by continual purchase of small prop-
erties in the immediate vicinity of the city is one of the most essential
and urgent tasks which a municipality can pursue. It would eventually
represent a tenfold return on the capital invested.

Industrial Quarters.[3]

51.   **Types of Buildings Employed.**   For business: sky-scrapers sixty
storeys high with no internal wells or courtyards. . . .

52.   Residential buildings with "set-backs," of six double storeys;
again with no internal wells: the flats looking on either side on to
immense parks.

53.   Residential buildings on the "cellular" principle, with "hanging
gardens," looking on to immense parks; again no internal wells.
These are "service-flats" of the most modern kind.

Garden Cities

Their Aesthetic, Economy, Perfection and Modern Outlook.

54.   A simple phrase suffices to express the necessities of tomorrow:
WE MUST BUILD IN THE OPEN. The lay-out must be of a purely
geometrical kind, with all its many and delicate implications.

55.   The city of to-day is a dying thing because it is not geometrical.
To build in the open would be to replace our present haphazard ar-
rangements, *which are all we have to-day,* by a *uniform* lay-out. Unless we do this *there is no salvation.*

56.   The result of a true geometrical lay-out is *repetition.*

57.   The result of repetition is a *standard,* the perfect form (*i.e.* the
creation of standard types). A geometrical lay-out means that mathematics play their part. There is no first-rate human production but
has geometry at its base. It is of the very essence of Architecture. To
introduce uniformity into the building of the city we must *industrial-
ize building.* Building is the one economic activity which has so far

---

[3] In this section I make new suggestions in regard to the industrial quarters:
they have been content to exist too long in disorder, dirt and in a hand-to-mouth
way. And this is absurd, for Industry, when it is on a properly ordered basis,
should develop in an orderly fashion. A portion of the industrial district
could be constructed of ready-made sections by using standard units for the
various kinds of buildings needed. Fifty per cent of the site would be reserved
for this purpose. In the event of considerable growth, provision would thus be
made for moving them into a different district where there was more space.
Bring about *"standardization"* in the building of a works and you would have
mobility instead of the crowding which results when factories become impos-
sibly congested.

resisted industrialization. It has thus escaped the march of progress, with the result that cost of building is still abnormally high.

The architect, from a professional point of view, has become a twisted sort of creature. He has grown to love irregular sites, claiming that they inspire him with original ideas for getting round them. Of course he is wrong. For nowadays the only building that can be undertaken must be either for the rich or built at a loss (as, for instance, in the case of municipal housing schemes), or else by jerry-building and so robbing the inhabitant of all amenities. A motor-car which is achieved by mass production is a masterpiece of comfort, precision, balance and good taste. A house built to order (on an "interesting" site) is a masterpiece of incongruity—a monstrous thing. 58.

If the builder's yard were reorganized on the lines of standardization and mass production we might have gangs of workmen as keen and intelligent as mechanics. 59.

The mechanic dates back only twenty years, yet already he forms the highest caste of the working world. 60.

The mason dates . . . from time immemorial! He bangs away with feet and hammer. He smashes up everything round him, and the plant entrusted to him falls to pieces in a few months. The spirit of the mason must be disciplined by making him part of the severe and exact machinery of the industrialized builder's yard. 61.

The cost of building would fall in the proportion of 10 to 2. 62.

The wages of the labourers would fall into definite categories; to each according to his merits and service rendered. 63.

The "interesting" or erratic side absorbs every creative faculty of the architect and wears him out. What results is equally erratic: lopsided abortions; a specialist's solution which can only please other specialists. 64.

We must build *in the open:* both within the city and around it. 65.

Then having worked through every necessary technical stage and using absolute ECONOMY, we shall be in a position to experience the intense joys of a creative art which is based on geometry. 66.

How City Planners Hurt Cities

City planners and rebuilders are killing our cities, not on purpose, but because they do not understand how cities work. Their 1.

Jane Jacobs, "How City Planners Hurt Cities," *The Saturday Evening Post,* CCXXXIV, No. 41 (October 14, 1961), 12–14. Copyright © 1961 by Jane Jacobs. Reprinted by permission of the publisher.

well-meant but ignorant actions, supported by public money and political power, can be fearsomely destructive.

2.   We are continually assured that planners are producing healthful city environments for us. But most planners and rebuilders do not recognize a healthful city environment when they see one, much less know how to create one. Consider, for example, a district called the North End, in Boston.

3.   Twenty years ago, when I first saw the North End, its buildings were badly overcrowded. Run-down brick houses had been converted into flats. Four- or five-story walk-ups had been built to house immigrants first from Ireland, then Eastern Europe and finally from Sicily. You did not have to look far to see that the district was taking a severe physical beating and was desperately poor.

4.   When I saw the North End again in 1959, I was amazed. Scores of buildings had been rehabilitated. Instead of mattresses against the windows, there were Venetian blinds and glimpses of fresh paint. Many of the small, converted houses were now occupied by one or two families instead of three or four. Some of the families in the tenements had uncrowded themselves by throwing two flats together, equipping them with new bathrooms and kitchens. Mingled among the buildings were splendid food stores. Small industries—upholstery making, metal working, food processing and the like—rimmed the neighborhood. The streets were alive with children playing, people shopping, strolling and talking.

5.   I had seen a lot of Boston in the past few days, most of it dull, gloomy and decaying. This place struck me as the healthiest district in the city. To find out more about it, I went into a bar and phoned a Boston planner I know.

"Why in the world are you down in the North End?" he said. "Nothing's going on there. Eventually, yes, but not yet. That's a slum!"

"It doesn't seem like a slum to me," I said.

"Why that's the worst slum in the city. It has 275 dwelling units to the net acre! [Excluding streets, nonresidential land, etc.] I hate to admit that we have anything like that in Boston, but it's a fact."

"Do you have any other figures on it?" I asked.

6.   He did. Statistics showed that the neighborhood delinquency, disease and infant-mortality rates are among the lowest in the city. The child population is just about average. The death rate is low, 8.8 per 1000, against the average city rate of 11.2.

"You should have more slums like this," I said. "Don't tell me there are plans to wipe this out. You ought to be down here learning as much as you can from it."

"I know how you feel," he said. "I often go down there myself just to walk around the streets and feel that wonderful, cheerful street life. You'd be crazy about it in summer. But we have to rebuild it eventually. We've got to get those people off the street."

7. My planner friend's instincts told him the North End was a healthful place. Statistics confirmed it. But his training as a city planner told him the North End had to be a "bad" place. It has little park land. Children play on the sidewalks. It has small blocks. In city-planning parlance, the district is "badly cut up by wasteful streets." It also has "mixed uses"—another sin. It is made up of the plans of hundreds of people—not planners. Such freedom represents, as one of the wise men of city planning put it, "a chaotic accident . . . the summation of the haphazard, antagonistic whims of many self-centered, ill-advised individuals."

8. Under the seeming chaos of a lively place like the North End is a marvelous and intricate order—a complicated array of urban activities. These activities support and supplement each other, keeping the neighborhood interesting and vital. The planners would kill it.

9. The North End is not unique. In city after city, there are districts that refuse to decay, districts that hold people even when their incomes rise and their "status" improves, districts that spontaneously repair and renovate in spite of discouragement by government officials and mortgage lenders. These interesting and vital areas are the ones that have everything possible wrong with them—according to city-planning theory. Equally significant, in city after city the districts in decline and decay are frequently the ones that ought to be successful—according to planning theory.

10. The Morningside Heights area in New York City is such an example. According to theory, it should not be in trouble. It has a great abundance of park land, campus areas, playgrounds and other open spaces. It has plenty of grass. It occupies high and pleasant ground with magnificent river views. It is a famous educational center. It has good hospitals and fine churches. It has no industries. Its residential streets are zoned against "incompatible uses."

11. Yet by the early 1950's Morningside Heights was becoming the kind of slum in which people fear to walk the streets. Columbia University, other institutions and the planners from the city govern-

ment got together. At great cost the most blighted part of the area was wiped out. In the torn-down area a middle-income project complete with shopping center was built. Nearby a fenced-off low-income project was erected. The projects were hailed as a great demonstration in city saving.

12.   After that Morningside Heights went downhill even faster. It continues to pile up new mountains of crime and troubles to this day. The "remedy" didn't work. Dull, sorted-out "quiet residential areas" in cities fail because they are inconvenient, uninteresting and dangerous. The dark, empty grounds of housing projects breed crime. And it is much the same with dark, empty streets of "quiet residential areas" in big cities.

13.   Our cities need help desperately. If places like Morningside Heights are to be helped, the help must be based not on imitations of genteel, "good" addresses, but on understanding the real needs of those who live in big cities. A little involvement with the life of city streets, a little recognition that empty grass festooned with used tissue paper is no treat for anyone, a little common sense—these are the first requirements.

14.   The New York City neighborhood where I live is considered a mess by planners. They have plans to sort out its differing land uses from one another and isolate residences from working places with a buffer strip. Such a strip would be useful primarily to muggers. For months residents and businessmen of the neighborhood have been combating the scheme to simplify and regiment the area with Federal funds. Simplification would be the avenue to its ruin.

15.   One need only watch the sidewalk to see how the neighborhood is built upon a complicated set of activities. Each day Hudson Street, my street, is the scene of an endlessly varied parade of persons, some of them neighbors, many of them strangers. This scene is all composed of interesting movement and change.

16.   I make my first entrance a little after eight A.M. when I put out the garbage can. Around me, droves of junior-high-school students and people coming to work in the district walk by the center of the stage. While I sweep the sidewalk, I watch the signs and rituals of morning. Mr. Halpert unlocking his laundry hand-cart from its mooring to a cellar door. Joe Cornacchia's son-in-law stacking out empty crates from the delicatessen. The barber bringing out his sidewalk folding chair. Mr. Goldstein arranging coils of wire that proclaim the

hardware store is open. The primary children, heading for St. Luke's to the south. The children for St. Veronica's heading west. The children for P.S. 41 heading east. Well-dressed and even elegant women, and men with briefcases, emerge now from doorways and side streets. Simultaneously numbers of women in house dresses emerge and pause for quick conversations. Longshoremen who are not working gather at the White Horse Tavern or the International Bar for beer and conversation.

As noontime arrives, the executive and business lunchers from the industries in the neighborhood throng the Dorgene Restaurant and the Lion's Head coffee house down the street. If there were no workers to support these places at noon, we residents would not have them to use at night. Character dancers come onstage: a strange old man with strings of old shoes over his shoulders; motor-scooter riders with big black beards and girl friends who bounce on the back of their scooters. Mr. Koochagian, the tailor, waters the plants in his window, gives them a look from the outside and accepts a compliment on them from two passers-by. The baby carriages come out. [17.]

As residents return home from work in other places, the ballet reaches its crescendo. This is the time of roller skates and stilts and tricycles and games with bottle tops and plastic cowboys. This is the time of bundles and packages and zigzagging from the drugstore to the fruit-stand. This is the time when teenagers, all dressed up, are pausing to ask if their slips show or their collars look right. This is the time when anybody you know in the neighborhood will go by. [18.]

As darkness thickens and Mr. Halpert moors the laundry cart to the cellar door again, the ballet goes on under lights. It eddies back and forth, intensifying at the bright spotlight pools of Joe's sidewalk pizzeria, the bars and the drugstore. On Hudson Street we do not barricade ourselves indoors when darkness falls. [19.]

I know the deep night ballet from waking long after midnight to tend a baby. Sitting in the dark I have seen the shadows and heard the sounds of the sidewalk. Mostly it is snatches of party conversation. When the bars have closed, it is the sound of singing. Sometimes there is anger or sad weeping; sometimes a flurry of searching for a string of broken beads. One night a young man came along bellowing invectives at two girls who apparently were disappointing him. Doors opened, a wary semicircle of men and women formed around him; the police came. Out came the heads, too, along Hudson Street, of- [20.]

fering opinion, "Drunk. . . . Crazy. . . . A wild kid from the suburbs." (It turned out he *was* a wild kid from the suburbs.)

21.   I have not begun to describe the many differences that keep our sidewalks bustling. Among businesses and industries alone there are more than fifty different kinds within a few blocks. On Hudson Street, just as in the North End of Boston, we are the lucky possessors of a complex city order that is anything but the chaos that city planners proclaim it to be. Such neighborhoods as ours engender intense affection among those who live and work in them. As a result, they are stable places where people of many different incomes and tastes remain permanently—by choice.

22.   The true problem of city planning and rebuilding in a free society is how to cultivate more city districts that are free; lively and fertile places for the differing plans of thousands of individuals—not planners. Nothing could be farther from the aims of planners today. They have been trained to think of people as interchangeable statistics to be pushed around, to think of city vitality and mixture as a mess. Planners are the enemies of cities because they offer us only the poisonous promise of making every place in a city more like dull and standardized Morningside Heights. They have failed to pursue the main point: to study the success and failure of the real life of the cities. With their eyes on simple-minded panaceas, they destroy success and health. Planners will become helpful only when they abandon what they have learned about what "ought" to be good for cities.

23.   When they learn how fulfilling life in a city really can be, then they will finally stop working against the very goals they set out to achieve.

DISCUSSION QUESTIONS

1. Le Corbusier's plans were formulated over forty years ago. Have cities since then used his ideas in any way?
2. Jacobs stresses that "The true problem of city planning and rebuilding in a free society is how to cultivate more city districts that are free." What is her concept of freedom here? What is Le Corbusier's?

3. Le Corbusier would replace the "ballet" of life which Jacobs sees from her window with more trees and open spaces. Having read the two articles, which would you prefer?

4. Jacobs feels that many city planners, influenced by theorists such as Le Corbusier, are sacrificing the lives of people to their own particular plans and visions. She accuses the planners of being more interested in their *idea* of what should be present in a healthy city rather than in the healthy conditions that are already there. Are her arguments convincing?

5. In another part of his book, Le Corbusier argues that for the sake of economy and convenience, architects must standardize structures. All buildings should be constructed according to a few basic plans. Evaluate the advantages and dangers of such a theory.

RHETORIC

1. Write a theme outlining any basic changes needed in your living area. Refer to Le Corbusier's section titles.

2. Notice that Jacobs has her organizing sentence for the entire essay in the first paragraph. How does she then develop her ideas?

3. Much of Le Corbusier's essay is more an outline than a coherently developed piece of writing. Expand or draw together in a clearer fashion the following groups of paragraphs: six through nine; eleven through fifteen; sixteen through nineteen; forty through forty-three; fifty-four through sixty-six. Be especially careful with your topic sentences and transitions.

4. In paragraphs sixteen through nineteen Jacobs describes the activity on her street. She uses a chronological organization; paragraph sixteen describes the activity at 8 A.M., while nineteen discusses the midnight hours. Write a similar theme describing the movements of people in your own neighborhood at different times of the day.

5. Paragraphs ten through twelve of Jacobs' essay deals with the Morningside Heights area. Defend her use of three separate paragraphs in this discussion. What kind of transitions are used? The entire discussion supports what previous statement?

VOCABULARY

Le Corbusier

fundamental (paragraph 1)	hub (28)
formidable (1)	augment (30)
compelled (1)	elevated (32)
cope (1)	spectacle (43)
allotted (7)	urgent (50)
elastic (8)	implications (54)
periphery (8)	essence (57)
reserved (9)	rendered (63)
deprived (14)	erratic (64)
delicate (14)	abortions (64)
internal (19)	technical (66)
traversed (23)	creative (66)

Jacobs

rehabilitated (paragraph 4)	rituals (16)
glimpses (4)	proclaim (16)
chaotic (7)	throng (17)
intricate (8)	crescendo (18)
array (8)	eddies (19)
supplement (8)	bellowing (20)
blighted (11)	invectives (20)
buffer (14)	wary (20)
isolate (14)	engender (21)
regiment (14)	cultivate (22)
varied (15)	standardized (22)
composed (15)	panaceas (22)

What Happened to Dream Town?

1.   Things seemed peculiar no matter where you looked. You had to approach the place on foot because no cars were allowed. No one was wearing plastic curlers in the Safeway. The WANTED DESPERATELY sign on the bulletin board was an inscrutable request for 420 forty-six-ounce juice cans and 38 one-pound coffee cans for a production of *Waiting for Godot.*

2.   The village itself was positively startling. The main square was paved in tawny brick, with an artfully off-center fountain, framed by

Anne Chamberlin, "What Happened to Dream Town?" *The Saturday Evening Post,* CCXLI, No. 11 (June 1, 1968), 64–68. Copyright © 1968 by the Curtis Publishing Company. Reprinted by permission of the publisher.

a horseshoe curve of handsome storefronts. The drugstore had outside tables, and pale cement steps as wide as a highway led to a boat
landing. To the right, rising straight out of the Virginia countryside,
was a 15-story apartment building, and further along the shore, nested
in the reeds, you could see clumps of town houses, with walled gardens, sun decks, docks and moorings. Beyond, the fields and trees
stretched in lazy green loops all the way to the horizon.

3. And it's not every Saturday afternoon that you run into a group
of teen-aged boys gathered with flute and trumpet in a town square,
tootling through three 16th-century airs by Pezel, with a chaser by
Giovanni Gabrieli. They had no sooner finished than a Baptist minister, a dentist, a patent attorney, a retired admiral and a dozen other
men and women in tweeds gathered around a Wurlitzer piano,
propped between a lamppost and the long tables where the Girl
Scouts were spreading their cookies and cider. Led ("Everybody
shush, now") by two spirited ladies with short fur jackets and red
purses, they navigated two verses of *America the Beautiful,* five verses
of an ode specially composed for the occasion and three trips through
an anthem that wound up:

> Lake and plaza and crystal fountain,
> Clustered houses and lakeside homes,
> You stand, a vision of life to be,
> Hail to your founder's plan!
> What a man, what a man!

4. Mr. Robert E. Simon, the man in question, who had been lurking
diffidently on the fringes, was propelled toward the microphones to be
thanked for his vision and courage, presented with a book containing
signatures of the community's first residents; a silver cigarette case
inscribed; "Where there is no vision, the people perish"; an honorary
membership in Troop 113 of the local Boy Scouts, and a facsimile of
a U.S. patent, as the "inventor" of the community.

5. He looked as though he might cry. It was to be his last appearance in the plaza before going into exile. The festival had been
prompted, in fact, by the news that he had just been fired.

6. Reston, Va., the dream town he had founded, whose devoted
residents had turned out to serenade him, was up to its ears in debt.

7. What had gone wrong? Designed by some of the nation's most

adventurous planners and architects, it was already a dazzling enclave of stylish town houses, model factories, fountains, towers and tennis courts, rising out of a lovely patch of field and forest about 20 miles from Washington. It was the talk of the art pages, a symbol of taste in a sea of slurbs. Mrs. Lyndon Johnson gave it a beautification award. The governor of Virginia compared it to Williamsburg. Tourists tramped through it on Sunday as though it were a shrine. Foreign visitors were taken to look at it as proof that the American building explosion was Not All Bad. People took its pulse and clucked over it as though it were a transplanted heart. Reston was as close as we had come lately to Camelot.

8.   But in the American Dream even Camelot has to break even. And as of last fall, Reston had 2,700 residents and a debt of $45 million. To protect its own $15 million investment, the Gulf Oil Company took control of the limping Utopia, fired its founder and put the whole tangle in the hands of Robert H. Ryan, a real-estate consultant from Pittsburgh. Mr. Ryan announced he intended to "listen to the market" and find a formula for the place that would make it sell.

9.   The gasps could be heard all the way to Chevy Chase Circle. Would "the market" reveal that what people really want is to live on small square lots with boxes on them? Would Camelot's fields and woods have to be given to the bulldozers to produce a profit? For those who hoped that New Towns like Reston would provide an alternative to the mindless destruction of the American landscape, the prospect of going back to business-as-usual was almost too ghastly to contemplate.

10.   Things had started downhill because of the desperate need for housing at the end of World War II. A new breed of merchant builders, stamping out assembly-line houses, started blanketing the land in acres of look-alike boxes. Then the centers of the cities began to crumble and their inhabitants fled to the suburbs at the rate of 4,000 a day—requiring more boxes.

11.   In the case of Washington, D.C., the slide-rule people figured that by the year 2000 the population would be five million—more than twice what it is today. And Washington doesn't even have a core to crumble. There is one conspicuous family bivouacked at 1600 Pennsylvania Avenue behind a fence of pickets, and the rest of downtown Washington empties out every night like a drained sink. If two million more people start looking for a place to sleep out there on the

An aerial shot of downtown Reston, Virginia.
Courtesy of Ollie Atkins

city fringes between rush-hour traffic jams, the whole remaining gentle green fuzz in Maryland and Virginia figures to be blocked out in tiny close-knit tufts, like a wall-to-wall waffle. A whole generation which now has to be led to a zoo to see what a cow looks like would have to lead *its* children to the National Arboretum to see their first tree. Assuming you can still get to the Arboretum in the year 2000 without a National Guard tank.

12. Meanwhile, however, people were beginning to discover what other countries were doing about their urban sprawl. Instead of blotching the land at random, some of them had begun to build self-contained communities. They weren't just dormitories for the nearest big city but places to work, live, shop and even have a little fun— sometimes without once climbing into an automobile.

13. Several experimental "New Towns" began to sprout in this country and even looked as though they might pay off. In fact, some of the great aluminum, oil, chemical, shipping, wood and insurance companies began to invest in them (just as Gulf put money into Reston).

14.   So the Washington landscape in 1961, though still being merrily carved into parcels and stripped of its trees, was nonetheless ripe for a fresh approach. And Robert Simon had just the unlikely background the situation seemed to require. A graduate of Harvard, a particularly strong recommendation in 1961, he had spent 22 years as head of the family corporation that owned Carnegie Hall. He was the former president of the National Music League and editor of something called "Be Your Own Music Critic." He played the piano and had composed an Indian War Dance by the time he was six. He was interested in swimming, boating, skiing, golf, riding and tree planting. He read books. And he had money.

15.   In March of 1961 he swept down from the polluted canyons of New York and paid out $13 million for 7,000 wooded acres in Fairfax County. As he had never actually tangled with a whole new community, he enjoyed a newcomer's uncluttered belief that it would be possible to build one that was attractive to look at, pleasant to live in and nonetheless financially successful.

16.   "The beginning of a plan for a New Town," Mr. Simon said, "must be philosophy, not topography—not existing zoning and other ordinances of the community, not FHA regulations or other factors dealing with the money market." In this New Town, it was announced to the startled multitudes, shopping and housing were to be within walking distance of each other and people would walk on special automobile-proof walkways. "This is an exciting thing," Mr. Simon said, conjuring up visions of museums, libraries, theaters—and "more tennis courts than anywhere east of California." Word soon got around the flint-eyed Washington real-estate industry that Mr. Simon was down with a case of creeping idealism.

17.   Whatever he was down with, it was highly personal. "I would rather play my own brand of tennis," he once said, "than watch any tennis tournament." The New Town's name, RESton, is formed from his initials. Its 30-acre, man-made lake is named for his wife, Anne. Another lake on the premises was renamed Lake Elsa for his mother.

18.   In 20 years Reston was to have a total population of 75,000. That's more people, the Richmond *Times* pointed out with awe, than there are in Danville or Lynchburg. And almost as many as there are in Roanoke. The plan called for seven interrelated but distinct villages of 10,000 people each, plus a "downtown Reston" with museums, shops,

restaurants, movie theaters, libraries, hospital, hotels and offices. The community was programmed for 35 churches and 21 schools.

There were plans for 4,000 single-family houses; 17,000 town houses; 3,000 apartment units. It was calculated that single people with incomes as low as $5,000 to $7,500 a year could rent the apartments—so that everyone who worked at Reston could live there if he wanted to.

As Mr. Simon saw it, in fact, a Reston resident could spend his whole life there and never once have to surface in the real world. Younger people, with no children, could rent some of the lower-priced apartments; later they could buy a house; when their children grew up and left home, they could move back to an apartment. The family breadwinner could strike out across the rolling hills to his job in the industrial park—on foot.

These were the guiding principles. Mr. Simon wore out several sets of planners before settling on a final Master Plan. He kept going places and seeing new things he wanted to incorporate. Whittlesey and Conklin of New York (now Conklin and Rossant), the firm which ultimately got the over-all planning job, had designed model cities in British Columbia and India, and Mr. Simon admired the fact that they planned big and built with style.

Lake Anne Village Center, the only one of the seven projected villages which has actually been built, is an example of some of the interlocking planning made possible by the new zoning worked out for Reston. Surrounding the plaza are a private club, stores, a pharmacy, hairdresser, barbershop, community center, library and the teen-agers "Rathskeller"—a domain no adult is supposed to penetrate without invitation. On the upper floors are apartments. On the roof of the Safeway market is the carpeted outdoor playground of the Lake Anne Nursery Kindergarten, which includes swings, ropes, rabbits, a turtle run and a place to roller skate. The whole village and the neighboring Heron House high-rise apartment building are cooled by the same air-conditioning system, and the top of the cement structure that houses the machinery for it doubles as an umpire's stand for two of Reston's tennis courts.

Groups of town houses and garden apartments curve along Reston's hillsides, wall to wall and back to back as though they were clustered in the thick of town. The acreage left over from eliminating front lawns and backyards runs to woods, meadows, streams, a golf course, stables, riding ring, swimming pools and tennis courts. One large segment, called Hunters Woods, is even divided into old-fashioned lots with single houses on them.

24.   In the industrial park, chaste and landscaped buildings in the new Think Tank school of design are spotted discreetly among the knolls and trees and live up to Reston's Protective Covenants and Restrictions, which guarantee no "smoke, smog, obnoxious odors or excessive noise."

25.   At the Inhalation Research Division of Hazleton Laboratories, Inc., Philippine monkeys are wheeled about in Plexiglas highchairs by men in clean white smocks, and the only bad smell in the place comes from the room where they've got a mouse smoking 17 brands of cigarettes. From the other smokeless endeavors which run to things like Electronics, Environmental and Behavioral Research, Communications Systems, Magnetic Devices, Consultants and Systems Analysis, only the pure steam of the human brain in furious concentration rises to mingle with the fleecy puffs from the friendly hearthfires of the distillery which was there before Mr. Simon arrived.

26.   Whenever a new company moved to the industrial park, there were lease-signing ceremonies, and Reston, Inc., presented a painting by a Virginia artist to hang in the front entrance. Early Reston ads in the Washington papers quoted Marcus Aurelius in the original Latin, an inscrutable Arab maxim from Lawrence of Arabia, remarks by Virginia Woolf, William Hazlitt, Samuel Butler, G. K. Chesterton, Salvador de Madariaga, Nietzsche, Robert Frost and Don Marquis. They drew a talented, unusual, interesting crop of settlers to Reston, but not *enough* of them.

27.   Those who did move there found themselves embarked on a whole way of life. "The *way* people live," Mr. Simon kept saying, "is at least as important to them as *where* they live."

28.   The trouble was that each of Reston's innovations and architectural adventures brought about a new fight with Fairfax County. Each culvert and storm drain somehow led to a new encounter with the Director of Streets and Drainage. Every stretch of road brought a traffic jam in the highway department. Mr. Glenn Saunders, who was project engineer in those days, and is now executive vice president of the new Gulf Reston, Inc., combines the faultless courtesy of the Old South with the tact and Buddhist restraint of U Thant. He remembers

these early months as one diplomatic and engineering cliff-hanger after another.

"Each one we thought was the most critical part of Reston's life," 29. he says, "And around the corner was always something just as big."

Each obstacle brought more delays. "We probably lost a year 30. that way," Mr. Saunders says. "And each delay brought more expense. But rather than compromise, Mr. Simon insisted we do it the way we started out."

For Reston to work, everything had to be done at once. If buyers 31. were to be lured to this new city-in-the-woods, some of the "amenities" had to be ready—a golf course, tennis courts, stables. If Restonians were not to spend their time commuting to the nearest shopping center like the rest of suburbia, they needed a few basic stores in the villages. But merchants were reluctant to move in until they could count on customers. Before companies would move to the industrial park they wanted a prospect of housing that their employees could afford. But since nearly everything in Reston was a departure from the norm, the usual assembly-line cost-cutting housebuilding techniques couldn't be used, so even low-cost houses became luxuries.

And there were nasty surprises around the fringes. The U.S. 32. Geological Survey, which was to build a $30 million headquarters on an 85-acre slice of the industrial park, ran into budget problems. And the new four-lane highway planned to link Washington and Dulles International Airport was envisioned as a traffic-free channel between Reston and Washington; when finally built, it slashed straight through the middle of the tract without a single exit or entrance ramp. Restonians commuting to Washington were left to grapple morning and night with one of the worst stretches of road outside of northern Thrace.

To achieve all the goals Mr. Simon had set for Reston finally 33. took more money than he was able to raise. The architectural critics loved him, but the bankers held back. No one felt like parting with massive doses of money that it would take so long to get back. As Simon rather poignantly remarked to a Yale Architecture Conference in 1965: "I doubt that the ancient Egyptians concerned themselves very much with payroll projections before they okayed a pyramid project."

But with all this crashing about his ears, Mr. Simon never al- 34. lowed Reston to waver from its sense of style.

35.   The Reston, Va., Foundation for Community Programs, Inc., was incorporated in 1962 to help coax the residents into Reston's many activities. It operates, among other things, the Community Center, the Rathskeller and the Lake Anne Nursery Kindergarten, whose students have ground their own corn to make corn bread and churned the butter to spread on it. They have fed fish, ducks, geese and themselves. They have found a woolly bear caterpillar, a beetle hole and an enormous hornets' nest, hatched some chicken eggs and even made a start on French.

36.   To help the city folk recognize something besides the slimy-leaved, monoxide-breathing ginkgo tree and the wild yammering of a squadron of starlings on a bombing run, a Nature Center was added to the Reston Foundation, with Vernon Walker as resident Nature Director.

37.   Mr. Walker, who wears corduroy trousers and a leather jacket, was soon neck deep in ecological activities all over Reston. As it was sliding toward bankruptcy, its dauntless inhabitants were gathering in damp glades at 8:30 Saturday mornings for Mr. Walker's Family Nature Walks. I joined them one day, and our little group identified a kingfisher, some lichen, a squirrel, a garter snake (round eyes, bad smell), a poison ivy vine with no leaves and some pokeweed.

38.   On another dawn patrol, when I stalked the wild asparagus with Mr. Walker's Adult Nature Seminar, we were sent out into a wind-tossed field with a mimeographed assignment sheet ordering us to re-turn in 20 minutes with: something fuzzy; something fragrant (describe the fragrance); something edible (*but,* do not eat it until it has been checked out!); something man-made. I managed to find something fuzzy and four man-made beer cans, but the others, who had already done time in Mr. Walker's tough school, found everything. That is, if you can *really* eat boiled pine cones.

39.   Most Restonians found this sort of thing just what they had been looking for. "On George Washington's birthday, two years ago, we just drove out," one of them told me. "We asked if there were any four-bedroom houses, took home a floor plan, told our sons about it, who said it 'sounds keen.' The next trip out we saw the house for the first time and signed a contract."

40.   Enthusiasm didn't seem to dim after they moved in. "The whole community is back to early American days where everybody works together," one Restonian said. "The other night," a young housewife

remarked over loud strains of Bach from the hi-fi, "we met a delight-ful couple in their sixties. If we'd stayed in Washington, we'd just be seeing the people our age, all doing the same things we're doing.

"Here the kids are safe to walk around the parks," the refugee 41. from suburbia went on. "The littlest boy can go and get bread at the grocery store. We're six hundred yards from the tennis court. In sum-mer I can play tennis and eat dinner by eight at night. We were happy in our old house, watching the power mowers go by outside the picture window, but we didn't know what we didn't have." Reston, a new-comer wrote to the local paper, "seems like a place where meanness and triteness and skepticism would soon wither on the vine. Reston is a land of Titans. We only hope we can make the grade."

Making the grade in Reston involves quite a lot. Property owners 42. are responsible for the parks, playgrounds, open spaces, walkways, tennis courts, swimming pools, lakes, bridle paths, streets, outdoor lighting—all that commonly held property made possible by the planned community zoning. Townhouse dwellers belong to Cluster Association, which is charged with maintaining commonly held land through dues ranging from $120 to $200 a year. Reston, Inc., has been paying the dues for unsold houses.

"There is a lot of pride in Waterview Cluster," their association's 43. secretary told me. "One fifth of the Waterview men volunteered to help build a wall. Sixty out of ninety members go to the general meet-ings." Hickory Cluster, near Lake Anne Village, is so gung-ho it even publishes a newsletter.

Restonians got to be as fiercely protective of their work-play 44. Eden as Mr. Simon. When young pranksters put sugar in someone's gas tank, heaved a rock at a pedestrian from the high-rise roof and threw a board down the air shaft, a fierce editorial in the Reston *Times* called them VANDALS IN VALHALLA. There were arguments about dogs and laundry and infringement of club rules regarding "behavior and sanitation" at the North Shore Swim Club. There was a tempest about putting low-cost housing near Lake Anne Village. One view held it would bring occupants with "low-level conduct." Other aroused Restonians retorted that "the belief that only people who can afford houses costing in the forty thousands are 'nice' is con-trary to our democracy. We hold Reston to the promise that there will be housing available for all persons who work here; otherwise, we will feel deprived and somehow cheated."

45.   Through it all, while Mr. Ryan and Gulf Oil were taking over, Mr. Walker was advising that putting pieces of string, yarn, horsehair and cotton batting in a wire basket hung in a tree would encourage the birds to nest and that 93 kinds of birds prefer dogwood.

46.   Mr. Ryan, despite the news accounts describing him as waving an unlit cigar and declaring that "town houses in the country are ahead of their time," turned out to be a Harvard man himself. He kept huge sheets of paper propped on an easel in one corner of his office and charged at it with a black felt-tipped marker like a picador at a bullfight. "I say you don't have good design and planning," he keeps saying, "until you meet the test of economic feasibility. We are *going* to save trees. We are *going* to use the contours of this land. We're not going to bulldoze this beautiful piece of land. It's not a question of contemporary versus traditional. But if there are to be any New Towns in America, they've got to make economic sense."

47.   Economic sense for Reston—its "survival pace"—is to produce and sell 1,000 housing units a year. They will have to cost less to build so that they will sell for less so that more people can afford to buy them.

48.   Ryan sent Mr. Saunders out to explain to the citizenry that "to listen to the market doesn't mean tearing pages out of a builders' magazine. The price range will have to get down so that we have more houses in the twenty-thousands. In the long run it's no more a question of detached house versus town house than it was under Simon. It's a matter of *when* you build each of the types. The overall mix has to stay or you lose the open spaces. All these are going to be retained. We have to build what people want. That still doesn't mean it has to be bad. Maybe we can lead the market a little bit."

49.   Gradually, Restonians have begun to ease around to Mr. Ryan's view. "Good design," said one, "is a minority taste. The premium at Reston was too high." Mr. Simon's overplanning may even have scared people away. As one resident points out: "Reston says, 'This is the way it should be. If you don't like it, you've got no taste.' Facts are so different from ideology. We disparage Los Angeles, but it is the fastest-growing city in America. People wouldn't be moving there if they didn't like it."

50.   This spring Reston opened three new sections of town houses, some of them redesigned to sell for less than $25,000. It is embarked on 200 new garden apartments, some 40 "patio houses"—a form of

slightly separated town houses—a new golf course, a health club, a convention-center complex, an office building. The drugstore is keeping longer hours. Lake Anne Inn has instituted Sunday brunch and there is a new Sunday buffet at the golf club. It now takes three full-time checkers to handle the crowds at the Safeway.

As the first of Hickory Cluster's 2,300 daffodil and crocus bulbs 51. began to sprout, the mighty Gulf was not only holding the bulldozers at bay but beginning to sound a bit like Mr. Simon. "A town that celebrated its opening with a review of the performing arts—songs, dances, and the poetry of Stephen Spender, and an ambitious display of sculpture," said an article in the handsome company magazine, "cannot but leave its quite considerable mark on the country."

DISCUSSION QUESTIONS

1. Jacobs and Le Corbusier are concerned with rebuilding our cities. The Reston developers feel it is best simply to construct entirely new ones. Which approach do you favor?
2. Reston has importance as one of the first ventures of its kind in the United States. Evaluate the lessons learned from such an experiment. Will more Restons appear in the future? Should they? Or should all our energies be focused on rebuilding the cities that now stand?
3. Discuss Mr. Ryan's statement: "But if there are to be any New Towns in America, they've got to make economic sense."
4. What were the major factors that damaged Mr. Simon's dream?
5. Formulate a list of the assets and liabilities of living in a community designed by Jacobs, Le Corbusier, and Mr. Simon. Which one would you prefer?

RHETORIC

1. The first five paragraphs dramatize the end of a dream. How is the transition made back to the basic discussion? What purpose does the rhetorical question in paragraph seven serve?
2. Write a theme listing the three essential requirements you would want in any new community.
3. In what way is paragraph eleven linked to paragraph ten? What is the topic sentence of the latter paragraph?
4. New communities such as Reston obviously need to be built in large

areas of open land. Check the maps and do other research into such areas near your hometown. Select an area as a possible site for a new city. Then write a theme defending your choice. Keep in mind the need for roads, trees, water, etc.

VOCABULARY

clumps (paragraph 2)
enclave (7)
tangle (8)
sprawl (12)
sprout (13)
uncluttered (15)
startled (16)
incorporate (21)
domain (22)
penetrate (22)
clustered (23)

mingle (25)
distillery (25)
innovations (28)
obstacle (30)
reluctant (31)
skepticism (41)
infringement (44)
tempest (44)
traditional (46)
disparage (49)

Mechanics
of Style

INTRODUCTION

You may feel that all the time and energy lavished upon grammar and rhetoric in the classroom is much ado about nothing. You usually have little trouble communicating with your friends and relatives. Further, you find that most of your communication is vocal and not written. Why, then, spend long hours laboring over sentences, paragraphs, essays?

To begin with, the world in which you now operate is always subject to change. If you could see the world you will have to contend with in a few years, it is very likely you would be positively frightened at its size and complexity. The responsibilities which others assume for you now, you will soon have to accept for yourself, and they are by no means simple ones. It is in this world—the world of adults—that spoken communication is no longer completely adequate. In this world, the people with whom you must deal and communicate will extend far beyond the circle of your friends and relatives—and they will not always be familiar with or sympathetic to the "jive" of your youth. Often you will have to write and not speak what you have to convey to others.

Confronted with this situation, you may refuse to learn the new language and knowledge required of you. You can retreat back into the old neighborhood and never get out. You can live all your life on a dead-end street. If you want to rise in this world, however, if you want to succeed in it and shape it, and thus enlarge and enrich your own life and that of your children, you must meet the world on its own terms. And one of the most important of those terms is Standard American English. Standard American English is what is called grammar and rhetoric in the classroom. It is because of its importance that so much time and energy are lavished upon it.

We called this Standard American English—this written form of communication—a new language, and so it is. A person's experience in spoken communication will not always help him in writing, and often it can be a definite hindrance. Certain words and ways of speaking, perfectly acceptable and even effective in conversation with friends, become inadequate and inadmissable when put down on paper. This is a social fact, a fact which everyone, no matter what his economic status or section of the country, must face and accept. As Langston Hughes says in the poem quoted in the introduction to this book, one must "learn all jive." Everyone, to stay alive, must know at least two languages, spoken and written English. You, for example, have used your own form of spoken English for years; now you must learn to use as well and as easily the form of written English employed by most Americans.[1]

Usually, the chief problem in learning expository writing is becoming aware of and accepting its limitations as well as its possibilities. A large part of your communication in a conversation or argument is carried by your tone of voice, facial expressions, gestures. None of these are communicable in written prose. New means for expressing things like irony, sarcasm, emphasis, and emotional tone must be found. Since the reader will not see you or hear your voice, you must find other ways to convey to him the subtleties of your meaning. These clues cannot simply be listed, but must be discovered through much reading and actual writing. One gets to know writing the way one gets to know a neighborhood, by living in it for awhile. And one of the basic ground rules for writing is that language and punctuation—only those things which can be written down on paper—must be made to communicate what you normally say through your eyes and hands and tone of voice when speaking.

---

[1] It is obvious, of course, that there is a spoken Standard American English, too, which very much resembles in idiom and vocabulary the written form and this also must eventually be mastered. But as the conscious discipline of writing becomes more and more a natural and familiar style, this style can more easily be transferred to speech, not replacing one's original speech habits, but supplementing them.

Again, much of your most effective speaking vocabulary, those words we call slang, must be surrendered and a new vocabulary acquired. Phrases like "sock it to me, baby," "gig," and "boss"—often the most frequently used expressions in conversation—cannot be used in written work. Slang is usually limited in usage to a particular group or even to one city. To outsiders these words are puzzling or meaningless. And because the meanings of slang words are not always widely known or change so frequently, they can be quite untrustworthy. A word or phrase which means one thing today may mean something far different six months from now, or it may be understood in quite a different way in Chicago than it is in, say, Birmingham. Written speech is far more permanent than conversation; it requires a stabler, more widely accepted language. The vocabulary of writing, however, is also very rich in vivid, suggestive words. One of your tasks in learning how to write more effectively will be to explore and discover this new vocabulary. The dictionary is filled with words; the more of them you know and are able to use, the more eloquent and powerful your personal voice will become.

Another advantage you have in speaking that is taken away when you begin to write is that of active interchange with your listeners. In conversation, the person you are talking to can always stop you at any point to ask you to clarify a phrase or a meaning in your argument. He can, for example, tell you that your evidence or examples are beside the point, to which you can reply by justifying them or citing new ones. How often in an argument between two people have you heard, "What do you mean by . . . ?" or "Hold on, man, that's got nothing to do with . . ." or "Well, if that's the case, then what about . . . ?" Such exchange, giving you a chance to change and to shape your argument or explanation to your particular listener's doubts and questions, is not available to you when writing. You must anticipate in advance what information your reader will want or need to know, what relevant questions he might ask. When your essay or report is before him, you will not be beside it to explain points of confusion. If your written words do not seem clear or convincing to him, he may simply toss your discussion aside, and that will be that. Thus you must put down all you have to say, as clearly and concisely and persuasively as possible, in your final written draft.

If such is the nature of written language, it is obvious that certain things must be agreed upon by the people who use that language if they are able to communicate with each other as clearly and effectively as possible. These agreed-upon things are the rules of grammar and the conventions of rhetoric. Because these rules are shared by everyone, men who have never seen or known each other can discuss with each other, perhaps without ever meeting personally, very complicated issues and ideas. Very often this kind of communication —between men who have never met—is required of everyone living in the adult, social world. It might be required, for example, of anyone writing to another for a job or job interview. If the letter were poorly written, the job-seeker might never get the opportunity of a personal meeting. And such written communication is a part of the daily life of lawyers, teachers, ministers, businessmen.

Much of what has been said about writing up to this point probably seems of a negative nature—we have dwelled on what in your spoken language you must give up; we have insisted on the obligation, the necessity of knowing how to write. This, however, is only half the story. To be able to write (and to speak) well is to have opened to you a world of opportunities and possibilities. It gives you a chance to overcome isolation and estrangement. Think of some of the men who have become great in our time: Martin Luther King, Jr., John F. Kennedy, Malcolm X. All were helped immeasurably by their ability to speak to all kinds of men through the written word. It was this ability that spread their thoughts and ideas far beyond the circle of their personal acquaintances.

In this section, the lessons will deal with problems in grammar and style. Here is the area where the distinctions between speaking and writing are most difficult to make. The run-on sentence is an example. As you meet each problem in grammar and style, try always to bear in mind the greater effort toward clarity that writing requires. Your sentences must say (all by themselves) what you want to say— to everyone.

I. RUN-ON SENTENCE

Below are some examples of the run-on sentence. What is wrong with these sentences; why are they inadequate? Rewrite them correctly to eliminate any awkwardness which may confuse what the writer of each is trying to say.

A.   The reason that I picked taste as my favorite sense is because I like to eat and when you are eating, for instance you are eating some chicken or strawberry pie you would like to get the best out of it, and when you are eating a piece of candy when you bite in it tastes so good in your mouth, and then a cold strawberry soda when it is fresh it tastes like some strawberries.

B.   The hardest decision that I have ever had to make was when I first came out of high school on whether to go to the service or go to school. This was a hard decision because I took the Air Force test before I came out and passed the test and I received some pamphlets telling me what different fields I could go into such as take a trade, or go to school it all sounded so good to me but I had to make up my mind of whether to go to school or to the service so I chose school, but sometimes I think I made the wrong decision.

C.   Cool is usually a term used to mean a swinger but not a loud-mouth, someone who's really "in" and has got his own style, but in my group we sometimes call a person cool who is anything but a swinger because the term has come to be kind of sarcastic for us, but I guess most people still use it in the old way, for example Ray Charles and Miles Davis and even Everett Dirksen are cool, but you don't have to be famous to be cool, even a teen-ager can be cool— like me.

II. COMMA SPLICE

A reminder: A *sentence* may be simply defined as a word or group of words which expresses a complete meaning to a reader:

Come here!
John went to the movies.

A *phrase* is a group of words, without a subject or predicate, that is used as a noun, or an adjective, or an adverb:

NOUN PHRASE: *Walking at night* is fun.
ADJECTIVAL PHRASE: The boy *walking the dog* is Jim.
ADVERBIAL PHRASE: He ran *down the wide track*.

A *clause* is a group of words with a subject and predicate:

I never saw the girl at the party.

An *independent* (also called *main*) clause can stand by itself.

A *dependent* (also called *subordinate*) clause depends on the independent clause to complete its meaning:

He is the player *who caught the ball.*

The dependent clause *who caught the ball* is dependent for its meaning on the independent clause: *He is the player.*

You may join two main clauses with a *coordinating conjunction* (and, but, or, nor, for):

They went to the store with Tim, *but* I remained at home.
Make certain you leave the dog home, *for* they will not let him in the theater.

Use a semicolon to separate main clauses joined by *conjunctive adverbs* (besides, hence, however, moreover, therefore) or *transitional phrases* (for example, in addition, on the other hand, in fact):

I don't want to go; *besides,* I really don't have any money.
Trust me this one time; *in fact,* trust me all the time.

A common error in student papers is the *comma splice* (that is, the joining of two complete sentences or independent clauses with only a comma between them). Examine the following paragraphs to see if such errors exist and then correct them:

A.   I dislike the dishonesty of politics, most politicians are qualified by their skill in deception. A candidate for office has no inhibitions whatever about the promises he makes, I have known men whose only intention seemed to be an attempt to out-promise their opponents. If candidates were more careful and intelligent in their promises I would be more convinced, a man with a program that is modest but possible could very well do the job. But politicians give no sincere thought to their election promises, they care only about winning an election.

B.   Most people think that as you get older you are better able to contribute to society and to make important decisions, I think that this is not always true. As people get older they do experience more and understand more of their experience, they also become more conservative, more uneasy about any kind of change, and more intent upon security for its own sake. Young people may not have much experience, they do have a great deal of vitality, courage, and ability. They have not learned to compromise their ideals with the real world, compromise is necessary to a certain extent but too much compromise is a sell-out. The rebelliousness of young people often forces their elders to reexamine their own fears and compromises.

C.   Making friends is not as easy as parents and teachers pretend it is, true friendships are really hard to discover and to develop. Anyone can have a number of acquaintances, they do not satisfy the needs that one genuine friend does. A friend knows you deeply and cares deeply about you, a friend knows when you have problems and he is interested not because he is curious or nosey but because he wants to help you as much as he is able to. This kind of understanding between people is not easy to come by, it is a rare thing to find and it takes much effort to develop and keep it.

D.   People think that they have much happiness in their lives, in reality they have very little. Much of the time we are neither happy nor unhappy, the emotion we most often feel is boredom. The other emotions are rarer but more memorable, a week of boredom is soon forgotten but the memory of ten hours of anger can linger in our minds for a lifetime. Even the experiences of anger and suffering, however, are much longer than the few brief moments of love and fulfillment that we have actually had, people take a few seeds of genuinely felt love or ambition and nurse them into vast imaginary gardens of memory and dream.

III. WORDINESS

Below are two character sketches. Which do you prefer reading? Is your preference due in any way to a superior use of language and detail by one of the writers? If you do find one of the sketches better than the other, defend your choice by comparing and contrasting the two.

A.   I guess of all the people I've ever known, the one who would get my vote for being the most unforgettable would be Jim Harris. Jim was shorter than most of us, and had a big mop of brown hair. He always wore the same pair of baggy dungarees and the same sneakers. He wore them every day. In fact, I don't think there was a

single time that I saw him that he wasn't wearing those same dungarees and sneakers.

Jim was always doing something far-out and unusual. He was always making jokes in class. Sometimes it got so bad the teacher had
to throw him out of the room. But he would be back the next day
—as bad as ever and still full of mischief. He would pour salt in your
lunch when you weren't looking and would write crazy poems on the
blackboard. One time he took books from six kids' desks and put
them all on different desks. Those kids sure were confused and mixed
up (a fight almost broke out between two of them!) until we found
out it was all a joke. And of course we knew right away who had
done it. Who else could it be? Jim Harris, naturally.

Jim and I were good friends in spite of his pranks, many of which
were played on me (like the one about pouring salt in my lunch). I
feel that if a friend is interesting and loyal, one should be able to
overlook a lot. We played ball together, went to the movies together,
and even studied together sometimes, though I didn't get much studying done when Jim was around, because he was such a cut-up. We
had completely different personalities, but we always got along well
and always stood up for each other, no matter what happened.

B.   Mr. Gore [a slave overseer] was a grave man, and, though a
young man, he indulged in no jokes, said no funny words, seldom
smiled. His words were in perfect keeping with his looks, and his
looks were in perfect keeping with his words. Overseers will sometimes indulge in a witty word, even with the slaves; not so with Mr.
Gore. He spoke but to command, and commanded but to be obeyed;
he dealt sparingly with his words, and bountifully with his whip,
never using the former where the latter would do as well. When he
whipped, he seemed to do so from a sense of duty and feared no
consequences. He did nothing reluctantly, no matter how disagreeable;
always at his post, never inconsistent. He never promised but to ful-
fil. He was, in a word, a man of the most inflexible firmness and
stone-like coolness.

His savage barbarity was equalled only by the consummate coolness with which he committed the grossest and most savage deeds
upon the slaves under his charge. Mr. Gore once undertook to whip
one of Colonel Lloyd's slaves, by the name of Demby. He had given
Demby but few stripes, when, to get rid of the scourging, Demby ran
and plunged himself into a creek, and stood there at the depth of his
shoulders, refusing to come out. Mr. Gore told him that he would
give him three calls, and that, if he did not come out at the third call,
he would shoot him. The first call was given. Demby made no re-

sponse, but stood his ground. The second and third calls were given with the same result. Mr. Gore then, without consultation or deliberation with any one, not even giving Demby an additional call, raised his musket to his face, taking deadly aim at his standing victim, and in an instant poor Demby was no more. His mangled body sank out of sight, and blood and brains marked the water where he had stood.[1]

IV. SENTENCE FRAGMENTS

A sentence fragment is an incomplete sentence; it lacks an essential element. If the problem behind a run-on sentence is the attempt to put too much into one sentence, the problem behind a sentence fragment is the failure to put enough into it. Every sentence must have at least two elements: a *subject* and a *verb*. *John runs.* Simple though this statement is, it is a correct sentence because it contains a subject and a verb. Many sentences, of course, need not only a subject and a verb, but a *direct object* and an *indirect object* as well: *John gave me his jacket.*

You should always make certain that each sentence you write contains at least a subject and a verb. Verbs can be tricky. *John running to win the race* is not a complete sentence because it lacks a verb. *Running* is a participle, and *to win* is an infinitive (see Chapter X). Subjects can be tricky too. In imperative statements the subject can be implied. *Go to work.* If this is a command, the implied subject is *you* and the sentence is correct. You will not usually use many imperative sentences, however, so the great majority of your sentences will have to contain an explicitly stated subject.

Many sentence fragments are really dependent clauses. Some dependent clauses contain a subject and a verb, but they do not state a grammatically complete thought. *If Jim took the 10:30 bus.* This fragment has a subject, *Jim,* and a verb, *took,* but it does not state a complete idea. If Jim took the 10:30 bus, then what?

Below is a brief story. There are two columns of optional statements. In each case, one is a complete sentence and the other is a sentence fragment. Write out the story, using only the complete sentences.

[1] Frederick Douglass, *Narrative of the Life of Frederick Douglass* (Garden City, N.Y.: Doubleday & Company, Inc., 1963), pp. 24–25.

1. Working in a national park seems exciting in the first month or two, but by the third month the routine begins to drag.
2. Which is the way Sam and Jack felt about their jobs at the ToHa Trading Post in Yellowstone National Park.
3. Because they were tired of selling Indian Maiden Slipovers to fat, middle-aged women who were not Indians at all. Probably had never been maidens either.
4. Life, they felt, was becoming as monotonous as Old Faithful Geyser down the road.
5. Every day gawking tourists herded around by a forest ranger. Gathering around a hole in the ground.
6. They waited patiently for a huge spurt of water. To leap into the air.
7. Then they would exclaim "ooh" and "aah." And walk away with contented smiles under their sun glasses.
8. Sam and Jack watched group after group do the same thing, day after day.
9. One day the two boys decided. Either quit their jobs at the ToHa Trading Post or lose their sanity.
10. The fat, middle-aged women in Indian Maiden Slipovers were really beginning to look like Indians to them.
11. They definitely had to move on.
12. Though they could not resign from their jobs in the usual, routine manner.
13. Somehow shake up the monotony of the place before leaving.
14. They wanted to be remembered. After they were gone.
15. They hitting upon a plan.
16. Every day for a week, one or the other of them sneaked away

1. Working in a national park exciting in the first month or two, but by the third month, what a drag!
2. At least that was the way Sam and Jack felt about their jobs at the ToHa Trading Post in Yellowstone National Park.
3. They were tired of selling Indian Maiden Slipovers to fat, middle-aged women who were not Indians at all, and probably had never been maidens either.
4. Life, they felt, was becoming as monotonous. Like Old Faithful Geyser down the road.
5. Every day they watched herds of gawking tourists, guided by a forest ranger, gather around a hole in the ground.
6. They waited patiently for a huge spurt of water to leap into the air.
7. Then they would exclaim "ooh" and "aah," and walk away with contented smiles under their sun glasses.
8. Group after group the same thing, day after day.
9. One day the two boys decided that they either had to quit their jobs at the ToHa Trading Post or lose their sanity.
10. The fat, middle-aged women in Indian Maiden Slipovers beginning to look like real Indians to them.
11. Definitely had to move on.
12. They felt, though, that they could not resign from their jobs in the usual, routine manner.
13. Somehow they had to shake up the monotony of the place before leaving.
14. They wanted to be remembered after they were gone.
15. They hit upon a plan.
16. Every day for a week, one or the other of them sneaked away

from work whenever he could and went down to Old Faithful Geyser.

17. They took watches and carefully timed the rhythm of the geyser.
18. They got precise measurements on when the geyser erupted. And on how long the fountain of water remained gushing.
19. Determining to the second when the peak of water would begin to recede.
20. Then the two searching around for a wagon wheel.
21. They finally located one and concealed it near the geyser one night.
22. Now were completed.

23. The next morning they dressed as Indians—real Indians, not Hollywood Indians.
24. They dragged the wagon wheel near the site of the geyser and waited.
25. Before long a ranger brought a large group of tourists up to the geyser at about the time of its scheduled eruption.
26. He explained to them, in a speech Sam and Jack had heard a hundred times, that the "magnificent column of hot water and steam vapor" was named by Gen. Henry D. Washburn in 1870, that the eruptions last from two and a half to five minutes, and that 10,000 to 12,000 gallons of water are discharged to an average height of 150 feet.

27. Finally the ranger concluded, "It should be going off any minute now and you will witness one of the most amazing spectacles of Nature."
28. Sam, a little apart from the group, and Jack squatting near the wheel.
29. Sam watched the hand of his

from work whenever he could. And went down to Old Faithful Geyser.

17. They took watches. Carefully timing the rhythm of the geyser.
18. They got precise measurements on when the geyser erupted, and on how long the fountain of water remained gushing.
19. They determined to the second when the peak of water would recede.
20. Then the two searched around for a wagon wheel.
21. Finally located one and concealed it near the geyser one night.
22. Now their preparations were completed.

23. The next morning they dressed as Indians. Real Indians, not Hollywood Indians.
24. Dragged the wagon wheel near the site of the geyser and waited.
25. Before long a ranger brought a large group of tourists up to the geyser. At about the time of its scheduled eruption.
26. He explained to them, in a speech Sam and Jack had heard a hundred times. That the "magnificent column of hot water and steam vapor" was named by Gen. Henry D. Washburn in 1870, that the eruptions last from two and a half to five minutes, and that 10,000 to 12,000 gallons of water are discharged to an average height of 150 feet.

27. Finally the ranger concluded, "It should be going off any minute now and you will witness. One of the most amazing spectacles of Nature."
28. Sam was standing a little apart from the group, and Jack was squatting near the wheel.
29. Sam watched the hand of his

watch. He saw the moment was right.

30. "All right, Joe," he said, raising his hand in the air.
31. Everyone turning and looking at him curiously.
32. "Let her go!" he shouted and brought his hand down quickly.
33. Started turning the wheel furiously.
34. Just then the water began to spurt from the ground.
35. Jack kept turning the wheel and the water rose. Higher and higher.
36. Reached its peak and remained there.
37. All this time, Sam paying close attention to his watch.
38. The tourists completely confused. They looked at the geyser, then at Sam, then at Jack.
39. Again at the right moment. Sam shouted, "OK, Joe, shut her off!"
40. Jack turning the wheel in the reverse direction and the water started to recede.
41. Then there was dead silence.
42. The tourists looked at the hole in the ground, at Jack, at Sam. Then turned to the ranger.
43. Stared at him in cold anger.

44. A voice came out of the crowd and broke the awful silence: "You must think we're pretty stupid."
45. Then thirty tourists walked away. Left the forest ranger standing there alone.
46. Whether the deep red coloring of the ranger's face was due to embarrassment or anger, Sam and Jack never found out.
47. Not waiting around to ask.

48. The next afternoon the two boys took a Greyhound bus. Out of Yellowstone.
49. They jobless, but happy.

watch. Until he saw the moment was right.

30. "All right, Joe," he said. Raising his hand in the air.
31. Everyone turned and looked at him curiously.
32. "Let her go!" he shouted. And brought his hand down quickly.
33. Jack started turning the wheel furiously.
34. Just then the water from the ground.
35. Jack kept turning the wheel and the water rose higher and higher.
36. It reached its peak and remained there.
37. All this time, Sam was paying close attention to his watch.
38. The tourists, completely confused, looked at the geyser, then at Sam, then at Jack.
39. Again at the right moment, Sam shouted, "OK, Joe, shut her off!"
40. Jack started turning the wheel in the reverse direction; the water began to recede.
41. Then dead silence.
42. The tourists looked at the hole in the ground, at Jack, at Sam; then they turned to the ranger.
43. Thirty pairs of eyes stared at him in cold anger.

44. A voice out of the crowd and the awful silence: "You must think we're pretty stupid."
45. Then thirty tourists walked away and left the forest ranger standing there alone.
46. Whether the deep red coloring of the ranger's face embarrassment or anger. Sam and Jack never found out.
47. They had not waited around to ask.

48. The next afternoon the two boys took a Greyhound bus out of Yellowstone.
49. They were jobless, but happy.

V. PARALLELISM

> And so, my fellow Americans: ask not what your country can do
> for you—ask what you can do for your country.

This line from John Fitzgerald Kennedy's Inaugural Address of
January 20, 1961, has since become a famous one. What is the
reason for its popularity? First of all, it was spoken by a very popular
American. Also, the *way* the sentence is constructed contributes to its
powerful and enduring effect. In this example Kennedy employs *antithesis,* a form of parallelism in which the parallel elements contrast
with each other.

We find other examples of parallel structure in Kennedy's
speech:

> We observe today not a victory of party but a celebration of freedom—symbolizing an end as well as a beginning—signifying renewal
> as well as change. (parallel phrases each beginning with a participle)
>
> Let every nation know, whether it wishes us well or ill, that we
> shall pay any price, bear any burden, meet any hardship, support any
> friend, oppose any foe to assure the survival and the success of liberty.
> (parallel clauses each beginning with a verb)
>
> Let both sides explore what problems unite us instead of belaboring
> those problems which divide us. Let both sides, for the first time,
> formulate serious and precise proposals for the inspection and control
> of arms—and bring the absolute power to destroy other nations under
> the absolute control of all nations.
>
> Let both sides seek to invoke the wonders of science instead of
> its terrors. . . .
>
> Let both sides unite to heed in all corners of the earth the command
> of Isaiah—to "undo the heavy burdens . . . [and] let the oppressed
> go free." (parallel sentences)

We can use parallel construction in arranging words, phrases, clauses,
or sentences. Most effective public speakers and writers realize the
value of good parallel construction; it makes the prose more coherent
and forceful. Be especially careful that when you use parallel construction, you are certain to carry it out in each item of the series;
otherwise, you spoil the effect and puzzle the reader. Also, in working

out a parallel sequence you will want to repeat certain "pointer" or guiding words, such as prepositions, as a way of keeping things clear for the reader.

Examples:

> I came, I saw, I conquered.
>
> He is a bum, a drunk, and a good friend.
>
> He became first in his class by attending all the classes, by taking good notes, and by learning his lessons.
>
> We were all ranked together at the valuation. Men and women, old and young, married and single were ranked with horses, sheep, and swine. There were horses and men, cattle and women, pigs and children, all holding the same rank in the scale of being, and all subjected to the same narrow examination.[2]

EXERCISE

Examine the following sentences and paragraphs for errors of any kind.

1. He was a slim man about thirty years old with light brown skin and thought to be a good preacher.

2. Ben's job was working in the garden, feeding the chickens, and to keep the grass cut.

3. Mrs. Jones was said to be quite superstitious, and proved herself to be just that to me and all the other students, she didn't believe that there should be the presence of a waste paper can in her classroom, nor was there the presence of an eraser to erase the blackboard.

4. Most of the children didn't know who their father was, they were severely beaten and their living condition is poor.

5. He is critical of the school. The condition of the seats and the building itself is nothing but an old barn.

6. A good education should teach one to read critically, to write clearly, and speaking to one's fellow man.

7. She instilled within me the idea of traveling along in with the authors and try to share all their emotions, she instilled so much within me that I decided to read more books to see if I could really do such a thing and in the course of reading several books I found out that I really could travel with the author feel his emotion and inspiration.

---

[2] Frederick Douglass, *Narrative of the Life of Frederick Douglass* (Garden City, N.Y.: Doubleday & Company, Inc., 1963), pp. 47–48.

VI. MODIFIERS

The position of words or phrases in a sentence is extremely important. This is particularly true of *modifiers*—words, phrases, or clauses in a secondary relationship to other words or phrases which they help to limit or define. For example:

We should all be grateful to the boy who organized this dance.

The clause *who organized this dance* is a modifier that helps to define boy. According to the sentence, we should be grateful not to all the boys or to any boy, but to one particular boy, the one *who organized the dance*. Notice how much the meaning of the sentence changes if we shift the position of the modifier:

We who organized this dance should all be grateful to the boy.

A modifier should refer to a specific word or phrase in the sentence and it should be placed near the word or phrase it modifies. A *misplaced modifier* is one that is in the wrong position in its sentence, usually because it is not close to the word it modifies. A *dangling modifier* is one that does not refer clearly and logically to another word in the sentence. For example:

An anxious stranger in town, the crowd seemed overwhelming.

Here the modifier *an anxious stranger in town* seems to modify *crowd*. Of course it does not, but there is no other word in the sentence it could refer to. It should be rewritten and made clearer:

An anxious stranger in town, I felt overwhelmed by the crowd.

Here *an anxious stranger in town* clearly and logically refers to *I*.

EXERCISE A

In the examples below, rewrite the sentence (a) so that it correctly contains the modifier (b):

1. (a) The party was held in the main ballroom.
   (b) which everyone attended

2. (a) He performed extremely well in the game against the Baltimore Colts.
   (b) as left end

3. (a) The author claims that the British almost defeated the Americans in the War of 1812.
   (b) in the first chapter of his book

4. (a) I drove my car to school Monday.
   (b) which I bought just last week

5. (a) Rick was the only one who came to visit him at the hospital.
   (b) of all his many friends

6. (a) The runner fell down just before the wire.
   (b) who was leading

7. (a) The mongrel dog won the affection of all of us.
   (b) with the long, floppy ears

8. (a) I was told that you had been awarded a varsity letter in basketball.
   (b) by your mother

9. (a) Jack decided to try out for the college football team.
   (b) after considering his chances

10. (a) The picture was painted by a famous artist.
    (b) which is hanging in the hall

EXERCISE B

In the examples below, you are given a modifier and a choice of two main clauses. In each case, write a complete sentence, using the modifier and the correct main clause:

1. Arriving five minutes late,
   (a) we missed the first scene of the movie.
   (b) the first scene of the movie was over.

2. With her big, brown eyes,
   (a) we all loved her.
   (b) she was the most beautiful girl in the room.

3. Alone in the middle of the dance floor,
   (a) the music caught up the couple in its rhythm.
   (b) the couple was caught up in the rhythm of the music.

4. Wishing him well,
   (a) I shook hands with John before he got aboard the train.
   (b) John shook hands with me and got aboard the train.

5. Believing that what she said was true,

     (a) she convinced Lou that his friends were angry with him.

     (b) Lou was convinced that his friends were angry with him.

6. Running down to the store as soon as she heard of the sale,

     (a) Sally found amazing bargains everywhere.

     (b) there were amazing bargains everywhere.

7. Outside the room at the time.

     (a) the voices of the women inside could still be heard by us.

     (b) we could still hear the voices of the women inside.

8. Too tired even to eat,

     (a) Jack took Sam's suitcase and showed him where he could take a nap.

     (b) Sam gave Jack his suitcase and asked if he might take a nap.

EXERCISE C

Below are examples of modifiers that are awkwardly placed in the middle of the sentence. Rewrite the sentences so that they read more smoothly:

1. John ought to, if he wants to get a good grade, spend much more time studying.
2. Lou and I after mother finally came home went to the movies.
3. I intend to as quickly as possible run to the drugstore and back again.
4. Joe had with fists hard as iron hit his opponent again and again.
5. If you are today or tomorrow going to Al's house, will you give him a message for me?
6. I am if my parents let me driving to Sanford next Saturday.
7. Sally told Mary and Ellen to as quickly as possible write to the others.
8. Jane will not because she is being punished by her parents be going to the dance next Saturday.
9. The boys wanted to without much expense repair their old Ford.
10. We will if you are not too late take you along.

VII. SENTENCE VARIETY

Compare the following paragraphs:

A.   Colonel Lloyd kept a large and finely cultivated garden. He needed four men to work in it. He also needed a chief gardener. This man was called Mr. M'Durmond. The garden was probably the greatest attraction of the place. People came from far and near to see it during the summer months. They came from Baltimore. They came from Easton and Annapolis. It abounded in fruits of every description. It had the hardy apple from the north. It also had the delicate orange of the south. The garden was not the least source of trouble on the plantation. Its fruit was a temptation to the boys. It was also a temptation to the older slaves. These people could not resist the temptation. These slaves were beaten for stealing fruit. This happened every day in the summer. The colonel tried to keep the slaves away. He tarred his fence all around. The slave caught with tar on him would be beaten. The colonel figured the tar showed the slave was in the garden. The colonel's plan worked very well. The slaves avoided the tar. They realized they would be beaten if they got tar on them.

——— .   ——————————————— .   ———————————

—— .   ————————————————————————— .

B.   Colonel Lloyd kept a large and finely cultivated garden, which afforded almost constant employment for four men, besides the chief gardener (Mr. M'Durmond). This garden was probably the greatest attraction of the place. During the summer months, people came from far and near—from Baltimore, Easton, and Annapolis—to see it. It abounded in fruits of almost every description, from the hardy apple of the north to the delicate orange of the south. The garden was not the least source of trouble on the plantation. Its excellent fruit was quite a temptation to the hungry swarms of boys, as well as the older slaves, belonging to the colonel, few of whom had the virtue or the vice to resist it. Scarcely a day passed, during the summer, but that some slave had to take the lash for stealing fruit. The colonel had to resort to all kinds of stratagems to keep his slaves out of the garden. The last and most successful one was that of tarring his fence all around; after which, if a slave was caught with any tar upon his person, it was deemed sufficient proof that he had either been into the garden, or had tried to get in. In either case, he was severely whipped by the chief gardener. This plan worked well; the slaves became as fearful of tar as of the lash. They seemed to realize the impossibility of touching tar without being defiled.[1]

—————————————————— , ———

————————————————— , ———————

——— (—————). ————————————

————————— . ———————— , ———————

—————— — —————— , ————— , ———————— — ———— .

——————————————— , ————————

——————————————— . ————————

————————————————— . ————————

[1] Frederick Douglass, *Narrative of the Life of Frederick Douglass* (Garden City, N.Y.: Doubleday & Company, Inc., 1963), p. 17.

————————————————————————, ——————

——, ———————————, ——————————

—————————. —————————, ——————, ——

——————————————————————. ————

—————————————————————————————.

——————————————————————————

——; ————, ————————————————

——, ————————————————————————

——————, —————————. ————, ——————————

——————————————. ——————; ————

——————————————. —————————————

————————————————.

The punctuation diagram is one way of indicating the structure of the individual sentences in each paragraph. Notice how paragraph A is monotonous and boringly uniform with its series of simple sentences, all of them about the same length. Paragraph B, however, avoids this machine-gun effect by using a variety of sentence structures. The diagrams suggest these differences.

Always remember that you have at your disposal three basic kinds of sentences:

1. SIMPLE SENTENCE.   The simple sentence consists of just one independent clause and no other clauses, though it may have a number of phrases. Example:

The slaves avoided the tar.

2. COMPOUND SENTENCE.   The compound sentence is made up of two or more simple sentences (or independent clauses) joined together to make one sentence. The reason for making up a compound sentence, rather than a number of simple sentences, is ordinarily to

make the prose smoother and less jumpy, and to show that the ideas in the different clauses are closely related, and are of equal importance. Ordinarily the main parts of a compound sentence are joined in one or two ways: by a comma plus a conjunction (and, but, or, nor); or by a semicolon. Example:

> He was said to own a thousand slaves, and I think the estimate well within the truth.
> This plan worked well; the slaves became as fearful of tar as of the lash.

3. COMPLEX SENTENCE. The complex sentence is made up of one independent clause and one or more dependent (subordinate) clauses. A writer uses a complex sentence when he has two ideas to express and he wants to:

(a) put them in the same sentence;
(b) show that one is more important than the other;
(c) show exactly how the two ideas are related to each other.

For example, take the following two ideas expressed in two sample sentences:

> Frederick Douglass became a great Negro leader. He was born a slave.

Here are three different complex sentences connecting these two ideas. Identify the main idea being stressed in each sentence. How do you know it is the main idea?

(a) Frederick Douglass, who was born a slave, became a great Negro leader.
(b) Frederick Douglass, who became a great Negro leader, was born a slave.
(c) Although Frederick Douglass was born a slave, he became a great Negro leader.

We have available to us three basic kinds of sentences—simple, compound, and complex—upon which we can build a number of variations for arranging our ideas.

> SIMPLE: Bill Demby refused to come out of the water. Mr. Gore shot him.

COMPOUND: Bill Demby refused to come out of the water, and Mr. Gore shot him.

Bill Demby refused to come out of the water; (so) Mr. Gore shot him.

COMPLEX: When (or because) Bill Demby refused to come out of the water, Mr. Gore shot him.

Here are some additional hints for adding variety to your sentences:

1. WORD ORDER.   Important ideas should be placed at the beginning and end of the sentence. Do not waste these positions on weak or unimportant words or ideas.

Scarcely a day passed but that some slave had to take the lash for stealing fruit during the summer.
Scarcely a day passed, during the summer, but that some slave had to take the lash for stealing fruit.

2. LOOSE AND PERIODIC SENTENCES.   In the periodic sentence the main idea is not complete until the end of the sentence. In the loose sentence the main idea comes at the beginning, and the rest of the sentence adds particulars. Though lacking the suspense of the periodic sentence, the loose sentence communicates the main idea early.

LOOSE: Colonel Lloyd kept a large and finely cultivated garden, which afforded almost constant employment for four men, besides the chief gardener (Mr. M'Durmond).

PERIODIC: During the summer months, people came from far and near—from Baltimore, Easton, and Annapolis—to see it.

3. PARALLEL CONSTRUCTION.   (See Chapter V, p. 231.) Notice how parallel structure makes the following selection smoother and more correct:

People came from far and near to see it during the summer months. They came from Baltimore. They came from Easton and Annapolis.
During the summer months, people came from far and near—*from Baltimore, Easton, and Annapolis*—to see it.

4. TRANSITION WORDS AND PHRASES.   (See Chapter IX, p. 245.)

In either case, he was severely whipped by the chief gardener.

5. PRONOUNS AS CONNECTING WORDS. (See Chapter VIII below.)

The garden was not the least source of trouble on the plantation. *Its* excellent fruit was quite a temptation to the hungry swarms of boys. . . .

EXERCISE

Apply these various ideas to the following selections. Do a punctuation diagram of the sentence patterns to justify possible corrections.

(A)   The most common sense I like is hearing. I like to listen to modern jazz. I try to find the mood in different jazz artists. Jazz has a sound to relax me. Jazz today has that groove sound most people like. It's a sound that is hard to express. Jazz is pleasing to me.

(B)   Harry is a character of great complexity. He has good characteristics as well as bad. He is a self-made man who worked hard to acquire his wealth. He can be admired for his desire to better himself. Harry is a mild mannered, friendly man. He is always willing to entertain others. His irrational manner of thinking is his chief downfall. He loves the past. This is his destruction. He emphasizes materialism too much. This is his major drawback in life.

(C)   I attended a very strict high school. I had few dates there for four years. I came to college. One day I got enough courage to ask Mary out for a date. She accepted my offer. I now feel great. I am going out now much more. I get better grades for two basic reasons. I no longer sit around feeling miserable about not dating. I am more relaxed. I have even stopped chewing on the ends of pens.

VIII. POINT OF VIEW

To make your writing as clear as possible, maintain a consistent and logical point of view throughout your essay. Avoid shifting needlessly from *he* to *you* to *we* to *they*. This does not mean that once you use a pronoun you can only use that same pronoun for the remainder of your paper. The point is never to shift a pronoun reference without a logical reason. For example:

> Many young people who live in cities frequently go to movies. They may see as many as one film a week. You know you like to see your favorite stars whenever you get the chance.

There is no good reason here for shifting suddenly from the third person to the second person pronoun (*they* to *you*). There are instances, however, when a shift is logical or even necessary:

> Many of the college students refused to make the compromise. I was one who felt this way. I thought that as a student I could reasonably expect more from the university than just so many hours of class lectures.

The shift here from the third person to the first person is justified. The writer moves from a general statement to a concrete illustration, with himself as the example. This shift in point of view is not a careless but a purposeful one.

Avoid careless shifting in verb tense too. For example, do not move back and forth between present and past tense without cause. Whenever you shift verb tense—from present to future or present to past—make certain that there is a good reason for doing so.

Below are two exercises dealing with point of view. When you have a choice of words or phrases to use, draw a line through those you do not want. The purpose is not to avoid completely pronoun and verb tense shifts, but to be consistent and, where you do shift, to have a good reason for doing so.

A. A man must develop the ability to think for himself. $\begin{bmatrix} \text{You} \\ \text{They} \\ \text{He} \end{bmatrix}$ should not rely on others to make the important decisions of $\begin{bmatrix} \text{your} \\ \text{their} \\ \text{his} \end{bmatrix}$ life for $\begin{bmatrix} \text{you} \\ \text{them} \\ \text{him} \end{bmatrix}$ Many $\begin{bmatrix} \text{people} \\ \text{of us} \end{bmatrix}$ would probably agree with this assertion, and yet $\begin{bmatrix} \text{they} \\ \text{we} \\ \text{he} \end{bmatrix}$ do not act in $\begin{bmatrix} \text{their} \\ \text{his} \\ \text{our} \end{bmatrix}$ personal lives as if $\begin{bmatrix} \text{they} \\ \text{he} \\ \text{we} \end{bmatrix}$ do. Actually, $\begin{bmatrix} \text{they} \\ \text{he} \\ \text{we} \end{bmatrix}$ frequently depend on others to decide the style of clothes [they/he/we] wear, the places [they/he/we] go to for entertainment, the people [they/he/we] have as friends.

John, for example, is a boy who considers himself an independent thinker. Yet [their/his/our] clothes are identical in style to those worn by [their/his/your] friends Jim, Bob, and Lou. [They/He/We] also enjoys the same music [they/he/we] do; [their/his/your] favorite popular songs also happen to be [their/his/our] favorite songs. Everything [they/he/you] do, [they/he/we] does with them.

One summer, while visiting some relatives in another city, John meets a girl named Sue, whom [they/he/we] likes very much. They date frequently for about three months. At the end of the summer, when John returns home, [he/she/you] is very sad at having to leave Sue and begins to think of ways in which [he/she/it] might make their relationship more secure.

Back at home, [he/she/they] shows a picture of Sue to his friends. [He/They/We] is surprised when [they/he/she] are unimpressed by [their/his/her] looks. [They/He/She] tell John not to waste [their/his/your] time with [them/it/her]. John begins to think over [their/his/her] reactions to [their/his/your] girl friend, and after a week or two he himself doubts that [they/he/you] really cares for Sue. After a month, [they/he/she] writes to [them/him/her] to break off [their/his/her] relationship. [You/John/They] starts out letting [their/his/your] friends make "little" decisions for [them/him/you], and before too long [they/he/you] is depending on them to make all [their/his/your] decisions for [them/him/you].

Though most [people/of us/of you] admire independent thinking in theory, [they/we/you] rarely practice it, even in making important decisions in [their/our/your] lives.

B. Human beings [expected/expect/will expect] far too much from life. They [expected/expect/will expect] too much from themselves, and they [overestimated/overestimate/will overestimate] their natural abilities, their courage, and their determination. They [wanted/want/will want] too much from common experiences. They [thought/think/will think] true love is a combination of intense and constant passion, deep happiness, and permanent security, and they [thought/think/will think] that everyone has a right to expect all of this. They [looked/look/will look] for a life filled with wealth and fame that [matched/matches/will match] their wildest dreams.

Alexander the Great, for example, [sat down/sits down/will sit down] and [wept/weeps/will weep] when he [was told/is told/will be told] that his armies [had conquered/are conquering/will conquer] the known world and there $\begin{bmatrix} \text{were} \\ \text{are} \\ \text{will be} \end{bmatrix}$ no more lands to subjugate. Napoleon $\begin{bmatrix} \text{destroyed} \\ \text{destroys} \\ \text{will destroy} \end{bmatrix}$ himself because he $\begin{bmatrix} \text{tried} \\ \text{tries} \\ \text{will try} \end{bmatrix}$ to extend his empire too far. Today we $\begin{bmatrix} \text{saw} \\ \text{see} \\ \text{will see} \end{bmatrix}$ movie stars marry as many as seven or eight times in their search for a "perfect" wife or husband. Even the most beautiful and the most gifted people $\begin{bmatrix} \text{asked} \\ \text{ask} \\ \text{will ask} \end{bmatrix}$ more from life than it can give them.

Will people of the future be any different? $\begin{bmatrix} \text{Did} \\ \text{Do} \\ \text{Will} \end{bmatrix}$ men ever set limits on their dreams and desires? It $\begin{bmatrix} \text{was} \\ \text{is} \\ \text{will be} \end{bmatrix}$ unlikely. People $\begin{bmatrix} \text{always looked} \\ \text{always look} \\ \text{will always look} \end{bmatrix}$ beyond what they $\begin{bmatrix} \text{had} \\ \text{have} \end{bmatrix}$ to what they $\begin{bmatrix} \text{did not have} \\ \text{do not have} \end{bmatrix}$. Because of this, men $\begin{bmatrix} \text{always struggled} \\ \text{always struggle} \\ \text{will always struggle} \end{bmatrix}$ to new achievements and new successes, but they $\begin{bmatrix} \text{were always} \\ \text{are always} \\ \text{will always be} \end{bmatrix}$ searching for more.

IX. TRANSITIONS

One way to give your sentences some variety and to increase the general coherence of your paragraphs is to use proper transitions. These are connectors which serve as links between sentences and paragraphs. They help the reader keep the order of your sentences. For instance, observe the simple but effective use of connectors in the following paragraph:

There are roughly three New Yorks. There is, first, the New York of the man or woman who was born here, who takes the city for granted and accepts its size and its turbulence as natural and inevitable. Second, there is the New York of the commuter—the city that is devoured by locusts each day and spat out each night. Third, there is the New York of the person who was born somewhere else and came to New York in quest of something.[1]

Here the use of "first," "second," and "third" help link one sentence to another while also establishing the division of subjects that the remainder of the essay will follow.

There are, of course, a variety of transition words and phrases. We suggest a few here. But always remember that your use of them depends on the particular sentence and paragraph.

A. Words and phrases to present contrast or express another view:

however	yet	otherwise
still	in contrast	on the contrary
even so	nevertheless	in spite of that
on the other hand	but	unlike

B. To express comparison or a similar development of ideas:

for example	namely	moreover
in fact	that is	likewise
furthermore	in the same way	similarly
in addition	besides	also

C. To express a result of summary:

as a result	consequently	so
therefore	in summary	after all
thus	because	hence
since	in short	in conclusion

D. Others:

as I have indicated	meanwhile	of course
second, third, etc.	in addition	finally

EXERCISES

A. Insert the proper connectors in the following blank spaces:

My home town is Birmingham, Alabama. It is the second largest industrial city in the United States. There are many steel mills in Birmingham. _____, it is the largest city in Alabama.

---

[1] E. B. White, "Here Is New York," *Holiday*. Copyright © 1949 by the Curtis Publishing Company. Reprinted by permission of *Holiday*.

_____ being the largest city and leading industrial center, Birmingham offers many sources of entertainment. _____, there is the municipal auditorium. Here one can see the great music groups. _____ the Academy of Music, which plays only classical sounds, the auditorium features Blues and Rock. _____, Ray Charles was there just the other night. Legion Field is another good place. Here we can see a variety of football games. Last week, _____, the Baltimore Colts were there for an exhibition game. _____, the stadium was filled to capacity. _____, there are a number of entertainment spots such as the Inn Club, the 401 Club, and many others.

_____, Birmingham offers major industry, music centers, good athletic facilities, and fine entertainment spots. _____ you can see why I like my city.

B. Assemble the following groups of sentences into logical, clear paragraphs. Use transitions where needed:

1. Every girl hopes and dreams about what she will become in her adult life. I have my hopes and dreams. I hope to become well educated. I do not want to be dependent upon others. I want to go to a good school. I want to marry a handsome young man. We will work hard together. We will own a beautiful house. I hope to have children. I want four of them. I want two boys and two girls. I guess my hopes and dreams are similar to every girl's.

2. My summer job was a good one. I worked at the Imperial Tobacco Company. The job influenced my knowledge of people. I learned a person can go through high school and never really meet people. I had friends in high school. At work a group of people must cooperate to get the job done. One must compromise to work with others. It is bad to work with someone you dislike. It is up to the individual to get along with his associates. A business man must make an impression on the public. I did not work with the public. I can understand the importance of a good impression. Work is tough if no one likes you and you are always by yourself. You only reap what you sow. A friendly smile and warm greeting can have its rewards.

3. I will marry a nice young man. I plan to major in Elementary Education. Paris must be beautiful. I want ten children. I will go to Smithfield College in September. It is summer now. I want to go to New York, California, Chicago, and Paris. We would first

buy our home. I would like to attend summer school every year. I really love children. I would like to see these cities and the people that live there. High school was fun. My friends say that college work is somewhat harder. I like to teach children. These are my plans. I want to travel around the world. We would first buy our own home and car.

X. ABUSE OF VERBS

The beauty of April mornings are something to behold.
Make certain you keeps me in cash.
Verbs has to agree with their subjects.

These sentences may sound all right, but the verb forms are nonetheless incorrect as written. If you are going to deal with these problems you must at least be aware of the basic rules for verbs. You have encountered these rules before. We here review the most important ones. Refer to them often when correcting your own writing.

A *verb* is a part of speech which denotes action (he *runs,* she *walks,* it *jumped*). A few verbs show state of being rather than action. These are usually forms of *to be* and are called copulative verbs (he *is* in the room).

The general characteristics of verbs are:

1. VOICE: ACTIVE AND PASSIVE.   In the active voice, the subject does the acting; in the passive voice, the subject is acted upon.

Active: Mike visited the United Nations.
Passive: The United Nations was visited by Mike.

2. TENSE: indicating the time of action.

PRESENT: He studies. (Action taking place now)
PAST: He studied.
(Action completed in the past)
FUTURE: He will study.
(Action will be completed in the future)
PRESENT PERFECT: He has studied very hard.
(Action begun in past and continuing to present)

PAST PERFECT: He had studied for a week.
(Action completed sometime in the past)
FUTURE PERFECT: He will have studied before next week.
(Action will have been completed at some time in the future.)

3. MOOD: the form of the verb that indicates the way or manner in which the action or state of being comes about.

INDICATIVE MOOD: (states a fact or asks a question):
Has John gone?
John has gone.
IMPERATIVE MOOD: (gives a command):
Leave this bus immediately.
SUBJUNCTIVE MOOD: (expresses wishes and conditions contrary to fact):
I wish he were here.
If I were you, I would leave him alone.
(Notice that in the subjunctive mood, active voice, you use the past indicative plural, even if the subject is singular.)

4. PARTICIPLE: a form of the verb, but by itself does not act as a verb. It requires an auxiliary (am, have) to make it into a verb. It also functions as an adjective. It forms its present by adding *-ing* and its past by adding *-d* or *-ed*.

	Participle as Adjective	*As Verb*
PRESENT:	Seeing me, he ran away. ("Seeing" modifies he.)	He was seeing me for the first time. (Present participle, part of predicate)
PAST:	The surrounded soldiers formed barricades against the Indians. (Past participle modifies "soldiers.")	The Indians have surrounded the soldiers. (Past participle, part of predicate)

5. PRINCIPAL PARTS: must be known, since they allow us to make up all forms of the verb. The principal parts include

(a) the present infinitive (*study*),
(b) the simple past form (*studied*),
(c) the past participle (*studied*).

Present Indicative	*Past Indicative*	*Past Participle*
I *study* now.	I *studied* yesterday.	I have *studied* often.
love	loved	loved
act	acted	acted
know	knew	known

You probably notice that *know* forms its principal parts differently. This is because it is an irregular verb, whose principal parts you must check in the dictionary or memorize. The following list provides a handy reference list of the most common irregular verbs:

Present	*Past*	*Past Participle*	*Present*	*Past*	*Past Participle*
arise	arose	(have) arisen	lay	laid	(have) laid
beat	beat	beaten	lead	led	led
become	became	become	lie	lay	lain
begin	began	begun	lose	lost	lost
break	broke	broken	make	made	made
bring	brought	brought	pay	paid	paid
buy	bought	bought	ride	rode	ridden
catch	caught	caught	rise	rose	risen
choose	chose	chosen	run	ran	run
come	came	come	say	said	said
do	did	done	see	saw	seen
drink	drank	drunk, drunken	send	sent	sent
			sing	sang	sung
drive	drove	driven	sit	sat	sat
eat	ate	eaten	speak	spoke	spoken
fall	fell	fallen	spring	sprang, sprung	sprung
fight	fought	fought			
flee	fled	fled	stand	stood	stood
fly	flew	flown	steal	stole	stolen
get	got	got, gotten	swim	swam	swum
			take	took	taken
give	gave	given	teach	taught	taught
go	went	gone	tear	tore	torn
grow	grew	grown	throw	threw	thrown
hold	held	held	wear	wore	worn
keep	kept	kept	write	wrote	written
know	knew	known			

If in doubt about the principal parts check your dictionary. It lists all verbs under the present form (the first of the three principal parts). It lists all irregular verbs with the past tense, the past participle, and the present participle (*know, knew, known, knowing*).

6. PERSON: changes in the form of verbs and pronouns to indicate if the "person" is the speaker (first person), the one spoken to (second person), or the one spoken about (third person).

NUMBER: change in the form of a word to denote one (singular) or more than one (plural).

PRESENT TENSE

	Singular	Plural
1st per.	I love	we love
2nd per.	you love	you love
3rd per.	he, she, it loves	they love

PAST TENSE

	Singular	Plural
1st per.	I loved	we loved
2nd per.	you loved	you loved
3rd per.	he, she, it loved	they loved

Such a grouping of verb forms is called a *conjugation*. Notice that in regular verbs such as *love,* just one form (the third person singular of the present tense) adds an *s* to indicate the person and number of the subject.

Always make certain that the verb agrees in number with the subject.

> WRONG: The *girls* (plural subject) *loves* (singular verb) their records.
>
> CORRECT: The *girls love* (third person plural of the present tense) their records.

7. INFINITIVE FORM: the first of the three principal parts of a verb. When used as a noun, adjective, or adverb, it is generally preceded by the word *to*.

> The boys like *to swim.* (infinitive as adverb)
>
> The game *to play* is basketball. (infinitive as adjective)
>
> *To win* in the lottery is not easy. (infinitive as noun)

8. GERUND FORM: a gerund is an *ing* form of a verb which functions as a noun in a sentence.

Swimming is a good sport.

Jogging can be fun.

Examine the following sentences to see if you can detect any errors in verb form:

1. They are very neatly dress, but both persons represents his or her occupation.
2. The fool in me said that gun ain't loading.
3. My surrounding friends has taught me a lot. They taught me that wrong doings isn't good. Many of the boys in the community has been placed in jail.
4. She has help me to understand English.
5. Mrs. Walker is a stern person who never get tired of working. She boss Mr. Walker around and she tell him what to do.
6. My ideal high school would be a high school that offer its students requirements for a good education. It also have modern facilities for their educational and social needs.
7. Being a student I have learn the importance of education.
8. You said that we should be concern about our future.
9. The harder I try to understand English the worse I get until Mrs. Smith became my English teacher.
10. These are the most important things that he talk about.
11. She have a day such as Friday when we could chosen what our assignment would be.
12. Your talk will help many students who were undeciden about continuing.
13. You mostly was talking to us. You ask why we want to go to college. And then you told us not to be scare of the draft.
14. This made me aware of the fact that I'm not settle for passing.
15. We is certain of victory today.

Student Papers

4

You have studied the *Mechanics of Style and Essay Development* sections and, hopefully, have learned how to deal with a variety of writing problems. Examine the following papers to see if you can apply what you have learned.

A.   *Kinds of Bores*

When one thinks of a bore, most of us think of a person or persons they have known who have boring personalities. Who is boring? Most bores can be summarized into three categories: something uninteresting, a person very tedious to the point of complete frustration, or something annoying. Lets try to analyze these three types of bores with relation to the types of people that go with them.

First, there is Mr. X. Mr. X is usually well-liked by everyone. He has very few faults that detract from his person, he gets along with people, likes people, and people like him. All this is true until he opens his mouth. He tells you that your best friend has stopped dating the girl he has gone steady with for two years. Of course, all this is very interesting to someone who has never heard it. It's just that you heard it a week ago and know the story in every detail yourself. Mr. X always means to say something interesting, but either his timing is off or he is unclear in trying to get the subject across to you.

Next, there is Mr. Y. Mr. Y is a know-it-all. If you ask him what the body temperature of duck-billed platypus is, he will know that and its life history besides. To a stranger or new acquaintance Mr. Y may appear to be a very interesting person. But this impression soon wears off after long being bombarded by countless bits of his endless range of information.

Last of all, there is Mr. Z. Mr. Z is a loudmouth or a pest. Everyone must have known one of them at least once in their life. He doesn't carry with him the air of intelligence that Mr. Y does. He is marked by his loud tone of voice and friendly attitude toward almost everyone. He is the guy that comes right up to you in a church meeting and asks you in a loud voice if you like the bottle of wine he sent you for your birthday. Always friendly in this way, we try to avoid him.

All of these people represent a type of person that can be easily associated with one of your personal experience. Each of these people represent a type of bore when the word "bore" is considered a person.

B.   *The Word Cool*

Adults often think of words as they have been thought of traditionally. The word "cool" is often taken as meaning something cold. However, when a teenager uses this term, he describes a person's or object's popularity. Granted that a person described as "cool" often possesses an air of coolness or collectiveness, but these traits alone do not make a person "cool." A boy may be cool because of his attire, his speech, his way of dancing, or his new car. A girl, on the other hand, is cool by dressing fashionably, talking fashionably, or by acting permissively and fashionably. As you can see, "coolness" is something which must be sought, not obviously sought after. Many times, while seeking coolness, the individual is trapped by society to do things to its liking and its moral code. You must sacrifice part of yourself in order to gain coolness or popularity. Therefore, do not judge a man or a woman, as some do even for marriage, by the coolness or lack of coolness which that person possesses.

Definition of "Cool"

Contemporary word definitions have acquired a most flexible degree of meaning to the extent that Mr. Webster would begin to wonder if such a word existed in his beloved English language. Such is the case with the ever-prevealent word "cool." A connotation of pseudo-sophistication, of trying to be something one is not, is my meaning of this trite word. The common cliché of Joe Cool supports this explanation. The person wearing modern clothes, associating with the in-crowd, knowing the places to go. One can go on and on. But once again, all contemporary definitions have that flexibility. Many definitions of this word are found on the other side of the fence. Coolness is pleasing in certain situations. This seems like a contradiction of terms, but it is merely a contemporary characteristic. A cool party, a cool idea, a cool kid, all expressions denoting an air of easygoing and pleasant surroundings. Words are many things to many varieties of people. Today individuals assign their own definitions to expressions, so that one must equate the individual with a word before concluding the meaning, which may be still arbitrary.

C. *Richard Cory*

In reading the poem "Richard Cory," I let my imagination take over and this is the result of the poem as I saw it.

Richard Cory was a wealthy man and in the sight of the small townspeople he was a king. The people probably were under the impression that money was everything and that money could buy everything. Doubtless, they respected Richard for his riches, but at the same time they were very envious.

Being well educated is not enough either a man has to be able to feel as well as think but he couldn't do this, not in a town this size.

They were so blinded by the wealth that they fail to realize that money can't buy everything. Money can't buy happiness or that inner peace or even love.

A good education is no good unless one is given a chance to put them to use. And finding no peace, and torn between life and death, Mr. Cory's only solution was suicide.

The Character of Richard Cory

In the poem "Richard Cory," the character Richard Cory seemed to have been a very intelligent man.

He was described as being a man of grace and a gentleman. He was also rich.

In the last line of the poem Richard went home and put a bullet through his head.

My explanation for his doing this is that no matter how rich or pleasant a man is or looks he may still be dissatisfied inside. Money is not everything.

I believe that he wanted to be friends with the people instead of them looking up to him.

D.   *Machines of Death—or Life?*

"The War Against the Trees" is a descriptive poem in which the poet, Stanley Kunitz, is critical of the destruction of nature by man and his machines. He compares this annihilation to the horrors of war by creating the atmosphere of a battle. This war imagery is accomplished by the appeal to hearing in lines such as the "hireling engines charged the trees." Kunitz also uses personification to arouse pity in the reader when he says that nature is completely defenseless to "forsythia-forays and hydrangea raids." The trees, or "great-grandfathers of the town," reminds the author of his childhood and how he had played in these woods. Now the enemy was attacking his "green world" and forcing his memories "into the suburbs of their grievous age."

The language employed by the poet is very concrete and conventional. The use of modern terms gives us an overall sense of industry and progress. We can almost smell the gasoline and hear the huge bulldozers. There are many key words which are immediately apparent: "overthrowing," "maimed," "charged," "struck," and "ripped." This recurrence of destructive terms is effective in portraying to the reader the evils of the industrial world.

The main idea of the whole poem is the conflict between romanticism and reality. The poet is attempting to show us that man's mercenary nature overshadows his appreciation for beauty. A man "sold his lawn to standard oil" and then "joked with his neighbors." It seems that Kunitz overdoes his love for nature, almost to the point of the absurd. For someone who is so engrossed in the beauty of nature, he appears to have forgotten that man is also a part of nature. He sees modern construction only as a destructive force, whereas much good can be produced from this. The building of hospitals, schools, and even industrial parks has to be more beneficial than the feeling one gets while viewing a beautiful landscape.

E. *Education First*

The decisions of my life are to further my education, to find a job, and then I would like some day to get married.

The main decision is to further my education. I have decided to attend Smithfield College for a year and for the next four years to attend Carter University. I hope to major in Business Administration and minor in Elementary Education. I also plan to do my graduate work at Carter.

Upon receiving my diploma, I hope to find a job as a private secretary. I have decided to work at least one year, and no longer than three years. I am not certain yet where I will work. I hope to work close to home. I want to be close to my mother and father. I might then work at the local newspaper office.

After finishing college and work I plan to marry, but at the moment I do not know who the lucky man will be. I would also like to live in my own home and be the mother of a set of twins.

F. *Cool Action*

"Cool" has two meanings one describes the temperature of the atmosphere, however, we are concerned with the more colloquial aspect of the word. "Cool," in this sense, has a definite and important meaning it can describe the mood of a crowd or the atmosphere of a riot. To the young adult, however, the primary meaning is that it describes a personality trait. For a person to be "cool" he has the gift of accepting problems as they come and the ability to handel them sufficently. Consider a person who has been stopped by a policeman for speeding he is now confronted with a problem. He does not become excited or nervous but simply dreams up a plausible excuse and gets away free. This is real "cool."

G.   *New Experience*

This summer, I left my sheltered home life and had my first experience with the business world. This job not only has helped me get
through my first year at college; it has also given me many valuable
experiences. I discovered some of the characteristics of a good business man. I would like to introduce to you my two individuals, Mr. X
and Mr. Y, who will help me back up this statement.

Mr. X and Mr. Y are two college boys earning some money for
college expenses. Both have the same responsibilities and authority.
Their first job is to manage the cashiers at a supermarket. The job
gets done by both and for this they are highly thought of by the
management.

Mr. X is quite nasty at times, especially when things aren't going
his way. For this, he shows his immaturity and isn't well liked by the
cashiers.

Mr. Y is always pleasant. His spirit is transmitted to us and the
atmosphere is good. He works with us and there isn't a definite tension as there is with Mr. X.

Mr. Y will succeed in business because he is more mature, while
Mr. X will always be considered immature for his changing moods.

H.   *Smooth or Fast?*

Since dissimilarities of style seem to outnumber the similarities
within a given sport, everyone is able to find his particular aspect. The
popular winter sport of ice skating, or the movement of two metal
blades on ice, can be approached in either of two ways. For those
who are patient and graceful, figure skating may be undertaken. The
skater is concerned with rhythm and coordination in all of his movements. The ease of the actions performed is the final product of many
long hours spent in order to accomplish a perfect action. Time becomes an important element in the split-second performances of the
acquired skills. For those who are not as flexible or seem to be a second too slow or too fast, there is the other aspect of speed skating. The
objective of this skater, to reach a certain destination before his opponents, is fulfilled after many long hours of practice, but he is con-

cerned not with acquiring his goal at a given time, but rather pushing ahead and performing in less time. While skating, he does not move with the grace of a figure skater, although a certain amount of grace is required to stay on top of the ice. His main objective is speed, and he moves with a rhythm pertaining to speed. Both the figure skater and speed skater share a love for the ice, but they utilize different methods to fulfill this love.

I.   *Teaching Styles*

Each teacher has a particular approach to his subject through which he imparts to his students a definite like or dislike of the subject. Good examples are my chemistry and biology instructors. The former makes mimeographs of her lecture notes and distributes them in advance. The students are able to review them and be prepared for the following lectures. Once the individual student is at the lecture, he need only note those concepts which he does not understand.

On the other hand, my biology instructor requires each student to copy all his notes from the projected screen. At the same time one is also supposed to listen to her explanations. It has come to a point where the students no longer listen to the lecture at all; they want to finish copying one page of notes before she switches to another. Because of these differences in approaches, I prefer attending a chemistry lecture to a biology lecture, even though I find the subject matter of the former more difficult than that of the latter.

J.   *The Perfect School*

The perfect school of my choice must meet several qualifications. The school must: (1) not be too far from home, (2) must have good accreditation, (3) must have strict (but not too strict) rules on the girls, and (4) must offer the subjects I want to take.

I would like for the school I chose to be close to my home. If the school is close to my home I can go home weekends. I, like most girls, get homesick often when I am away.

My chosen school must have good accreditation, so that when I apply for a job, no matter where, I will not have any trouble.

This school must also have strict rules for girls, but not too strict. I strongly believe that no girl should be allowed to run free or have too much freedom. But I also believe that no girl should be kept too close. Strict dorms will eliminate most of the excess freedom.

And last of all, this college must offer the subjects I wish to take. I also must be able to complete these subjects within four years with normal study.

This concludes my concept of a perfect college.

My School

I think all schools should have regulations. All regulations should be obeyed. To have a good school, there must be good regulations.

Regulations for girls are somewhat hard. They must be in early. The rules are to fit the school. Sometimes strict rules helps to develop a good school.

The environment sometimes makes the school better. Such as a library, gym, and recreation room. Since a good school is a popular school. Where there is football, baseball, and basketball.

K.   *The Heroic 60's*

For years the American public had no one to look up to. No one to admire or be proud to copy. Of course, there were always Superman and The Lone Ranger for the children, but a true hero could not be found. At the turn of the last decade, however, there was much promise. The 60's were to bring new light, new faces, and brave bold heroes on the American scene.

The first hero or image to be admired was a man named Kennedy. A handsome, young, and determined senator, he smashed all roadblocks and bypassed all pitfalls, and in the most exciting contest in American history, was elected President of the United States in 1960. Kennedy immediately won the appraisal of all. His manner, technique, athletic appearance, and Irish-American accent, all accompanied by a beautiful wife and lovely children, brought sparkle and pride to the eyes of Americans. Kennedy handeled himself in a most worthy way. The affairs of the Presidency were not easy, yet the world seemed confident and relied most heavily on this statesman. Many new programs were introduced in order to give the United States a new face. The Peace Corps, Vista, Physical Fitness Programs, and many more were to be in progress or in the making before his reign would end. Kennedy seemed a perfect target for the Communists. They were to test this American hero, and attempt to prove that he was fallable. However, the President stood firm, the American public right behind him, in Cuba and Germany. Communism was checked, and the faith in our hero was retained. Kennedy seemed to be the man to get things done. Thus, the American Negro felt that this man could help them in their battles. The President did much for the Negro, yet time did not allow him to complete his job, he was viciously murdered in Dallas. Yet no hero would be a true hero if not crushed by some ill fate. America's hero was crushed, and the eyes of the world were filled with tears at this tremendous loss.

There were other heroes of the 60's. The world cannot forget the gallant astronauts who courageously dared to enter the limits of outer space. The most famous of these was John Glenn. The third American in space, he was the second human ever to orbit the earth. His smile, masculine features, and witty nature gained America many friends. He traveled the country and the world, spreading good will wherever he went.

There are others: Martin Luther King, Robert Kennedy, and Cassius Clay. But the 60's surely did bring to America what it lacked. A good solid hero.

L.   *20th Century Hero*

In December, 1941, a small squadron of P.T. boats left their base to perform perhaps the most decisive task of World War II. Their orders were to carry General Douglas MacArthur to safety away from the advancing forces of Japan. If this mission had failed, the war might have lasted longer than it did, and the price of victory could have been much higher.

Although MacArthur may not be considered as being strictly in our age, in my opinion he is the model of our generation, and a true hero.

He stood firm, without wavering and without compromise, for what he believed was right. In Korea, he disagreed with President

Truman concerning the conduct of the war, and he made his disapproval public. As a result, he was relieved of his command. But rather than do what he thought was wrong, he risked his position as Commander in the Pacific before compromising.

In our age, the theory of "civil disobedience" is a controversial subject. MacArthur practiced "civil disobedience"; however, when he practiced it the only person he hurt was himself. He invaded, in no way the rights of any other citizen.

MacArthur was also an intellectual. He graduated first in his class at West Point and also achieved one of the finest academic records in the history of the academy.

Personal bravery was also one of the General's many attributes. A lieutenant at the start of World War I, he became the nation's youngest general by 1934; and his promotions were not political ones.

Douglas MacArthur was an American who exercised his rights as a citizen in the correct manner. He, more than many today, can honestly be called a "concerned citizen." For he was concerned about the welfare of the United States; while many so-called "concerned citizens" of this age are concerned about themselves, and abuse rather than use their rights as citizens of the United States.

M.   *The American Man*

The American man is slowly being pushed out of his high and mighty position in our society. For hundreds of years the American man has been thought of as a big tough guy with a pioneering spirit. This image is epitimized in the TV Western where the Indian has to lose. The woman never plays an important part in these shows, but she is now coming into her own. The American man has come to realize that women are capable of doing many jobs he does. Men would still like to feel superior, but women are coming up on them. Women now compete with men for their jobs and when they come out on top the man's ego is crushed. The American man still likes to think of himself as that tough pioneer.

Foreigners see the American man as a very aggressive, fast-moving person. To them, the men here have no desire but to make money and get ahead. They will let no one get in their way, not even their family. They also see them as cold, unromantic people who don't know how to appreciate life.

American men can't cry. This is almost a law in our society. American men are supposed to be too tough for any of that silliness. We find that quite evident everywhere: TV, newspapers, books, and we find it in everyday life. If something really tragic happens, he still can't cry. He must turn his head and be brave.

If the American man were to live up to all his images he couldn't be human. As we come in closer contact with the American man we find he is human. He can be romantic and he can cry. American men are great, but the legends should cease so as to let them come down to the level where they really are.

N.   *The American Image of Femininity*

The image that America puts forth through the various media of the all-American woman is not a true one. Through magazines, the woman is transformed into a beautiful and flawless being. No model in any magazine is ever a true representative of the average American wife or student. She is usually the epitome of beauty, both in features and figure.

Through various television shows, the American woman is represented as a person with much time to do nothing except solve other peoples' problems. The daily afternoon soap operas are prime examples of this. They always have many problems but no real purpose to their life.

Movies further discredit the American female. These give the impression, especially abroad, that all Americans are rich and sexy. That everyone runs around on their husband at least once.

This image should be changed or at least modified, for although these traits of American woman are in some cases true, it is not a universal thing. I don't think there should rightfully be an American image of femininity. Any image of femininity is universal throughout the Western world, for all women strive for grace and beauty in some form. Basically, they strive for acceptance of themselves as they are. This is true beauty.

O.   *The Cool One*

The word "cool," although an abstract idea, is commonly used by the modern-day tongue as though it were concrete. When one hears this word, one immediately recognizes it, but does not actually know the meaning of it. In order for one to grasp the meaning of "cool" fully, one must compare the word on a concrete level. An individual, for instance, can be classified as "cool." "Cool" in the sense that he impresses or draws a reaction from people because of his actions. He appears to be calm and nerveless; he knows how to handle things in stride, correspondingly people obtain an impression about his cool-ness. It is from this impression that the word draws its meaning. Be-cause this person possesses this calm atmosphere, people associate him as being "cool" or one who attracts some type of attention.

Cool Under Fire

"Cool" is a quality that very few people possess. It is an abstract thing that manifests itself only in times of stress or uneasiness. When things are tense and time is running out, the person who has "cool" will make the right decision. These people are usually leaders, rich in other qualities such as courage and strength. A perfect example of this was the late John F. Kennedy. During the Cuban missile crisis, he took a bold stand and held his position firmly until the Russian mis-siles were removed from Cuba. He was under great pressure, but he brought the nation through this danger. Other examples are seen in wartime when commanders call down artillery fire almost on top of themselves and continue to fight the enemy. In the sports world "cool" is easily seen. It is exhibited by players like John Unitas and Joe Na-math every Sunday in a desperation drive in the waning minutes of an important game. It is displayed by the National Basketball Associa-tion greats such as Oscar Robertson and Jerry West, who can hold the ball for the final shot and make it. "Cool" is what the great ones have and that is why they are great.

P.   Mind Benders

Advertising, as a whole, tends to try to capture the minds of the viewers and readers. Modern-day advertising is nothing more than letting one know how much greater a person he would be if he bought the advertised article. Sex, culture, and youth seem to be the three main categories of today's advertising.

Sex tends to be the most versatile advertising motive. Beautiful girls are seen advertising articles from televisions to men's shaving cream. The sponser wants the viewer to believe he will have a greater love life if he buys or uses that particular article. To the advertiser, personality and character are trivial; the main idea is that their product enables and permits a greater love life in any person.

Culture is implied in many instances. The use of one single product, according to the advertisers, may develop a person and give him an instantaneous cultural background. The drinking of beer even gives culture if it is the advertiser's beer. The usage of certain articles, supposedly makes a man more versatile. Advertisements tends to reflect that a man can become renowned if a single product is used. Everything is tagged either the "style" or the "in" look. According to advertisements, a person can never succeed in popularity or fame if the advertised product is not used. Everything is implied in the article.

The youth motive is used mainly to capture the minds of the older generation. Everyone wants to become more lovely, but without certain articles it is impossible, according to sponsors.

The capture of the viewer's mind is more effective than any other advertising scheme ever improvised. The advertising is good; nevertheless, I have yet to see a person's sex life broadened, cultural background widened, or youth restored by the use of a single article.

Q. *The Art of Advertising*

The art of advertising is a very widely exploited business. It is used by both the smallest and the largest companies and helps to serve the same purpose for both. Its desired effect is to put before the consumer's mind a motto, song, or slogan that he will associate with their product. This works very often, as I have even found myself singing little songs that I have heard from advertisements on the radio or television.

There are many methods of advertising, one of which is the newspaper. The newspaper is used mainly by local stores and companies and usually tells of specials or sales. The purpose of these is to attract the consumer to the thought of saving money. I have seen this method send my parents into a frenzy as they try to hurry to the grocery store to buy groceries that are on sale.

Another method of advertising is billboards. Billboards are usually placed in strategic spots and try to draw your attention by use of either a picture or a peculiar heading. These can usually be found on major highways on the outskirts of a city. They are put out mainly by large companies that are located in the city, such as automobile dealers and soft drink companies.

Television and radio are the two greatest means of advertising. Their very existence depends on advertising. It is their sole source of income. These advertisements are both local and nationwide and are the most successful of the modes of advertising.

Everyone must agree that the advertisement is a very basic component of a capitalistic society and is important to us all as it helps to foster competition and thus helps to keep prices down and quality up. Advertising in some form has reached and will continue to reach you as long as you live, whether you resist it or not.

R. *Loneliness*

Loneliness is a feeling that carries you into personal thoughtfullness. The beauty of the campus and the excitement of the students around you are insufficient in comparison with that nagging suspicion that you are being watched intensely and that you are only one of such a great number. Your life revolves around yourself for the moment until you are able to acquire friends. Then trust and warmth give you confidence and there is sureness in what you say. You can smile on impulse because having someone to depend upon puts you completely at ease. Often two persons are brought together by a sense of relief from their loneliness. An equal trust in each other creates a strong bond. From loneliness grows a simple kindness and an understanding of petty embarrasments that another has been through. The most considerate will recognize one who is alone and make an effort to accustom him to the glare of many faces and the maze of paths before him that will lead into his future.

One Times One

The idea that the Smithfield co-ed is immediately beseiged by numerous young men and befriended by other young ladies the moment she arrives on campus is a very misleading one. From the first aukward attempt at conversation with her roommates she is continually faced with feelings of loneliness. She wants desperately to see a friendly smile and would love to encounter a familiar face from home. She feels a little twinge of jealousy when she walks past the Circus Café and sees crowds of laughing people. While sitting alone in the hall waiting for her Modern Civilization class to begin, she inwardly hates her Spanish professor for dismissing class early. After receiving notes, class assignments, and teachers' names, she returns to her room and hopes for a better day tomorrow.

S.   *The Perfect City*

The perfect city will materialize if the problems of crime, overpopulation, and food shortage are eliminated.

Crime, committed in the streets, back alleys, movie theaters, comic book stores; must be sought out and destroyed. A complete wipe-out can only be accomplished if every citizen takes a one-week leave of absence from his place of employment, and combats crime twenty-four hours a day with every container of ammoniated ammunition available. If a firm effort is put forth, crime will be eliminated. All the people in the city will also be thoroughly exhausted.

While the citizens of the city are recuperating from their crime fighting, they must be informed that their love making has caused overpopulation, and is dangerous to their health. Conception causes problems, and anyone giving birth will be immediately expelled from the confines of the city. Babies will continue to be born; people will not believe such a rediculous statement. Therefore, people will be methodically removed from the city, and with less people living there less food will be needed.

Food shortage, the perfect city's third problem, will be easily overcome since farms, livestock, and supermarkets will not be permitted in the city, once the sources and the outlets for food consumption are removed people will either stop eating or leave the city. The latter will be the desired effect.

With no people living in the city, there will no longer be present the problems of crime, overpopulation, and food shortage. Thus the perfect city appears.

T.   *A Comparison of the Ideas of Booker T.*
                                           Washington and W. E. B. DuBois

These are a few of the ideas that started the historical differences of Booker T. Washington and W. E. B. DuBois. Mr. Washington was considered the most striking thing in the history of the American Negro. His ideas were highly praised and followed by the Negroes. But he made three statements that caused Mr. DuBois to flare up. They were: (1) give up political power, (2) stop the insistance on civil rights, and (3) the higher education of Negro youth.

Mr. DuBois stated that because of this peace offering, the Negroes status was lowered and this caused their disfranchisement. He wanted the Negroes to give up the vote. True this vote wasn't worth much but at least they had it. If the Negro people had kept the vote they might have been able to get someone on their side by having the vote. And a lot of today's voting issues would not be so serious.

Second, Mr. Washington wanted the Negroes to give up their civil rights where Mr. DuBois didn't. Washington felt that they were not ready; DuBois felt that they were ready and should keep them. Because civil rights would be a necesity in their struggle for equality.

And finally Mr. Washington wanted the Negroes to give up their bid for college education. Mr. DuBois strongly disagreed. How could the Negro get anywhere without a college education, how could they be prepared to teach and go out into society without an education. Mr. Washington stressed industrial education. He figured that if a man is to go somewhere he must have something that would help to build himself up. He wanted to train the Negro in industries and in this way help them to make money at his trade and then send his children to college.

Both of these men were great men in wisdom and stature. Both wanted the best for the Negro. Mr. Washington and Mr. DuBois in my opinion were both on the right track and should be honored for their mistakes as well as their success. Both of them had in my opinion the right idea.

U.   *Parental Punishment*

There is a great difference in the method or style my parents use to correct my mistakes.

My father, as head of the family, feels that it is his duty to punish me when I do something wrong. His method of punishment is to prevent me from going somewhere or to cut off my allowance for a certain amount of time. This type of punishment can be very effective at certain times, but it doesn't always work. The reason for this is because at times I may not need my allowance or perhaps I may not really want to go out. In cases such as these my father is not really punishing me.

My mother's style is quite the opposite of my father's and in my opinion much more effective. When my mother corrects me she just talks with me. She explains what was wrong and asks me if I agree with her. In this way I have a chance to defend myself, although usually I end up agreeing with her. The style my mother uses always makes me think about what I did and usually makes me regret my actions.

Both of these methods are in their own way effective. When they are combined it is impossible to get away with anything.

V. *Soul*

Standing out as the most popular and meaningful utterance of emotion in America, "soul" is the one word that signifies the sincere inner motivations of today's youth. It most likely stems from the separation of the body and the soul, whereby the soul has become that beautiful spirit of one's personality. The search for self, preached by all teen-agers, finds it's answer to be "soul." We always look into ourselves for some attractive quality which will prove our acceptance with others. Hence, the Black youths have classified themselves as "Soul Brothers" because they see the one quality among them—their color —which proves their own acceptance. The unity so imperative to the Black movement today can be attained by the greeting of "Soul Brother." It can thus be seen that the word "soul" immediately turns one's attention to the quest for unity and personal brotherhood so imperative to our nation.

W. *The Donkey for Me*

Although I am not of voting age, I have noticed a strong inclination on my part to lean towards the Democratic Party. This is a com-

plete reversal of my earlier feelings, when I was under the influence of
my father who was quite active in the local Republican Party. This
switch is due mainly to the fact that I am liberal and the Democratic
party has come, in my opinion, to represent the left, both in ideals and
leadership.

I have come to the conclusion that the Democratic Party is the
more liberal by comparing the two major candidates in past elections.
I can go all the way back to Franklin Roosevelt who was a great
progressive, while his various adversaries always advocated conven-
tionalism. Truman, who came next, in defeating Wilkie in an upset,
proved that the people still wanted Rooseveltian Progressive leadership. In 1952 and 1956, however, Democrat Adlai Stevenson was defeated by war hero and conservative General Eisenhower. In 1960, in
a very close election, John F. Kennedy defeated his conservative Republican adversary Richard Nixon. In the election of 1964, while certainly President Johnson could never be called a standard bearer of
the New Left, he was a few hundred years to the left of Republican
Barry Goldwater. And President Nixon is more conservative than his
defeated foe, Hubert Humphrey. So for the last thirty-five years the
Democratic Party has offered the more liberal of the two candidates,
hence this is the reason for my present allegiance to the donkey.

This situation might seem to call for a renaming of the two
parties. The Democratic Party would become known as the Liberal
Party and the Republicans as the Conservative Party. I realize, however, that there are many conservative Democrats and liberal Republicans these people would simply realign themselves to the party that
conforms more closely with their ideals. If this system were adopted
the voters would be afforded more of an opportunity to vote for a
man's beliefs rather than a party. Unfortunately, this innovation is at
best years away in the meantime I will continue to support the Democratic party as long as it remains the more liberal.

X.   *My Party*

Patriotism! Why does everyone seem to ignore that topic today?
In television, in the papers, on the news broadcasts, the big thing they
are concerned about is dissent. Movies, too are joining the movement
towards the spread of dissent. Everybody seems totally allied in the

one goal to make people realize what is wrong with our country. Thankfully, there are still some people around, a vast, vast majority, who are, or seem to be, united towards a single goal in a positive instead of a negative attitude. They are trying to rekindle the passionate fire of patriotism that was widespread through the 40's and 50's. The people united, or at least more united than their counterparts, are known by the title, "The Republican Party."

You may point out that it is totally impossible to have a political party in which everyone is united in every aspect of the platform. People being people and thinking differently from one another, this is not totally possible. But people can compromise, alienating their beliefs just a little to make for a unified party, a strong party. The Democrats accentuate my point. There are factions not willing to give in a little, to prostitute their beliefs in order to make their party strong. Like spoiled children crying over "spillt milk." And, like the immature, irrational, irreverent, assinine children that they are, they offen demonstrate, cause violence to result, and then blame it on everybody but themselves.

Which brings me to another point. Demonstrations are great for the American system. Where else can you do it so freely and on every aspect of American life, political or otherwise. It is a way of showing your personal freedom. All well and good. But when, as a direct or indirect result, you infringe on another person's rights, then that is when the demonstrations should stop or be dispersed, by violence if necessary. This is the one big reason, the important reason, why I stand behind the Republican Party. They do not let professional agitators goad them into unwise and unreasonable decisions.

Perhaps I am a little different than most or some young people. I believe in the old saying "My country right or wrong," and I let nothing alleviate myself from this line of thought.

Y. *A Political View*

Since I believe strongly in the principles this country was founded on I generally support the Republican Party.

One of the major difficulties encountered in the establishment of the Federal Government was how to keep the Federal Government from becoming too powerful. The Republican Party is the party which believes in curtailing the power of the Federal Government to interfere in state and local issues. By curtailing this power the people in small towns have a greater say, which is the way our founding fathers wanted their government to function. The trend today is to increase the federal programs and thus increase the federal control over each individual state. This trend is against the principle on which this country was founded.

Another reason I support the Republican Party is that it believes in a strict interpretation of the Constitution, which increases the personal freedom of the individual. Such items as the draft and the gun control bills are considered unconstitutional because they violate the rights of individuals. The draft is really involuntary servitude while gun control bills violate the right to carry firearms. Republicans also do not believe it is constitutional to legislate social behavior and that one should be allowed to do as he wishes so long as he doesn't harm others or himself.

A third reason I support the Republican Party is that it believes in the free enterprise system. Since the depression of the thirties there has been a increase in welfare programs. While I believe that some are necessary I feel that an effort should be made to get private industry to help in the "War on Poverty." This would lead to a sounder economy and might help taxes and inflation.

Z.   *The Major Change*

During my first semester at school, I experienced a great transformation in my behavior towards the adult world.

In my childhood, I was taught by my own parents and many of my adult friends and relatives that the word sex, or any subject that would have any relationship to it, was obscene and should never be a topic of conversation. I believed them and I could never understand how some of my friends could live with themselves after telling dirty jokes. I was always terribly apprehensive when I was with any of them in adult company for fear that they would say something that would mean trouble for all of us. However, I soon learned that not all adults felt this way, but I still remained nervous around them. This problem followed me for a long time and it bothered me so much that I developed a two-faced personality. I presented the pretentious side to the adults and my true side to my friends. I was very similar to an actor who is called upon to portray a character who is almost an exact opposite of his own character. By this statement I do not mean to infer that I went around telling dirty jokes all of the time, but that I simply didn't see any justification for the views held by the adults.

I really changed my attitude towards the way I would act around adults sometime about the middle of last semester. I had become quite tense from continually suppressing my own opinion. I decided that if I were to retain my sanity I must stop my pretending and reveal my true nature to everyone. I realized that if I didn't change this habit now that I would have to live with it building up inside me for the rest of my life.